Financial
Wisdom
English

金融英语阅读与听力训练 ○ 附光盘

金融睿智英语

沈素萍／系列主编

2 金融危机
Financial Crisis

张懿馨／编著

中国金融出版社

责任编辑：杨　敏
责任校对：孙　蕊
责任印制：程　颖

图书在版编目（CIP）数据

金融危机（Jinrong Weiji）：汉英对照/张懿馨编著．—北京：中国金融出版社，2009.10
（金融睿智英语/沈素萍系列主编）
ISBN 978 - 7 - 5049 - 5166 - 3

Ⅰ. 金…　Ⅱ. 张…　Ⅲ.①英语—汉语—对照读物②金融危机—简介—世界　Ⅳ. H319.4：F

中国版本图书馆 CIP 数据核字（2009）第 118817 号

出版
发行　中国金融出版社

社址　北京市丰台区益泽路 2 号
市场开发部　（010）63272190，66070804（传真）
网上书店　http：//www.chinafph.com
　　　　　　（010）63286832，63365686（传真）
读者服务部　（010）66070833，82672183
邮编　100071
经销　新华书店
印刷　北京市松源印刷有限公司
尺寸　169 毫米 ×239 毫米
印张　19.25
字数　375 千
版次　2009 年 10 月第 1 版
印次　2009 年 10 月第 1 次印刷
定价　35.00 元
ISBN 978 - 7 - 5049 - 5166 - 3/F. 4726
如出现印装错误本社负责调换　联系电话（010）63263947

在金融英语的教学生涯中，笔者编写了不同层次和侧重点的金融英语教材二十余部，此次"金融睿智英语"系列丛书的策划，是应中国金融出版社的邀请，编写有关金融英语听力方面的教材，但在同出版社的孟威锋主任进一步讨论和策划中，正值笔者受邀到美国哈佛大学参与研究，所以，结合做中外银行历史体制的比较，最后确定编写一套了解金融历史的发展过程并兼顾英语语言学习的丛书。

本套系列丛书题材广泛，涵盖了一些不同类型的专题。首先在世界金融名家（World Financial Celebrities）中我们选择了银行家、诺贝尔奖获得者、投资大师、证券分析家等金融界杰出人物。其次在金融危机案例（Cases of Financial Crisis）中我们沿着历史上全球金融危机典型案例的轨迹来介绍金融历史。其中有17世纪荷兰的郁金香泡沫事件（Tulip Mania），18世纪英国的南海泡沫事件（South Sea Bubble），1929年美国经济大萧条（Great Depression）以及1997年的亚洲金融危机（Asian Financial Crisis）。特别是2008年9月雷曼兄弟公司破产（Bankruptcy of Lehman Brothers）成为美国历史上最大的倒闭案件。另外，本套丛书还包括金融改革、法律、电子金融、银行管理、金融人物励志案例等专题。

本系列读物均按照由浅入深、循序渐进的原则系统而连贯地编写完成。每册各自在内容上互相渗透，融会贯通。同时，每册又各具特色，风格迥异。

本套丛书语言设计新颖。每册编写共分20个单元左右，每个单元分七个部分："主题札记"、"阅读长廊"、"财经宝库"、"DIY工作室"、"归类记忆卡片"、"听力广场"和"非常点拨"。另外，丛书的语言生动活泼。"主题札记"是每单元的导读部分。我们用中文简单介绍本单元所要谈及的主题，便于读者阅读和进行听力学习。我们又在英文全文后加入了对应的中文翻译，并配有相关的人物照片及事件图例，让读者在轻松活泼的氛围中了解金融。同时，我们也注重语言设计的严谨。"阅读长廊"是一个单元的主要部分，采取中英文对照方式，同时对于生词采用注脚方式，标明音标、词性和文中含义。"财经宝库"主要针对文中涉及的与金融知识相关的词条做注释，方便读者直观快速了解金融背景知识。"DIY工作室"针对阅读材料提问题，便于读者思考总结。"听力广场"以中英文对照方式出现，其中的难点还在"非常点拨"中做了注释。

这套丛书可作为系列金融英语读物和教材（含配套听力），旨在帮助金融专业学生和金融从业人员在了解金融专业知识的同时，提高金融英语听说和阅读能力。在丛书的策划和出版过程中，中国金融出版社的孟威锋主任和肖炜、杨敏编辑为我们提供了很多宝贵的建议，在此谨致谢忱。

系列主编　沈素萍
2009年5月于哈佛园

作为中国金融出版社"金融睿智英语"系列的作品，《金融危机》精心遴选二十件具有代表性的金融泡沫事件，编写二十个单元，每个单元通过"主题札记"、"阅读长廊"、"财经宝库"、"DIY工作室"、"归类记忆卡片"、"听力广场"和"非常点拨"七项内容，介绍这些金融泡沫事件的起因、经过及结果。所用材料具有权威性，同时兼顾趣味性和可读性。

全书共分三部分。第一部分通过介绍历史上著名的金融泡沫事件，使读者对资本主义金融泡沫的产生发展过程有一个感性的认识，同时认识到金融泡沫并不是一个新生事物，它从某种程度上说与资本主义经济发展紧密相连。比如英国的南海泡沫与法国的密西西比公司泡沫，为什么在同一时间爆发，推动泡沫产生的根本原因是什么，读者可以从政治和经济两个角度去思考这个问题。第二部分通过介绍20世纪几次大型的国际和地区经济金融危机来使读者认识到在新的市场环境下，经济金融危机有哪些特征，同时各国如何能够共同预防金融危机，这是读者需要着重思考的问题。第三部分介绍目前正在恶化的由美国次级房贷市场引发的全球性的金融危机和经济衰退，谁是这场危机的罪魁祸首？几家大型投资银行的影响力为什么会有那么大？希望读者在读后有所收获。

由美国次级房贷引发的金融危机不断加深，一场全球性的经济危机似乎已经不可避免。希望这本书可以让读者对金融危机有一个全面清晰的认识。在此，我要感谢"金融睿智英语系列"主编、正在美国哈佛大学做访问学者的沈素萍教授的信任和鼓励，也要感谢中国金融出版社孟威锋主任等同志的大力帮助，同时还要感谢家人的理解和支持。

最后，欢迎读者对本书提出意见和建议，编者将认真听取并尽可能地加以改进。

作者：张懿馨
2009年4月于加拿大麦吉尔大学

Contents

目录

Financial Crisis

Topic One   Historical Financial Crisis

Tulip Mania
Unit 1

Tulip Mania
郁金香疯狂

主题札记

　　1593年，一位荷兰商人从康士坦丁（今土耳其）进口了第一株郁金香花根并种植。由于此花为进口商品，因此一跃为财富的象征，于是这种风气由荷兰扩散到德国。这时郁金香正好染上花叶病，郁金香花瓣产生了一些色彩对比非常鲜明的彩色条纹或如火焰，于是染病郁金香引起一股抢购风潮。从最初的郁金香行家赏其美到投机分子炒作，交易市场形成并热闹起来，如同股市。

　　1634年，郁金香热潮蔓延至中产阶级，后又成为全民运动，家家户户都倾一家之产，只为买一朵郁金香。1,000美元一个郁金香球茎，不到一个月就变为2万美元。最疯狂的时候，1个郁金香球茎＝4吨小麦＝1张床＝4头牛＝8头猪＝12只羊。

　　1636年，郁金香在欧洲一些股市上市，有的设选择权以降低投机者的门槛，使投机者可以买到几分之一的郁金香，于是价格又往上推，从购买一个月可获利20倍，到透过选择权获利可放大100倍。

A tulip, known as "the Viceroy", displayed in a 1637 Dutch catalog
一株郁金香，也称"总督花"，展出于1637年荷兰编目

　　最高点时，一位大户全数卖出；荷兰政府开始采取刹车行动；土耳其大量郁金香将抵达。郁金香的价格开始下滑，六个星期下跌了90%，此时，不管政府如何护盘都无力回天，郁金香价格持续探底，许多股市交割无法完成，而荷兰政府宣布这一事件为赌博事件，豁免交割，从而结束了这一场疯狂的郁金香泡沫事件。

阅读长廊

Mackay's Madness of Crowds

The modern discussion of Tulip Mania began with the book *Extraordinary Popular Delusions and the Madness of Crowds*, published in 1841 by the Scottish journalist Charles Mackay. The thesis of Mackay's work was that crowds of people often behave irrationally, and Tulip Mania was, along with the South Sea Bubble and Mississippi Company Bubble, one of his prime examples.

Mackay's vivid book was extremely popular among generations of economists and stock-market participants. Thus Mackay's popular, but flawed, description of Tulip Mania as a speculative bubble remains prominent even though since the 1980s economists have debunked[1] many aspects of his account.

麦基的群众性癫狂

对于郁金香疯狂的讨论开始于苏格兰记者查尔斯·麦基于1841年出版的《非同寻常的大众幻想与群众性癫狂》一书。该书的主题是大众群体往往失去理性，如荷兰的郁金香疯狂、南海泡沫和密西西比公司股票泡沫，并称为三大群体性不理智的经典案例。

麦基的书在几代经济学家和股市参与者中十分流行。尽管自20世纪80年代以来，许多经济学家都对麦基的观点从多方面提出质疑，但该书中对郁金香疯狂的描述还是值得肯定的。

---

1 debunk: [diːˈbʌŋk] *v.* 揭穿真相，暴露

According to Mackay, the growing popularity of tulips in the early 1600s caught the attention of the entire nation: "the population, even to its lowest dregs, embarked in the tulip trade".By 1635, a sale of 40 bulbs[2] for 100,000 florins was recorded. By way of comparison, a ton of butter cost around 100 florins[3], a skilled laborer might earn 150 florins a year, and "eight fat swine" cost 240 florins.

By 1636, tulips were traded on the stock exchanges of numerous Dutch towns and cities. This encouraged trading in tulips by all members of society; Mackay recounted people selling or trading their other possessions in order to speculate in the tulip market, such as a single bulb of the Semper Augustus that was purchased in exchange for 12 acres of land.

Many individuals grew suddenly rich. Every one imagined that the passion for tulips would last for ever, and that the wealthy from every part of the world would send to Holland, and pay whatever prices were asked for them. The riches of Europe would be concentrated on the shores of the Zuyder

根据麦基的描述，郁金香的流行始于17世纪初并迅速风靡全国："即使是社会的最底层也对郁金香贸易津津乐道。以至于到1635年，40枝郁金香卖到10万荷兰盾。而当时1吨黄油也不过100荷兰盾，一个技术工人一年的收入也不过150荷兰盾，8头肥猪也只要240荷兰盾。

1636年，荷兰的一些城镇开始允许郁金香在股票交易所进行交易，这也使得社会各界的人投入到郁金香交易中。麦基的书中指出，许多人将其自身的产业变卖来购买郁金香，如一枝Semper Augustus郁金香能够交换12英亩土地。

许多人因此一夜间暴富。每个人都梦想郁金香热潮能够永久持续下去，全世界的富人都将集中到荷兰，郁金香的价格不管要价多高，他们都愿出价购买。Zuyder Zee海滩将成为欧洲财富的集中地，贫穷将从此消失。贵族、市民、农民、技工、渔民、脚夫，甚至依靠扫烟

---

2 bulb: [bʌlb] n. 电灯泡，球状物
3 florin: ['flɔrin] n. 荷兰盾

Zee, and poverty banished from the favoured clime of Holland. Nobles, citizens, farmers, mechanics, seamen, footmen, maidservants, even chimney-sweeps and old clotheswomen, dabbled in tulips.

囡为生的人和靠洗衣为生的老妇人都投入到倒卖郁金香的狂潮中去。

People were purchasing bulbs at higher and higher prices, to turn them around and sell them for a profit. In February 1637, tulip traders could no longer get inflated prices for their bulbs, and they tried to sell. As this realization set in, the demand for tulips began to collapse, and prices began to plummet. The bubble burst. Some were left holding contracts to purchase tulips at prices now ten times greater than those on the open market, while others found themselves in possession of bulbs now worth a fraction of the price they had paid.

人们开始以越来越高的价格收购郁金香并转手抛售来套利。直到1637年2月，郁金香投机者们发现郁金香的价格不再上涨，他们开始抛售手中的郁金香。当这种意识在人群中传播的时候，郁金香变得不再受欢迎，需求的下降导致价格的下降。泡沫破裂了。尽管有些人手中持有10倍于市场价的郁金香期货合同，另外，许多人手中的郁金香只值他们之前所支付价格的一小部分。

Panicked, the tulip speculators sought help from the government of the Netherlands, which responded by declaring that anyone who had bought contracts to purchase bulbs in the future could void their contract with a 10 percent fee. Attempts were made to resolve the situation to the satisfaction of all parties, but these were unsuccessful. Ultimately, individuals were stuck with the bulbs they held at the end of the crash—no court would enforce payment of a contract, since judges regarded the debts as contracted through gambling, and thus not enforceable

恐慌的郁金香投机者们开始求助于荷兰政府。荷兰政府允许郁金香期货合同的持有者可以交10%的违约金来取消合同。尽管政府试图平衡各方利益，但最终还是失败了。许多人手中的郁金香变得一文不值，因为法院将郁金香交易裁定为赌博，因此郁金香债务不受法律保护。

in law.

According to Mackay, lesser versions of Tulip Mania also occurred in other parts of Europe although matters never reached the state they had in the Netherlands. The aftermath of the tulip price deflation led to a widespread economic chill throughout the Netherlands for "many years".

据麦基介绍，在欧洲的其他国家也出现了郁金香风潮，但都没有荷兰那么激烈。郁金香风潮犹如一股先热后冷的狂风吹过荷兰，达多年之久。

An allegory of Tulip Mania by Hendrik Gerritsz Pot
一幅由赫德里克·格利茨·波德创作的关于郁金香狂潮的讽刺画

财经宝库

1. **泡沫经济**　是指资产价值超越实体经济，极易丧失持续发展能力的宏观经济状态。泡沫经济经常由大量投机活动支撑。由于缺乏实体经济的支撑，因此其资产犹如泡沫一般容易破裂，因此经济学上称为"泡沫经济"。泡沫经济发展到一定的程度，经常会由于支撑投机活动的市场预期或者神话的破灭，而导致资产价值迅速下跌，这在经济学上被称为泡沫破裂。20世纪出现过多次泡沫经济浪潮，其中较为著名的是日本80年代的泡沫经济。其主要体现在房地产市场和股票交易市场等领域。但是一旦泡沫经济破裂，其影响将波及一个国家的大多数产业甚至国际经济的走势。

2. 荷兰盾（Dutch gulden） 用符号f或fl来表示，于13世纪开始流通的荷兰货币，至2002年被欧元所取代。在1999年到2002年，荷兰盾曾被官方定义为欧元在荷兰的"国内货币单位"；但支付时采用的是荷兰盾，因为此时欧元的纸币和硬币还没有被印制出来。在荷属安的列斯至今仍然流通安的列斯荷兰盾。另一个使用盾作为货币的国家苏里南，在2004年将苏里南盾替换为苏里南元。

3. Goods Exchanged for a single root of the Viceroy[4] 郁金香的价值

two lasts of wheat 两石小麦	448f	four lasts of rye[5] 四石黑麦	558f
four fat oxen 四头肥牛	480f	eight fat swine 八头肥猪	240f
twelve fat sheep 十二只肥羊	120f	two hogsheads[6] of wine 两大桶酒	70f
four tuns of beer 四大桶啤酒	32f	two tons of butter 两吨黄油	192f
1,000 lbs. of cheese 1,000磅奶酪	120f	a complete bed 一张床	100f
a suit of clothes 一套衣服	80f	a silver drinking cup 一尊银质酒杯	60f

DIY工作室

1. How did the Tulip become so valuable? (Two factors)

2. What role did the Dutch government play in this game?

---

[4] Viceroy: ['vaɪsrɔɪ] *n.* 黑色蝴蝶（郁金香的一种）

[5] rye: [raɪ] *n.* 黑麦、裸麦

[6] hogshead: ['hɔgzhed] *n.* 一种大桶(容量自238～530公升不等)，若干种容积单位的通称,常相当于238公升。

归类记忆卡片

贫困 poverty
投机 speculate
期权合同 option contract

赌博 gamble
期货合同 future contract

听力广场

Tulip Mania

Could a mere tulip bulb be worth $76,000? It is if people are willing to pay for it! It may sound preposterous, but this is exactly what happened in Holland in the 1630's.

Initially, only the true connoisseurs bought tulip bulbs, but the rapidly rising price quickly attracted speculators looking to profit. It didn't take long before the tulip bulbs were traded on

郁金香疯狂

一株郁金香球茎可以价值76,000美元吗？这么高价格居然会有人买！这也许听上去像天方夜谭，但这恰恰发生在17世纪30年代的荷兰。

最初，郁金香还只是富人们玩的游戏，但是飞涨的郁金香价格吸引了大批投机者，没过多久，郁金香交易便风靡全国，这与今天的

local market exchanges, which were not unlike today's stock exchanges. By 1634, Tulip Mania had feverishly spread to the Dutch middle class. Pretty soon everybody was dealing in tulip bulbs, looking to make a quick fortune. The name of the game was to buy low and sell high, just like in any other market. The whole Dutch nation was caught in a sweeping mania, as people traded in their land, livestock, farms and life savings all to acquire 1 single tulip bulb!

In less than one month, the price of tulip bulbs went up twenty-fold! To put that into perspective, if you had invested $1,000 and came back one month later, your investment would have ballooned to $20,000! Now you can understand the mad rush to buy tulip bulbs at any cost. Tulip bulb mania affected the public psyche to an extreme. One drunk man in a bar started peeling and eating what he thought was an onion, while it was in fact it was the bar owner's tulip bulb on display. This man was jailed for many months!

In 1636, tulips were trading hands on the Amsterdam stock exchange. These exchanges started to offer option contracts to speculators. These option contracts allowed tulip bulbs to be speculated upon for a fraction of the price of a real tulip bulb. This allowed people of lower means to speculate in the tulip market. Additionally, options allowed for leverage. Due to leverage, option buyers were able to control

股票市场相似。到1634年，郁金香风潮吹到荷兰中产阶级中，过不多久，人人为了一夜暴富而进入郁金香交易市场，这种低买高卖的游戏使得许多人将手中的土地、家畜、农场和毕生的积蓄变卖兑现来获取一枝郁金香球茎。

一枝郁金香的价格可以在一个月内翻到20倍。也就是说，如果你今天投资1,000美元买郁金香，一个月后你可以挣到20,000美元。现在你也许理解人们为得到一枝郁金香不惜一切代价的痴狂了吧。你也许很难想象，一个醉汉因为误食了一枝郁金香球茎而被判刑数月。这位倒霉的醉汉由于在酒吧里误把酒吧老板的郁金香装饰品当做洋葱吃掉，而遭受好几个月的牢狱之苦。

1636年，郁金香交易进入阿姆斯特丹股票交易所，并且开始出现适合投机者口味的郁金香期权交易。这不仅使得杠杆操作（只需付一部分价钱即可控制大量交易）成为可能，并且使得许多手头并不宽裕的人们进入市场。就像我们前面提到的例子，1,000美元的投资可以在一个月内获得20,000美元的回报。似乎这还不够，杠杆效应使得

larger amounts of tulip bulbs, allowing a greater profit. In a previous example, we showed how a $1,000 investment would have yielded $20,000 in one month. As if this weren't enough, option leverage allowed this same investment of $1,000 to balloon into $100,000!

Unfortunately, leverage is a double-edged sword. If the tulip bulb price moved downwards ever so slightly, the option buyer's investment would be lost and they might even owe money! Talk about risky. But at this point, it was commonly believed that the tulip market was immune to crashing and that it would "always go up".

After some time, the Dutch government started to develop regulation to help control the tulip craze. It was at this point that a few informed speculators started liquidating their tulips bulbs and contracts. It was these people, or the smart money, that secured large profits that were now in the form of cold hard cash. In addition, more tulip bulbs were added to the supply due to people harvesting new tulip bulbs. Suddenly tulip bulbs weren't as quite as rare as before. The tulip market began a slight down trend, but shortly after started to plummet much faster than prices went up. Suddenly the market began a widespread panic when everyone started realizing that tulips were not worth the prices people were paying for them. In less than 6 weeks, tulip prices crashed by over 90%.

同样的1,000美元投资能像滚雪球般变成100,000美元！

不幸的是，这种杠杆操作是一把"双刃剑"，当郁金香的价格下跌时，投机者同样要为此埋单，不仅原来的投资损失殆尽，并且还可能欠债。然而许多投机者普遍认为郁金香价格会永远走高。

这时荷兰政府也开始对郁金香狂潮进行法规约束，因为此时已经有一些信息灵通的投机者开始抛售手中的郁金香来套现。正是这些信息灵通的人，或者说正是聪明的钱罐子，获得了高额利润，手里握着大宗硬通货。同时由于人们大量种植郁金香，供给的增加导致价格的下降。突然间，郁金香已经不像以前那么希罕了。郁金香市场在经历早期小幅的下跌后开始大跌。更可怕的是大跌造成了市场的恐慌，人们开始争相变现。当人们开始意识到郁金香已经不值钱了，市价已经降至比他们以前买入时还低的价位了。6周内，郁金香的价格狂跌90%以上。

Fortunes were lost. Wealthy became paupers. Bankruptcies were everywhere due to the negative side of option leverage. People that traded in farms and live savings for a tulip bulb were left holding a worthless plant seed. Many defaults occurred, where speculators couldn't pay off their debts.

The Dutch government avoided intervening, only to advise tulip speculators and owners to form a council[7] to attempt to stabilize prices and mend public confidence. Every one of these plans failed miserably, as tulip prices plummeted even lower than before.

The supreme[8] judges of Amsterdam declared all tulip speculation to be gambling, and refused to honor these contracts. As a result, payments were not enforced by any of Holland's courts. This further fueled the market crash.

The price of tulips at the height of the mania was $76,000; 6 weeks later they were valued at less than one dollar! The only people who prospered from the insanity were the smart money who liquidated at the top.

In market manias, the investors are acting irrationally. This process occurs regardless of

财富的大幅缩水也导致许多人一夜间从富翁变成穷人。由于杠杆操作，许多投机者无法偿还债务，违约事件无处不在。许多人变卖土地和毕生积蓄所换来的只是一些不值钱的郁金香种子。

荷兰政府采取了不干预的政策，只是建议投机者和郁金香持有者建立协会来稳定郁金香价格和投资者信心。荷兰政府所有的这些政策都遭到了惨痛的失败，因为郁金香的价格无情地继续大幅下跌。

由于阿姆斯特丹最高法院宣布所有的郁金香投机都被视为赌博，因此，所有的郁金香期权合同都被视为无效。结果，所有郁金香交易的卖方都不能在荷兰的法庭执行他们要求买方付款的权利。这进一步加剧了市场的恐慌。

尽管郁金香价格最高达到七万六千美元，仅仅6周后就变得不值1美元。只有在最高价位时抛售的投机者能够从中获利。

由于投资者的不理性造就了市场疯狂。这一过程无论在商品市场

---

[7] council: ['kaunsil] *n.* 理事会,委员会
[8] supreme: [sjuː'priːm] *a.* 最高的

the fact whether the market is a commodity market or a paper market like stocks. The moral is clear; the only way to survive is to be the smart money.

还是票据市场（如股票市场）都会发生。规则却很简单：只有聪明的投机者才会获利。

非常点拨

1. "郁金香疯狂"由何而来迄今没有定论，之后有人提出这是因为民众的贪婪和疯狂所引发的事件，也有人说价格大幅波动是一般市场机制使然。当时荷兰是经济大国，也是引发热潮和泡沫化的旗手，但处于下等阶层的民众则过着贫穷的生活苟且度日。

当时的荷兰北部七州因为对抗西班牙取得胜利，在17世纪初取得了实质上的独立，自此荷兰一跃成为了海上帝国君临欧洲。又从葡萄牙手中夺取了香料贸易生意，再加上中欧身处三十年战争的阴霾下，让商业活动都集中在了阿姆斯特丹，同时荷属东印度公司经营巴达维亚也取得了相当可观的利益。在这样的时代背景下，荷兰有着当时最高的收入水准，连海外的美术品也都集中在荷兰。另外，荷兰的物价也比其他的地区高，一个工匠的年收入推算约250荷兰盾，这个数字只够让一家四口单求糊口。普通劳动者在泡沫经济的时候，只得把家里所有的财物如家畜、生产用的工具都拿去变卖。

2. 当地流行的喀尔文教派以勤俭持家为美德，因此荷兰人避免穿华服，富人穷人的服装并无二致，光从外观很难察觉这个人是否富有。以此为信念的荷兰人为什么会走上投机的道路，至今尚未解开这个谜。

Admirael van der Eijck from the 1637 catalog of P.Cos., sold for 1,045 florins on February 5,1637 P.Cos.1637年编目中展出的 Admirael van der Eijck，这株郁金香于1637年2月5日以1,045荷兰盾被卖出

The South Sea Company
Unit 2

The South Sea Company
南海公司

主题札记

南海泡沫事件

南海泡沫事件是世界证券市场首例由过度投机引起的经济事件。"泡沫经济"或"气泡经济"一词也是源于南海泡沫事件。

南海泡沫事件的始作俑者是英国的南海公司。南海公司成立于1711年，成立之初，为支持英国政府债信的恢复，该公司认购了总价值近1,000万英镑的政府债券。作为回报，英国政府对该公司经营的酒、醋、烟草等商品实行了永久性退税政策，并把对南美的贸易垄断权给予了它。南海公司在成立之初就有一个众所周知的企图，这就是攫取蕴藏在南美东部海岸的巨大财富。当然，人人都知道秘鲁和墨西哥的地下埋藏着巨大的金银矿藏，只要能把英格兰的加工商送上海岸，数以万计的"金砖银石"就会源源不断地运回国内。社会公众对南海公司的发展前景充满了信心，同时股票供求关系严重失衡，使得南海公司的股票多年来一直十分抢手，价格不断上涨。

1719年，英国政府允许中奖债券与南海公司股票进行转换。同年年底，南美贸易障碍的扫除，加上公众对股价上扬的预期，促进了债券向股票的转换，进而带动了股价上升。从1720年1月起，南海公司的股票价格直线上升，从1月的每股128英镑上升到7月的每股1,000英镑以上，6个月涨幅高达700％。

在南海公司股票价格扶摇直上的示范效应下，全英170多家新成立的股份公司股票以及所有的公司股票，都成了投机对象，社会各界人士，包括军人和家庭妇女，甚至物理学家牛顿都卷入了这股旋涡。人们完全丧失了理智，他们不在乎这些公司的经营范围、经营状况和发展前景，只相信发起人说他们的公司如何能获取巨大利润，人们唯恐错过大捞一把的机会。一时间，股票价格暴涨，平均涨幅超过5倍。

然而，南海公司的经营并未如愿，盈利甚微，公司股票的市场价格与上市公司实际经营前景完全脱节。

1720年6月，为了制止各类"泡沫公司"的膨胀，英国国会通过了《泡沫法案》（*Bubble Act*）。自此，许多公司被解散，公众开始清醒过来。对一些公司的怀疑逐渐扩展到南海公司身上。从7月开始，外国投资者首先抛出南海股票，撤回资金，军队下达了要求军人回到岗位的命令。随着投机热潮的冷却，南海公司股价一落千丈，9月直跌至每股175英镑，12月最终跌为124英镑。"南海泡沫"终于破灭。

1720年年底，政府对南海公司资产进行清理，发现其实际资本已所剩无几，那些高价买进南海股票的投资者遭受了巨大损失。"南海泡沫"事件使许多地主、商人失去了资产，也引发了政治问题。此后较长一段时间，民众对参与新兴的股份公司闻之色变，对股票交易也心存怀疑。直到一个世纪以后，股份公司和股票市场才得以正名。

阅读长廊

The South Sea Company

The South Sea Company (1711 –1850s) was an English company granted a monopoly to trade with South America under a treaty with Spain. Following the *South Sea Company Act of 1720*, it became better known for the "South Sea Bubble", an economic bubble that occurred through overheated speculation in the company shares. The stock price collapsed after reaching a peak in September 1720.

Initial Stage

The company, established in 1711 by the Lord Treasurer, Robert Harley, was granted exclusive trading rights in Spanish South America. (The British at that time applied the term "South Seas" to South America and surrounding waters, not to the South Pacific, an area that was still mostly unknown to

南海公司

南海公司（1711年到19世纪50年代）是一家在与西班牙签订的条约下与南美洲进行垄断贸易的英国公司。根据1720年的《南海公司法案》，南海公司因为南海泡沫而更加出名。由于对南海公司股票的狂热投机，南海公司的股价在1720年9月达到顶峰后一落千丈。

最初阶段

1711年，英国财政大臣罗伯特·哈里建立了南海公司并得到与西属南美洲（当时英国人所称的"南海"是指南美洲及其周围的水域，但不包括南太平洋地区，因为该地区在那时并不为欧洲人所熟知）贸易的垄断经营权。这一法令也是西班牙王位继承战争1713年结

Europeans.) The trading rights were pre-supposed on the successful conclusion of the War of the Spanish Succession, which did not end until 1713, and the actual granted treaty rights were not as comprehensive as Harley had originally hoped.

Harley needed to provide a mechanism for funding government debt incurred in the course of that war. However, he could not establish a bank, because the charter of the Bank of England made it the only joint stock bank. He therefore established what, on its face, was a trading company, though its main activity was in fact the funding of government debt.

In return for its exclusive trading rights the government saw an opportunity for a profitable trade-off. The government and the company convinced the holders of around £10 million of short-term government debt to exchange it with a new issue of stock in the company. In exchange, the government granted the company a perpetual[9] annuity from the government paying £576,534 annually on the company's books, or a perpetual loan of £10 million paying 6%. This guaranteed the new equity owners a steady stream of earnings to this new venture. The government thought it was in a win-win situation because it would fund the interest

束的结果，尽管实际的垄断权并没有哈里预想的那样大。

哈里需要为战争所带来的（英国）政府债务提供基金支持，然而，按英格兰银行法，英格兰银行是唯一的股份制银行，因此哈里不能开设银行，只能够开设贸易公司，尽管该贸易公司实际上的主要职责是为政府债务融资。

尽管失去了贸易垄断权，英国政府却看到了另一个赚取利润的机会。英国政府和南海公司说服短期政府债券的持有者（约一千万英镑）来换取南海公司新发行的股票。作为交换，英国政府承诺付给南海公司永久年金，政府每年支付576,534英镑的利息，相当于一千万英镑永久性贷款总额的6%。这也保证了新的股份持有者稳定的回报。英国政府认为这是一个双赢的局面，因为它可以在从南美洲进口的商品上加税来支付利息。

---

[9] perpetual: [pə'petjuəl] *a.* 永恒的，永久的

payment by placing a tariff on the goods brought from South America.

The Treaty of Utrecht of 1713 granted the company the right to send one trading ship per year （though this was in practice accompanied by two "tenders"） and the "Asiento", the contract to supply the Spanish colonies with slaves.

The company did not undertake a trading voyage to South America until 1717 and made little actual profit.Furthermore, when ties between Spain and Britain deteriorated in 1718, the short-term prospects of the company were very poor.Nonetheless, the company continued to argue that its longer-term future would be extremely profitable.

Debt for Equity

In 1717 the company took on a further £2 million of public debt. The rationale in all these transactions was to the:

Government: lower interest rate on its debt

South Sea Company (owners): a steady stream of earnings

Government Debt Holder: upside potential in a promising enterprise

In 1719 the company proposed a scheme by which it would buy more than half the national

1713年的《乌得勒支条约》授权南海公司在西班牙殖民地进行奴隶贸易并且每年可派遣一艘商用船（尽管在实践中，这艘商用船伴有两艘护卫舰）。同时，该条约还授予南海公司从事（向西班牙殖民地）奴隶贸易的权利。

然而直到1717年，南海公司才派遣商用船到达南美洲并且实际利润很少。1718年，英国和西班牙的关系恶化，使得南海公司的短期前景十分不被看好。然而南海公司仍宣称公司的长期前景仍然十分向好，仍有巨额利润可图。

债转股

1717年南海公司增购了200万英镑的公共债券。这笔交易对各方来说都是合算的：

政府：利率降低（债务负担减轻）

南海公司：稳定的收益来源（利息收入）

债券持有者：南海公司巨大的增长潜力

1719年南海公司提议将认购一半以上的政府债券（30,981,712英

debt of Britain (£30,981,712), again with new shares, and a promise to the government that the debt would be converted to a lower interest rate, 5% until 1727 and 4% per year thereafter.

The purpose of this conversion was similar to the old one: it would allow a conversion of high interest, but difficult to trade debt, into low interest, readily marketable debt/shares of the South Sea Company. All parties could gain.

For a clarification of the situation the total government debt in 1719 was £50 million:

• £18.3 million was held by three large corporations.

• £3.4 million by the Bank of England.

• £3.2 million by the British East India Company.

• £11.7 million by the South Sea Company.

• Privately held redeemable debt amounted to £16.5 million.

• £15 million consisted of irredeemable annuities, long fixed-term annuities of 72–87 years and short annuities of 22 years remaining maturity.

Crucial in this conversion was the proportion of holders of irredeemable annuities that could be tempted to convert[10] their

镑），并承诺债券利息1727年前只有5%，在1727年后，只有4%。

这样做的目的和以前相同，为了降低政府债券的利率和为南海公司融资提供更多资源，达到双赢。

1719年，五千万英镑的政府债券主要分派给：

三家大公司持有1,830万英镑。

英格兰银行持有340万英镑。

英国东印度公司持有320万英镑。

南海公司1,170万英镑。

私有可赎回债券 1,650万英镑。

不可赎回年金，长期定期年金（72年到87年），短期年金（22年）1,500万英镑。

值得一提的是，这也使得不可赎回年金的持有者能够将其手中的债券转化为高价股票（事实上，不

---

[10] convert: [kən'və:t] v. 使转变，使……改变信仰，倒置

securities at a high price for the new shares (Holders of redeemable debt had effectively no other choice but to subscribe). The South Sea Company could set the conversion price but could obviously not diverge[11] a lot from the market price of its shares

可赎回债券的持有者除了认购，别无选择）。南海公司可以自行制定转化价格，但不可以与市场价格相差太多。

财经宝库

1. 证券（securities） 是一种表示财产权的证明文件。常见类型包括股票、债券及认股权证等。

2. 在中国，债转股是指国家组建金融资产管理公司，收购银行的不良资产，把原来银行与企业间的债权债务关系转变为金融资产管理公司与企业间的控股(或持股)与被控股的关系，债权转为股权后，原来的还本付息就转变为按股分红。国家金融资产管理公司实际上成为企业阶段性持股的股东，依法行使股东权利，参与公司重大事务决策，但不参与企业的正常生产经营活动，在企业经济状况好转以后，通过上市、转让或企业回购形式回收这笔资金。

DIY工作室

1. Why is the debt to equity transaction ending up with a failure?

2. As a comparison, what are the differences and similarities between South Sea and Tulip Mania (Unit 1)?

---

[11] diverge: [dai'vɜːdʒ] v. 分歧

归类记忆卡片

贸易垄断权 exclusive trading right	股份公司 joint stock company
永久年金 perpetual annuity	可赎回债务 redeemable debt
不可赎回债务 irredeemable debt	稳定收入来源 steady stream of earnings

听力广场

Buoy[12] the Share Price

支持股价

The company then set to talking up its stock with "the most extravagant rumors" of the value of its potential trade in the New World which was followed by a wave of "speculating frenzy". The share price had risen from the time the scheme was proposed: from £128 in January 1720, to £175 in February, £330 in

随着南海公司"最夸张的谣传"和它在新世界(南美洲)贸易的潜力,人们开始疯狂地投机。南海公司的股票价格从1720年1月的128英镑/股升到2月的175英镑/股再到3月的330英镑/股,最后达到5月底的550英镑/股。

---

[12] buoy: [bɔi] *v.* 使……浮,支撑

March and, following the scheme's acceptance, to £550 at the end of May.

What may have supported the company's high multiples (its P/E ratio) was a fund of credit (known to the market) of £70 million available for commercial expansion which had been made available through substantial support, apparently, by Parliament and the King. Shares in the company were "sold" to politicians at the current market price; however, rather than paying for the shares, these lucky recipients simply held on to what shares they had been offered, "sold" them back to the company when and as they chose, and received as "profit" the increase in market price. This method, while winning over the heads of government, the King's mistress, etc., also had the advantage of binding their interests to the interests of the Company: in order to secure their own profits, they had to help drive up the stock. Meanwhile, by publicizing the names of their elite stockholders, the Company managed to clothe itself in an aura of legitimacy, which attracted and kept other buyers.

Bubble Act

A number of other joint-stock companies then joined the market, making usually fraudulent claims about other foreign ventures

议会和国王都大力支持为商业扩张提供信贷融资（七千万英镑），人们更加看好南海公司，南海公司的市盈率居高不下。此外，南海公司按市价，将股份"卖给"这些高官，这些幸运儿高官不用花钱买股，只要持有南海公司给他们的股份，然后"卖还给"南海公司，从市场价格的增额中获得"利润"。南海公司这样做实际上有着更深远的打算。这样做不仅可以让大众看到南海公司的持股人中有很多达官显贵，从而更加相信南海公司的实力，而且还可以将这些达官显贵的利益与南海公司捆绑在一起，共同抬高南海公司的股价。与此同时，凭着达官显要作为公司的持股人，南海公司给自己披上合法的外衣，以此吸引并套住其他买家。

泡沫法案

几家其他股份公司进入市场，并谎称其他外国风险资本为"泡沫"。

or bizarre schemes, and were nicknamed "bubbles".

In June, 1720, the Royal Exchange and London Assurance Corporation Act required all joint-stock companies to have a Royal Charter. This became known as the "Bubble Act" later after the speculative bubble had burst. The real purpose of the Act was to prevent other companies competing for capital against the South Sea Company.

The South Sea Company held a charter providing exclusive access to all of Middle and South America. However, the areas in question were Spanish colonies, and Great Britain was then at war with Spain. Even once a peace treaty had been signed, relations between the two countries were not good.

The best terms that the South Sea Company was able to obtain allowed them to send only one ship per year to Spain's American colonies (not one ship per colony; exactly one ship), carrying a cargo of not more than 500 tons. Additional wrangling won the company the right to transport slaves although steep import duties made the slave trade entirely unprofitable.

The price of the stock went up over the course of a single year from one hundred pounds a share to over one thousand pounds per share. Its success caused a country-wide frenzy as citizens of all stripes——from peasants

1720年6月，皇家交易和伦敦保险公司法要求所有股份公司都需要皇家授权（后来在投机性泡沫破裂后，该法称之为"泡沫"法案）。而这项法案的真正目的是为了阻碍其他公司与南海公司争夺资本。

尽管南海公司在中美洲和南美洲享有特权，但是这些地区大都是西班牙殖民地，而英国和西班牙却处于战争状态，即使战后签署了和平协议，两国的关系也不见好。

尽管南海公司享有每年向西班牙的美洲殖民地运送一艘商船的特权（不是每块殖民地一艘商船，是整个西属美洲殖民地一艘商船），货载不得超过500吨，包括运送奴隶的特权，但是高额的进口关税使得南海公司的奴隶贸易并无利润可图。

仅用一年时间，南海公司股票价格就从100英镑/股升到1,000英镑/股。从农民到地主，人人都对炒股、投资爆发出极大的兴趣，他们投资于一般性股票，而主要投

to lords——developed a feverish interest in investing; in South Sea primarily, but in stocks generally. Among the many companies, more or less legitimate, to go public in 1720 is famously one that advertised itself as "a company for carrying out an undertaking of great advantage, but nobody to know what it is".

The price finally reached £1,000 in early August and the level of selling was such that the price started to fall, dropping back to one hundred pounds per share before the year was out, triggering bankruptcies amongst those who had bought on credit, and increasing selling, even short selling——selling borrowed shares in the hope of buying them back at a profit if the price falls.

Furthermore, the scramble for liquidity appeared internationally as "bubbles" were also ending in Amsterdam and Paris. The collapse coincided with the fall of the Mississippi Scheme of John Law in France.

By the end of September the stock had fallen to £150. The company failures now extended to banks as they could not collect loans made on the stock, and thousands of individuals were ruined. With investors outraged, Parliament was recalled in December and an investigation began. Reporting in 1721, it revealed widespread fraud amongst the company directors. The newly appointed First

资于南海公司的股票。1720年，在众多多少有点合法的上市公司中，一家公司为自己打广告上市，说本公司"有很大的优势，但没人知道"。

8月伊始，南海公司的股价达到1,000英镑/股，此后由于投资者大量抛售，年底时股价降回到一年前的100英镑/股的水平，直接引发了借钱买股票的投资者的破产潮，甚至包括很多做空的投机者——投资者依靠自己的信用借到了股票到市场上卖掉，等股价下降后再到市场上买回同一种股票赚钱。

而且，投资者的仓促兑现也使得阿姆斯特丹的郁金香泡沫和巴黎的密西西比公司泡沫开始破灭。密西西比公司泡沫的破灭与约翰·劳恩的密西西比模式的终结，正好凑合在一起。

到9月底，南海公司的股价已跌至150英镑/股。公司的破产也造成了大批银行坏账，成千上万的人遭受打击。12月议会介入，开始调查。1721年，南海公司众多高层被指控欺诈。新任政府财政大臣罗伯特·沃波尔尽管最初不同意南海公司的获利模式，此时也不得不采取一系列新举措来重铸公众信心。

Lord of the Treasury Robert Walpole, who had argued against the scheme from the beginning, was forced to introduce a series of measures to restore public confidence.

The company continued its trade (when not interrupted by war) until the end of the Seven Years' War. However, its main function was always managing government debt, rather than trading with the Spanish colonies. The South Sea Company continued its management of the part of the National Debt until it was abolished in the 1850s.

南海公司继续经营贸易直至七年战争结束（未因战争而中断）。但它的主要功能变成了管理政府债券，而不是与西班牙殖民地进行贸易。此后，南海公司继续行使其管理国债的职责，直到19世纪50年代公司被撤销为止。

非常点拨

1. **股票的市盈率**（P/E） 指每股市价除以每股盈利（Earnings Per Share, EPS），通常作为股票是便宜抑或昂贵的指标(通货膨胀会使每股收益虚增，从而扭曲市盈率的比较价值)。市盈率把企业的股价与其制造财富的能力联系起来。

投资者计算市盈率，主要用来比较不同股票的价值。理论上，股票的市盈率越低，表示该股票的投资风险越小，越值得投资。比较不同行业、不同国家、不同时段的市盈率是不大可靠的。比较同类股票的市盈率比较有实用价值。

2. **国债（又称公债、政府债券、金边债券）** 即国家借的债，是国家为筹措资金而向投资者出具的借款凭证，承诺在一定时期内按约定的条件，按期支付利息和到期归还本金。在美国，一般以国债利率为无风险收益率。中国的国债专指财政部代表中央政府发行的国家公债，由国家财政信誉作担保。相对其他债券，其信誉度非常高，一般属于稳健型投资者喜欢投资的债券。其种类有凭证式、实物券式（又叫无记名式国债或国库券）、记账式三种。

3.1713年在乌德勒支签署的一系列旨在结束西班牙王位继承战争的和约。根据和约规定，各国承认法王路易十四的孙子——腓力五世为西班牙国王。西班牙的欧洲属地被瓜分——萨伏依获得西西里和部分米兰公国的土地；神圣罗马帝国皇帝查理六世获得西属尼德兰、那不勒斯王国、撒丁尼亚和米兰公国的剩余部分。此外，西班牙割让直布罗陀和米诺卡岛给英国，并给予英国奴隶专营权。

在北美，根据第10款至第13款，法国放弃对英国哈得孙湾公司在鲁珀特、纽芬兰和阿卡迪亚地区的领地要求。法国保留圣吉恩岛（现在的爱德华王子岛）和布雷顿角岛（此地建立了路易斯堡要塞）。

乌德勒支和约签订后，法国与查理六世皇帝和神圣罗马帝国之间仍处于战争状态，直到1714年拉什塔特和约及巴登和约签订为止。西班牙和葡萄牙之间的战争状态直到1715年《马德里条约》签订才告正式结束。西班牙与神圣罗马帝国则在1720年方才签署和约。

乌德勒支和约的一方是路易十四和腓力五世，另一方是英国的安妮女王、联省和萨伏依公国。

4. **西班牙王位继承战争（1701～1714年）** 是因为西班牙哈布斯堡王朝绝嗣，法国的波旁王室与奥地利的哈布斯堡王室为争夺西班牙王位而引发的一场欧洲大部分国家参与的大战。

Battle of Vigo Bay
维果湾战争

William Cecil, 1st Baron Burghly
威廉·赛西尔，波弗利第一男爵

Mississippi Company

Unit 3

Mississippi Company
密西西比公司

主题札记

密西西比公司是一家18世纪时的法国公司，当时它主要的目的是要在隶属于法国的北美地区密西西比河流域从事贸易和开发等商业活动，该公司的经营状况极差但是股价却暴涨到发行价格的40倍以上，是近代三大泡沫经济事件之一。

1717年8月，由一名叫做John Law 的商人所买下，当时法国政府承诺给他25年的垄断经营权。密西西比公司先后以其雄厚的财力发展出了法兰西东印度公司和法兰西银行。在这段时间之内，该公司的股票由500里弗涨到15,000里弗。但是在1720年夏天时，投资者对这家公司的信心大减，结果一年之内股票价格跌回500里弗。

Investors outside the Offices of the Mississippi Company in Quincampoix Street (1720)
昆坎波斯大街密西西比办公室外的投资者（1720年）

阅读长廊

Mississippi Company（I）

密西西比公司（上）

In August 1717, Scottish businessman John Law acquired a controlling interest in the then derelict Mississippi Company and renamed it Compagnie du Mississippi. Its initial goal was to trade and do business with the French colonies in North America, which included much of the Mississippi River drainage basin, and the French colony of Louisiana.

As he bought control of the company, he was granted a 25-year monopoly by the French government on trade with the West Indies and North America. In 1719 the company acquired the Compagnie des Indes Orientales, the Compagnie de China, and other French trading companies and became the Compagnie des Indes. In 1720 it acquired the Banque Royale, which was founded by John Law as Banque Générale in 1716.

Law exaggerated the wealth of Louisiana with an effective marketing scheme, which led

1717年8月，苏格兰商人约翰·劳恩收购了密西西比公司并将其重新命名。该公司最初以经营法国在北美地区殖民地贸易为主，包括密西西比河流域的大部分地区和法属殖民地路易斯安那地区。

收购密西西比公司使得约翰·劳恩获得了法国政府授予的在西印度地区和北美进行垄断贸易的25年特权。1719年公司兼并了东印度公司，中国公司和其他几家法国贸易公司合并成为印度公司。1720年公司还兼并了皇家银行（该银行于1716年由约翰·劳恩建立起名为兴业银行）。

约翰·劳恩通过有效的市场手段吹大了路易斯安那地区的财富，

to wild speculation on the shares of the company in 1719. Shares rose from 500 to 15,000 livres, but by summer of 1720, there was a sudden decline in confidence, and the price was back to 500 livres in 1721.

Debt Conversion

The number of outstanding shares of the company was probably around 500,000 in 1720. A stock price of 15,000 livres would have given the company a market capitalization of 7.5 billion livres. After the share price collapsed to 500 livres in September 1721, the company was valued at only 250 million livres. As a comparison, the French government expense was 150 million livres in 1700, while their debt in 1719 was 1.6 billion livres.

With the demand for company shares being high, the government and John Law set out to buy back the whole 1.6 billion livres government debt for shares in the company. The plan was successful and in 1720 the whole government debt was acquired by the company, before the company's market capitalization began to collapse during 1720 and 1721.

Compare this with the debt acquisition by The South Sea Company of England that acquired 80% of the 50 million pound government debt during 1720. The South Sea

招来了1719年大量对公司股票的投机行为。公司股价从500里弗升到15,000里弗，然而到1720年夏季由于投资者信心骤跌，1721年公司股价回落到500里弗。

债券转换

1720年公司的股本大约为五十万份，每股15,000里弗可以使得公司融资75亿里弗。当股价于1721年9月回落到500里弗时，公司市值仅为两亿五千万里弗。作为比较，1700年法国政府支出为一亿五千万里弗，然而1719年时，政府负债高达16亿里弗。

鉴于公司股票需求旺盛，政府和约翰·劳恩买回全部法国政府16亿里弗的政府债务换成了公司股份。 这项计划在1720年取得了成功，政府债务全部被密西西比公司收购，然而随后，密西西比公司市值在1720年和1721年开始跳水。

把以上情况与同期（1720年）英国南海公司收购了80%（5,000万）的政府债务，其股价于当年8月达到1,000英镑的历史最高点，

Company reached a highest share price of 1,000 pounds in August 1720, a few months later than the Compagnie des Indes.

As the creditors bought shares in the company with their Bonds and debt papers, the whole government debt became property of the company (debt-for-equity transaction). And the company became property of the former creditors, but effectively controlled by the government. Primarily the government paid an annual 3% interest to the company, which amounted to 48 million livres. Through these transactions the French government had successfully unloaded their whole gigantic debt of 1,000% the annual budget (perhaps 200% – 400% of GDP) and was basically debt free.

Reopened in 1722

The company sought bankruptcy[13] protection in 1721. It was reorganized and opened for business in 1722. In 1723 it was granted fresh privileges by Louis XV. Among these were the monopoly[14] of sale of tobacco and coffee, and the right to organise national lotteries. It could again tap the capital markets and raise capital by issue of shares and bonds[15].

仅比印度公司晚了几个月。

　　当债权人用手中的政府债券买公司的股份时，政府债券就变成了公司的资产（债转股交易），而公司成了前债权人的财产，但为政府有效控制。总之，政府每年只付给公司3%的利息，合4,800万里弗。这样，法国政府通过这些交易将身上的巨额负债（10倍的年度政府预算，也许相当于GDP的2到4倍）卸掉。

1722年的重建

　　1721年公司申请了破产保护，并在重组后于1722年重新开业。1723年，路易十五授予公司新的特权，其中有烟草和咖啡的垄断销售权和开展全国彩票业的特权。这使得公司通过发行债券和股票的方式重新进入资本市场筹集资本。

---

[13] bankruptcy: ['bæŋkrəp(t)si] *n.* 破产
[14] monopoly: [mə'nɔpəli] *n.* 垄断，专利
[15] bond: [bɔnd] *n.* 结合债券，黏结剂，黏合剂

After 1746 the spendthrift policies of the French Government began to hurt the Company, and the Seven Years' War (1756 - 1763) brought severe losses. In February 1770, an edict required the Company to transfer to the state all its properties, assets and rights, then valued to just 30 million livres while the King accepted to pay all the Company's debts and annuity (rente) obligations. The company was officially dissolved in 1770 although its liquidation dragged on into the 1790s.

1746年以后，法国政府的挥霍政策终于伤害到了公司，七年战争（1756～1763年）更是带来了严重的损失。1770年2月，一项命令规定公司将其所有财产、资产和权益国有化（当时价值仅3,000万里弗），而国王同意偿还公司的所有债务和年金。1770年，公司正式宣布解散，而清算工作一直拖到18世纪90年代才进行。

财经宝库

1. 债券是投资者凭以定期获得利息、到期归还本金及利息的证书。发债人须于债券到期日前按期支付早前承诺的利息，并在到期日以指定价格向债券持有人赎回债券（即归还本金）。根据发行方不同，可分为政府债券、金融债券以及公司债券。投资者购入债券，就如借出资金给政府、大企业或其他债券发行机构。这三者中，政府债券因为有政府税收作为保障，因而风险最小，但收益也最小。公司债券风险最大，可能的收益也最大。债券持有者是债权人(creditors)，发行者为债务人(debtors)。与银行信贷不同的是，债券是一种直接债务关系。银行信贷通过存款人—银行，银行—贷款人形成间接的债务关系。债券不论何种形式，大都可以在市场上进行

Jackson Square – Andrew Jackson Statue (The site of the original settlement of New Orleans by the French Mississippi Company in 1721)
加克森广场——安德鲁·加克森像（原址于1721年建于新奥尔良的法国密西西比公司）

买卖，并因此形成了债券市场。

2. 投机（speculation），不同于投资，是指货币所有者将其所持有的货币购买非货币资产，主要以期望未来将早先购买的非货币资产转换为货币资产时获得比原先购买时所支付的价格高的差额，即差价。

1. Why do you think the French government would like the debt-to-equity transaction with Mississippi Company?

2. In the end, who do you think suffer most from the stock bubble breaking down?

3. Why do you think the bubble happens from a wider perspective?

债券 bond
投机 speculation
破产保护 bankruptcy protection

彩票 lottery
垄断 monopoly
特权 privilege

Mississippi Company (II)
Company Profits and Dividends

密西西比公司（下）
公司利润和分红

In 1705, John Law had sketched a financial system and monetary theory in which an emission of paper currency would expand real commerce permanently (Money and Trade Considered With a Proposal for Supplying the Nation with Money). He argued that metallic money was unreliable in quality and quantity. Bank notes issued and managed by a public bank would remove the brakes on the economy. Demand for the new currency was thought to increase sufficiently to preclude pressure on prices. Although the theory clearly did not work in practice, Law's theory was considered plausible and has many modern manifestations even today (he is frequently considered to have been the world's first Keynesian).

Investors observed Law's expanding commercial enterprise and must have factored in the possibility of success. Apart from the

1705年，约翰·劳恩在他的贸易与国家货币供给的论述中提出了他关于货币和金融系统的主张。他认为发行货币可以永久性地带动商业活动。他认为金属货币无论是质量和数量上都不可靠。公共银行发行和管理的银行券会消除经济发展的阻碍，而对新货币的需求也会对价格产生压力。尽管在实际中行不通，劳恩的理论有很多值得肯定的地方，甚至在今天还有很多闪光的地方（他经常被认为是世界上最早的凯恩斯主义者）。

投资者们只要关注劳恩的商业扩大计划就有可能取得成功。除了政府债券转化项目和商业项目获利

profits from commercial enterprise and the government debt conversion program, the de facto expansionary monetary policy could also be perceived as stimulating economic activity and substantially increasing the profits from tax collection as well.

One estimate of the possible annual net revenues of the Compagnie looked as follows.

Interest paid by the King on loans 1,600 million livres (3% annual interest)   48,000,000

Profits from collection of indirect taxes	15,000,000
Profits from collection of other taxes	1,500,000
Profits from tobacco	2,000,000
Profits from the mint	4,000,000
Profits from trading	10,000,000
Total	80,500,000

Net present value calculations depend on the discount rate. At that time the Banque Royale was lending money at 2% interest, which suggests a NPV of 80.5/0.02=4,025 million livres, on the assumption that profits continued in perpetuity.

With between 312,000–600,000 shares actually in circulation this implies a share value of 6,700 – 12,900 livres (it is not clear how

外，劳恩的货币扩张政策还可以刺激经济增长并大幅提高税收。

有人估算了当时公司的年净收益。

来自对国王的十六亿里弗贷款利息收入（贷款3%的年利率）48,000,000

间接税收	15,000,000
其他税收	1,500,000
烟草	2,000,000
薄荷	4,000,000
贸易	10,000,000
总计	80,500,000

因为计算折现净值需要折现率，以皇家银行2%的利率来计算，假如收益可持续，当时公司的折现净值为四十亿两千五百万里弗（以永久年金为例）。

当时大概有31.2万到60万股份在流通，这意味着每股的价值为6,700~12,900里弗（我们不清楚究

many of the authorised shares were actually sold and/or repurchased).

Another calculation takes the announcement by the Compagnie in August 1719 of a dividend per share of at least 200 livres. Share value would be 200 / 0.02 = 10,000 livres. Historical research shows that financial investors at the time were fully aware of present value calculations for stock and bond prices.

Of course, these calculations cannot establish the true fundamental value; such a concept does not exist in reality. Financial market prices on the upside are determined by the so-called marginal optimistic investors, ready to buy at high prices. These calculations can only show that their expectations were not without consideration of fundamental value.

Without doubt, some or even many investors disagreed and decided not to participate in Compagnie shares. They were proven right, but with proof available only after the share price collapse.

Monetary Policy Aspects

The Mississippi Bubble is partly a story about inflation and subsequent deflation (i.e., misguided monetary policy). Starting with the July 1719 stock issue, each stock issue of the

竟有多少注册的股份在交易）。

另外一种方法是根据公司在1719年8月的红利来计算（每份200里弗）。股价约为一万里弗。历史研究表明，当时的金融投资者已经谙熟计算股票和债券价格现值的方法。

当然，这些计算方法并不能反映公司当时全部的状况，因为它们只是理论上的概念。金融市场上的价格是由投资者的边际效用决定的。投资者在作出预期时只是对这些基本概念加以考虑。

毫无疑问，有些甚至很多投资者都会有不同的看法而且不会购买密西西比公司的股票。结果证明他们是对的，因为密西西比公司股价之后狂跌。

货币政策方面

密西西比泡沫可以理解为一场错误的货币政策导致的通货膨胀和之后的通货紧缩（即误导性的货币政策）。从1719年7月密西西比公

Compagnie was accompanied by a note issue of the Banque Royale. In July 1719 a note issue of 240 million livres was authorized to more than double the 159 million notes previously in circulation. Note issue expanded with share issues in September/October 1719 (240million), December 1719 (360million) and February 1720 (200million) to a total of 1,199 million livres.

From February 1720 Banque Royale's notes were made legal tender for payments above 100 livres. Furthermore, from February 1720, any person was forbidden to have possession of more than 500 livres in coins. From March 1720 share prices were pegged at 9,000 livres because the Banque Royale intervened to exchange its notes for Compagnie stock. Pegging continued until May 1720 but caused note expansion of 1,490 million livres between March and May.

In May 1720 total specie[16] stock of France was estimated at 1.2 billion livres. Therefore, money circulation of specie and notes had increased by 186% within one-year(3,889/1,359-1). As a result of the increase in money, prices (measured as the price level in Paris) also doubled between July 1719 and December 1720. Therefore, a substantial part of the increase in the nominal share price of the

司股票发行以来，每份公司股票都有皇家银行发行的纸币与之对应。因此，发行价值2亿4千万里弗的股票也就意味着将有新的2亿4千万的货币进入市场流通，这超过之前流通量（1亿5千9百万）的两倍。而之后的几次新货币发行都伴随着股票的大量增发。1719年9月和10月（2亿4千万里弗），12月3亿6千万里弗和1720年2月2亿里弗，共计11亿9千9百万里弗。

1720年2月，皇家银行的票据成了支付100里弗以上的法偿。1720年2月之后，任何人不得持有500里弗以上的硬币。1720年3月，由于皇家银行的介入（购买密西西比公司股票），密西西比公司的股价被维持在9,000里弗之上。然而这也导致了3月到5月，票据增长了14亿9千万里弗。

1720年5月，法国硬币股票的价值估算为12亿里弗，因此流通的货币一年之内便增长了186%，这也导致了物价（以巴黎的物价水平衡量）从1719年7月到1720年12月翻了一倍。因此，密西西比公司名义股价的上涨其中一个重要的原因便是通货膨胀，而公司股价的真正上升是由其他因素决定的。

---

[16] specie: ['spi:ʃi] *n.* 正币，硬币

Compagnie must be considered inflation[17]. The remaining increase in the real share price must be explained by other fundamentals.

非常点拨

    1. 在18世纪初，由于法国国王路易十四连年发动战争，使得法国国民经济陷入极度困难之中，经济萧条，通货紧缩。当时法国的税制极不健全，不仅对法国王室贵族豁免税收，而且其他地方的漏洞也很多，尽管法国政府不断提高税率，穷征暴敛，依然入不敷出，国库空虚，债台高筑，百姓怨声载道，国家危机重重。

    2. 就在这个关头，一代怪杰约翰·劳恩（John Law）的货币理论应运而生。约翰·劳恩出生于英国爱丁堡，青年时代接受了良好的政治经济学教育。年轻时的约翰·劳恩血气方刚，他在1694年一场决斗中杀了人而不得不逃亡他乡。约翰·劳恩在欧洲流浪时期仔细观察了各国的银行、金融和保险业，从而提出了他独特的金融理论。

    3. 和许多18世纪的经济学家一样，约翰·劳恩认为在就业不足的情况下，增加货币供给可以在不提高物价水平的前提下增加就业机会并增加国民产出。一旦产出增加之后，对货币的需求也会相应跟上来。在实现了充分就业之后，货币扩张能够吸引外部资源，进一步增加产出。他认为纸币本位制要比贵金属本位制更好，纸币本位制具有更大的灵活性，给了发行纸币的银行更多的运转空间和控制宏观经济的能力（参见Law，1760）。说白了，采用贵金属本位制，发行货币要看手上有多少金银。

    4. 之所以被称为贵金属，是因为金银在世界上的储量有限，几乎不可能在短时间内增加金银的供给量。纸币本位制就没有这个限制。如果金融当局愿意的话，启动银行的印钞机，要印多少就可以印多少。纸币本位制的这个特点使之像一把"双刃剑"，在增强了金融货币政策影响力的同时，也带来了导致通货膨胀的危险。

    5. 约翰·劳恩认为拥有货币发行权的银行应当提供生产信贷和足够的通货来保证经济繁荣。他所说的货币供给中包括了政府法定货币、银行发行的纸币、股票和各种有价证券（参见Michael Bordo，1994）。不难看出，在约翰·劳恩的理论中已经蕴藏了当代供给学派和货币学派的一些基本观点。著名的经济学家熊·彼得曾经高度赞扬说，约翰·劳恩的金融理论使他在任何时候都可以跻身于一流货币理论家的行列。

---

[17] inflation: [inˈfleiʃən] *n*. 通货膨胀

Topic Two　Recent Financial Crisis

The Great Depression

Unit 4

The Great Depression
大萧条

主题札记

大萧条

大萧条，是指1929年至1939年全球性的经济大衰退。

1929年经济大萧条的影响比历史上任何一次经济衰退都要深远。这次经济萧条是以农产品价格下跌为起点的：首先发生在木材的价格上（1928年），这主要是由于苏联的木材竞争的缘故，但更大的灾难是在1929年到来的，加拿大小麦的过量生产，美国强迫压低所有农产品产地基本谷物的价格。不管是欧洲、美洲还是澳洲，农业衰退由于金融的大崩溃而进一步恶化，尤其在美国，一股投机热导致大量资金从欧洲抽回，随后在1929年10月发生了令人恐慌的华尔街股市暴跌。1931年法国银行家收回了给奥地利银行的贷款，但这并不足以偿还债务。这场灾难使中欧和东欧许多国家的制度破产了：它导致了德国银行家为了自保而延期偿还外债，进而也危及到了在德国有很多投资的英国银行家。资本的短缺在所有的工业化国家中都带来了出口和国内消费的锐减：没有市场必然使工厂关闭，货物越少，货物运输也就越少，这必然会危害船运业和造船业。在所有国家中，经济衰退的后果是大规模失业：美国1,370万人，德国560万人，英国280万人（1932年的数据）。大萧条对拉丁美洲也有重大影响，使得一个几乎被欧美银行家和商人企业家完全支配的地区失去了外资和商品出口。据估计，大萧条时期，世界的钱财损失达2,500亿美元。

阅读长廊

The Great Depression

大萧条

The Great Depression was a worldwide economic downturn starting in most places in 1929 and ending at different times in the 1930s or early 1940s for different countries. It was the largest and most important economic depression in modern history, and is used in the 21st century as a benchmark in how far the world's economy can fall. The Great Depression originated in the United States; historians most often use as a starting date the stock market crashed on October 29, 1929, known as Black Tuesday. The end of the depression in the U.S. is associated with the onset[18] of the war economy of World War II, beginning around 1939.

The depression had devastating effects in the developed and developing worlds. International trade was deeply affected, as were personal

经济大萧条是指始于1929年止于20世纪30年代或40年代早期（不同国家结束时间不同）的波及大部分地区的世界性经济衰退。它是现代历史上规模最大最为重要的一次经济衰退，并被用来作为衡量21世纪经济下滑幅度的基准。此次大萧条始于美国，历史学家常把1929年10月29日美国华尔街股市的大崩盘作为其起点，那一天被称为"黑色星期二"。大萧条在美国的结束常与始于大约1939年的第二次世界大战中的美国战时经济的开端联系在一起。

这次大萧条在发达国家和发展中国家都产生了摧毁性的影响。国际贸易深受其害，个人收益，

---

[18] onset: ['ɔnset] *n.* 攻击，进攻，肇端

incomes, tax revenues, prices, and profits. Cities all around the world were hit hard, especially those dependent on heavy industry. Construction was virtually halted in many countries. Farming and rural areas suffered as crop prices fell by 40 percent to 60 percent. Facing plummeting demand with few alternate sources of jobs, areas dependent on primary sector industries such as farming, mining and logging suffered the most. However, even shortly after the Wall Street Crash of 1929, optimism persisted; John D. Rockefeller said that "These are days when many are discouraged. In the 93 years of my life, depressions have come and gone. Prosperity has always returned and will again".

The Great Depression ended at different times in different countries; for subsequent history see Home front during World War Ⅱ. The majority of countries set up relief programs, and most underwent some sort of political upheaval, pushing them to the left or right. In some states, the desperate citizens turned toward nationalist demagogues[19]—— the most infamous being Adolf Hitler——setting the stage for World War Ⅱ in 1939.

The Snowball Spiral

The Great Depression was not a sudden

税收收入，物价和利润也同样受到波及。大萧条对世界上大部分的城市打击沉重，尤其是那些依赖重工业的城市。很多国家的建设实际上被迫停止。农业和农村也因农作物价格40%到60%的大幅下跌损失惨重。由于需求大幅下跌，工作机会剧减，依赖第一产业如农业、采矿业和伐木业的地区损失最为惨重。然而，继华尔街1929年股市崩盘后不久，乐观主义情绪开始出现；约翰·D.洛克菲勒曾说："这些天是大多数人颇为沮丧的日子，在我93年的生命历程中，萧条现象反复出现，繁荣总会再次到来，这次也不例外"。

大萧条在不同国家结束的时间各不相同，随后见证了第二次世界大战中各个国家的应对措施。大部分国家建立了援助项目，很多都经历了某种程度上的政治动荡，促其转向左翼或转向右翼。在一些国家，绝望的民众顺从了民族主义者的煽动——最为臭名昭著的当属阿道夫·希特勒——他为1939年开始的世界大战筑好了舞台。

滚雪球般的连锁反应

大萧条并非是一种突然的全盘

---

[19] demagogue: ['deməgɔg] *n.* 煽动者，群众煽动者

total collapse. The stock market turned upward in early 1930, returning to early 1929 levels by April, though still almost 30 percent below the peak of September 1929. Together, government and business actually spent more in the first half of 1930 than in the corresponding period of the previous year. But consumers, many of whom had suffered severe losses in the stock market the previous year, cut back their expenditures by 10 percent, and a severe drought ravaged the agricultural heartland of the USA beginning in the northern summer of 1930.

In early 1930, credit was ample and available at low rates, but people were reluctant to add new debt by borrowing. By May 1930, auto sales had declined to below the levels of 1928. Prices in general began to decline, but wages held steady in 1930, then began to drop in 1931. Conditions were worst in farming areas, where commodity prices plunged, and in mining and logging areas, where unemployment was high and there were few other jobs. The decline in the American economy was the factor that pulled down most other countries at first, then internal weaknesses or strengths in each country made conditions worse or better. Frantic attempts to shore[20] up the economies of individual nations through protectionist policies, such as the 1930 U.S. *Smoot-Hawley Tariff*

崩溃。事实上，股市在1930年初期转好，并到4月重新回到1929年时的水平，尽管比1929年9月高峰时期的水平低30%。跟1929年同期相比，政府和企业一起在1930年上半年同比增加更多消费开支。但许多消费者由于在1929年的股市崩盘中损失严重都缩减了10%的消费开支，与此同时，始于1930年夏天美国北部的一场严重的干旱给美国的农业中心地带造成严重破坏。

1930年年初，美国信贷充足且利率较低，但人们不愿意通过借贷而增加债务。到1930年5月，汽车销售量降至1928年时的水平以下。1930年，物价总体上开始下降，工资水平稳定，但从1931年开始下跌。在农业区，由于商品价格猛跌，境况最为悲惨；在采矿和伐木区，失业率很高且无其他工作可找。起初美国经济的下滑拖累了很多国家，随后由于每个国家国内境况的不同从而使得情势变好或更糟。个别国家通过保护主义政策企图提振经济的疯狂尝试比如1930年美国的《斯穆特—霍利关税法》和其他国家的报复性关税的实施加剧了全球贸易的崩溃。到1930年年底，稳定下滑局面开始出现并于1933年3月滑至最低点。

---

[20] shore: [[ɔː],[ɔə] *n.* 岸，滨

Act and retaliatory tariffs in other countries, exacerbated[21] the collapse in global trade. By late 1930, a steady decline set in which reached bottom by March 1933.

Causes

U.S. industrial production (1928–1939)

There were multiple causes for the first downturn in 1929, including the structural weaknesses and specific events that turned it into a major depression and the way in which the downturn spread from country to country. In relation to the 1929 downturn, historians emphasize structural factors like massive bank failures and the stock market crash, while economists (such as Peter Temin and Barry Eichengreen) point to Britain's decision to return to the Gold Standard at pre-World War I parities (US$4.86: £ 1).

Recession cycles are thought to be a normal part of living in a world of inexact balances between supply and demand. What turns a usually mild and short recession or "ordinary" business cycle into a great depression is a subject of debate and concern. Scholars have not agreed on the exact causes and their relative

起因

美国1928～1939年的工业生产

美国1929年的经济初步下滑原因众多，包括经济结构薄弱和使经济下滑转为大衰退的具体事件以及经济衰退从一国向另一国传递的方式等原因。关于1929年的经济低迷，史学家们强调的是结构性因素，如大量银行倒闭、股市崩盘，而经济学家们（像Peter Temin 和 Barry Eichengreen）则归咎于英国政府作出的回归到第一次世界大战以前的金本位制的决定（4.86美元兑1英镑）。

在一个供求均衡并不精确的世界里，经济衰退周期性出现实属正常。促使一次温和而短期的经济衰退或"平常的"经济周期转向大萧条的因素往往是人们争论和关注的话题。学者们对大萧条的确切起因及其相关重要性并没有达成一致意见。对于大萧条起因的找寻和未来

---

[21] exacerbate: [ik'sæsəbeit] *vt.* 使加剧，使恶化

importance. The search for causes is closely connected to the question of how to avoid a future depression, and so the political and policy viewpoints of scholars are mixed into the analysis of historic events eight decades ago. The even larger question is whether it was largely a failure on the part of free markets or largely a failure on the part of governments to curtail widespread bank failures, the resulting panics, and reduction in the money supply. Those who believe in a large role for the state in the economy believe it was mostly a failure of the free markets and those who believe in free markets believe it was mostly a failure of government that compounded the problem.

Current theories may be broadly classified into three main points of view. First, there is orthodox classical economics: monetarist, Austrian Economics and neoclassical economic theory, all of which focus on the macroeconomic effects of money supply and the supply of gold which backed many currencies before the Great Depression, including production and consumption.

USA GDP annual pattern and long-term trend, 1920–1940, in billions of dollars at constant prices.

Second, there are structural theories, most importantly Keynesian, but also including those of institutional economics, that point

如何避免新的衰退的问题常常是紧密相连的。所以现在学者们政治和政策的视角与80年前对于历史事件的分析结合在了一起。现在更为重大的一个问题是这次大萧条在很大程度上是自由市场的失败还是政府干预（诸如减少银行的大量倒闭，控制由此引起的恐慌情绪和削减货币供应等）的失败。那些相信国家在自由市场上起主导作用的人认为这主要是自由市场的失败而那些信仰自由市场的人认为这主要是政府的失败从而使得问题复杂化。

当前的理论大致可以分为三种观点。第一，正统的古典经济学理论：货币主义者、奥地利经济学和新古典经济学理论，他们都主张要重视货币供给的宏观经济影响和在大萧条以前支撑着很多种货币的黄金供给，包括生产方面和消费方面。

美国GDP的年度模型和其长期趋势，1920～1940年，以数十亿美元的不变价格计。

第二，结构主义理论，最主要的是凯恩斯主义者，但也包括制度经济学，其研究消费不足和过度投

to underconsumption and overinvestment (economic bubble), malfeasance[22] by bankers and industrialists, or incompetence by government officials. The only consensus viewpoint is that there was a large-scale lack of confidence. Unfortunately, once panic and deflation set in, many people believed they could make more money by keeping clear of the markets as prices got lower and lower and a given amount of money bought ever more goods.

Third, there is the Marxist critique of political economy. This emphasizes contradictions within capital itself (which is viewed as a social relation involving the appropriation of surplus value) as giving rise to an inherently unbalanced dynamic of accumulation resulting in an overaccumulation of capital, culminating in periodic crises of devaluation of capital. The origin of crisis is thus located firmly in the sphere of production though economic crisis can be aggravated by problems of disproportionality of over-production in the manufacturing and related production sectors and the underconsumption of the masses.

资（经济泡沫）以及银行家和工业家的不法行为问题，或者是政府官员的无能。大范围的缺乏信心是唯一达成的共识点所在。不幸的是，一旦恐慌和通货紧缩开始出现，很多人认为随着物价越来越低，定量的钱将能够买到更多的商品，从而他们能够通过远离市场而赚到更多的钱。

第三，马克思主义者对政治经济学的评论。强调资本自身的矛盾（被看成是一种包括对剩余价值占有的一种社会关系）随着产生一种固有的积累的动态不平衡导致资本的过度积累，并导致资本贬值的周期性危机达到极点。危机产生的根源被看做在生产环节，尽管危机会因为在制造业中过度生产的分配不均和相关的生产环节以及大众的消费不足而恶化。

---

[22] malfeasance: [mæl'fi:zəns] n. 不正当，不法行为，坏事

财经宝库

1. Black Tuesday "黑色星期二"　1929年10月29日，美国华尔街股市大崩盘，这一天被称为"黑色星期二"。黑色星期四、黑色星期一，也经常用来形容这次股市风暴。1929年10月24日，即黑色星期四，股市首次出现崩盘，并于10月28日和29日继续恶化，造成灾难性经济衰退，引起全民恐慌，美国经济陷入困境。

2. U.S. *Smoot-Hawley Tariff Act*美国《斯穆特—霍利关税法》　该关税法案于1930年6月17日正式签署为法律，规定对20,000多种美国进口货物征收关税。法案实施后，许多国家对美国进行报复，提高了进口美国货物的关税。因而，美国的进出口总额下降了一半以上。许多经济学家认为，该法案是在大萧条中，美欧贸易从1929年高水平下降到1932年低水平状态的催化剂。

3. Gold Standard 金本位　金本位是一种金属货币制度。在金本位制下，每单位的货币价值等同于若干重量的黄金（即货币含金量）；当不同国家使用金本位时，国家之间的汇率由它们各自货币的含金量之比——金平价（Gold Parity）来决定。金本位制于19世纪中期开始盛行。金本位制总共有三种实现形式，它们是金币本位制、金块本位制、金汇兑本位制，其中金币本位制最具有金本位制的代表性。

4. Business Cycle 商业周期　也称为经济周期，是指经济活动在长期增长中出现的波动。此过程涉及经济从较快增长期（复兴与繁荣）到停滞或下降期（收缩或衰退）的发展变化。这些波动经常用实际国内生产总值来衡量。尽管被称为周期，在经济增长与衰退的过程中，这些波动并不完全遵循机械的、可预见的周期模式。

DIY工作室

1. Why was the Great Depression spreading within the industrialized countries?

2. Why does each school of economists disagre with others?

3. What do they mostly agree on?

归类记忆卡片

primary sector 第一产业
retaliatory tariff 报复性关税
classical economics 古典经济学

relief program 救助计划
business cycle 经济（商业）周期
monetarist 货币学派/货币主义者

听力广场

Debt Deflation

Irving Fisher argued that the predominant factor leading to the Great Depression was overindebtedness and deflation. Fisher tied loose credit to over-indebtedness, which fueled speculation and asset bubbles. He then outlined 9 factors interacting with one another under conditions of debt and deflation to create the mechanics of boom to bust. The chain of events proceeded as follows: (1) Debt liquidation and distress selling. (2) Contraction of the money supply as bank loans are paid off. (3) A fall in the level of asset prices. (4) A still greater fall in the net worths of business, precipitating bankruptcies. (5) A fall in profits. (6) A reduction in output, in trade and in employment. (7) Pessimism and loss of confidence. (8) Hoarding[23] of money. (9) A fall

债务通缩理论

欧文·费雪认为导致这次大萧条的主要因素是过度负债和通货紧缩。费雪认为松散的信贷与过度负债导致了投机和资产泡沫。然后他描述了在债务和通货紧缩的情况下相互作用的、造成由繁荣转向破产的机制的9个因素。这一系列的事件按如下步骤进行：(1)债务清偿，销售受阻；(2)随着银行贷款的偿付，货币供应开始收缩；(3)资产价格水平下降；(4)企业净值的大幅下跌加速了破产；(5)利润下降；(6)产出减少，贸易和就业水平下滑；(7)悲观主义大行其道，信心丧失；(8)贮藏货币；(9)名义利率下降，通货紧缩调整后的利率上升。

---

[23] hoard: [hɔːd] *vt.* 贮藏

in nominal interest rates and a rise in deflation adjusted interest rates.

During the Crash of 1929 proceeding the Great Depression, margin requirements were only 10%. Brokerage firms, in other words, would loan $9 for every $1 an investor had deposited. When the market fell, brokers called in these loans, which could not be paid back. Banks began to fail as debtors defaulted on debt and depositors attempted to withdraw their deposits en masse[24], triggering multiple bank runs. Government guarantees and Federal Reserve banking regulations to prevent such panics were ineffective or not used. Bank failures led to the loss of billions of dollars in assets. Outstanding debts became heavier because prices and incomes fell by 20%– 50% but the debts remained at the same dollar amount. After the panic of 1929, and during the first 10 months of 1930, 744 U.S. banks failed. (In all, 9,000 banks failed during the 1930s). By 1933, depositors had lost $140 billion in deposits.

Bank failures snowballed as desperate bankers called in loans which the borrowers did not have time or money to repay. With future profits looking poor, capital investment and construction slowed or completely ceased.

在大萧条前的1929年股市大崩盘中，保证金仅为10%。换句话说，经纪公司每得到一个投资者所存的1美元就要借入9美元。当市场不景气时，经纪商借入的这些贷款无法收回。当债务人拖欠贷款而存款人又大量取回存款而引发大量银行挤提时，银行开始倒闭。政府担保和联邦储备银行有关防止此类恐慌的规章效果不佳或者这些规定并没有被有效使用。银行倒闭致使数亿美元的资产损失。因为物价和收入水平下滑了20%~50%，但债务却保持在同量的美元水平从而使未清偿债务变得更为巨大。在1929年大恐慌之后的1930年的头10个月里有744家美国银行倒闭（20世纪30年代总共有9,000家银行倒闭）。到1933年，储户损失了1,400亿美元的存款。

随着绝望的银行家们收回贷款，然而借款人却没有时间或没有钱偿还时，银行倒闭就像滚雪球般的多起来。随着未来的收益不被看好，资本投资和建设放慢或完全停止。面对不良贷款和日益恶化的前

---

[24] en masse: [aŋ'mæs] ad. 全体地，一同地

In the face of bad loans and worsening future prospects, the surviving banks became even more conservative[25] in their lending. Banks built up their capital reserves and made fewer loans, which intensified deflationary pressures. A vicious cycle developed and the downward spiral accelerated. This kind of self-aggravating process turned a 1930 recession into a 1933 great depression.

The liquidation of debt could not keep up with the fall of prices which it caused. The mass effect of their stampede to liquidate increased the value of each dollar they owed, relative to the value of their declining asset holdings. The very effort of individuals to lessen their burden of debt effectively increased it. Paradoxically, the more the debtors paid, the more they owed.

Macroeconomists including Ben Bernanke, the current chairman of the U.S. Federal Reserve Bank, have revived the debt–deflation view of the Great Depression originated by Fisher.

Trade Decline and the U.S. *Smoot-Hawley Tariff Act*

Many economists have argued that the

景，幸存的银行在借贷方面变得更加保守。银行建立了资本储备，并减少贷款，这样做加剧了通货紧缩压力。如此就形成了一个恶性循环并且螺旋下降趋势加快。这种自我恶化的过程导致1930年的经济衰退转变为1933年的大萧条。

债务清偿不能跟由其导致的物价下降保持一致。民众蜂拥挤提的大规模效应反而增加了他们所欠的债务的价值（相对于其所持有的下滑的资产价值而言）。个人想减轻自己债务压力的努力反而有效地增加了压力。自相矛盾的是，债务人偿还的越多，他们欠的也就越多。

宏观经济学家们包括美联储现任主席本·伯南克已经接受了由费雪提出的大萧条的债务–通货紧缩的观点。

贸易下滑和美国《斯穆特—霍利关税法》

不少经济学家认为，1930年

---

[25] conservative: [kən'sə:vətiv] *a.* 保守的

sharp decline in international trade after 1930 helped to worsen the depression, especially for countries significantly dependent on foreign trade. Most historians and economists partly blame the American *Smoot-Hawley Tariff Act* (enacted June 17, 1930) for worsening the depression by seriously reducing international trade and causing retaliatory tariffs in other countries. Foreign trade was a small part of overall economic activity in the United States and was concentrated in a few businesses like farming; it was a much larger factor in many other countries. The average ad valorem rate of duties on dutiable imports for 1921–1925 was 25.9% but under the new tariff it jumped to 50% in 1931–1935.

In dollar terms, American exports declined from about $5.2 billion in 1929 to $1.7 billion in 1933; but prices also fell, so the physical volume of exports only fell by half. Hardest hit were farm commodities such as wheat, cotton, tobacco, and lumber. According to this theory, the collapse of farm exports caused many American farmers to default on their loans, leading to the bank runs on small rural banks that characterized the early years of the Great Depression.

后的国际贸易急剧下降加剧了大萧条的恶化，特别是对那些严重依赖外贸的国家而言。大部分历史学家和经济学家谴责美国《斯穆特—霍利关税法》（实施于1930年6月17日）责备该法通过大幅削减国际贸易和导致其他国家的报复性关税而使大萧条恶化。对外贸易对美国整个经济活动而言只是一小部分并且集中在小范围经济中例如农业上，然而在许多其他国家却是一个很大的因素。1921～1925年对可征进口商品的征税的从价税率为25.9%，但1931～1935年在新关税规定下跃升到了50%。

以美元计算，美国的出口额从1929年的52亿美元下降到1933年的17亿美元，但物价也同样出现下滑，因此实际出口量仅下降了一半。遭受打击最大的是农产品诸如小麦、棉花、烟草和木材。根据这一理论，农产品出口的崩溃引发美国许多农民拖欠贷款，导致小型乡村银行的挤提，这就是大萧条最初几年的特点。

U.S. Federal Reserve and Money Supply

美联储与货币供应

Monetarists, including Milton Friedman and current Federal Reserve System chairman Ben Bernanke, argue that the Great Depression was caused by monetary contraction, the consequence of poor policymaking by the American Federal Reserve System and continuous crisis in the banking system. In this view, the Federal Reserve, by not acting, allowed the money supply as measured by the M_2 to shrink by one-third from 1929 to 1933.

Friedman argued that the downward turn in the economy, starting with the stock market crash, would have been just another recession. The problem was that some large, public bank failures, particularly that of the New York Bank of the United States, produced panic and widespread runs on local banks, and that the Federal Reserve sat idly by while banks fell. He claimed that, if the Fed had provided emergency lending to these key banks, or simply bought government bonds on the open market to provide liquidity and increase the quantity of money after the key banks fell, all the rest of the banks would not have fallen after the large ones did, and the money supply would not have fallen as far and as fast as it did. With significantly less money to go around, businessmen could not get new

货币主义学派，包括弥尔顿·弗里德曼和美联储现任主席本·伯南克认为大萧条是由银根紧缩引起的，是美联储的决策失误和银行系统的持续危机导致的结果。在这种观点指导下，美联储任由狭义货币供给量从1929年到1933年缩减了三分之一。

弗里德曼认为始于股票市场崩溃的经济下行有可能仅是一种经济衰退。问题在于一些大型国有银行的倒闭，尤其是美国纽约银行的倒闭制造了恐慌并在地方银行造成了大范围的银行挤提。与此同时，美联储却对银行的倒闭不闻不问。他说，如果美联储能提供紧急贷款给那些主要银行或是在主要的银行倒闭后在公开市场上购买政府债券以提供流动性和增加货币供给量的话，那么在一些大银行倒闭之后，剩下的银行本来可以不倒闭，并且货币供给量也本不会下滑快到如此程度。随着货币流通的大幅减少，商人们得不到新的贷款，而他们以前的贷款也不能再续贷，这样就迫使很多商人停止了投资活动。这种观点谴责了美联储尤其是其下属的纽约联邦储备银行的不作为

loans and could not even get their old loans renewed, forcing many to stop investing. This interpretation blames the Federal Reserve for inaction, especially the New York branch.

One reason why the Federal Reserve did not act to limit the decline of the money supply was regulation. At that time the amount of credit the Federal Reserve could issue was limited by laws which required partial gold backing of that credit. By the late 1920s the Federal Reserve had almost hit the limit of allowable credit that could be backed by the gold in its possession. This credit was in the form of Federal Reserve demand notes. Since a "promise of gold" is not as good as "gold in the hand", during the bank panics a portion of those demand notes were redeemed for Federal Reserve gold. Since the Federal Reserve had hit its limit on allowable credit, any reduction in gold in its vaults had to be accompanied by a greater reduction in credit. Several years into the Great Depression, the private ownership of gold was declared illegal, reducing the pressure on Federal Reserve gold.

的做法。

美联储没有采取措施限制货币供应量减少的原因之一是管制。当时美联储所能发放的贷款数额是受法律限制的，要求贷款要有部分的黄金支持才行。到20世纪20年代末，美联储几乎是达到了由其黄金储备支持下的所能够放贷量的最大限额。这种贷款当时是以美联储的即期票据形式发放的。由于"期许黄金"没有"持有黄金"好，在银行恐慌期间，一部分的即期票据被赎回成联邦储备的黄金。因为美联储已经达到它所能放贷的最大限额，它储备库的黄金的减少必将要求更大幅度地减少信贷。大萧条期间几年，私人持有黄金被视为非法，从而减轻了联邦储备黄金的压力。

非常点拨

1. **新古典经济学（Neoclassical Economics）** 新古典经济学是19世纪70年代由"边际革命"开始而形成的一种经济学流派。它在继承古典经济学经济自由主义的同时，以边际效用价值论代替了古典经济学的劳动价值论，以需求为核心的分析代替了古典经济学以供给为核心的分析。新古典经济学形成之后，代替了古典经济学成为当时经济理论的主流。新古典经济学派主要包括奥地利学派、洛桑学派和剑桥学派，认为边际效用递减规律是理解经济现象的基础，利用这一规律可以解释买主面对一批不同价格时所采取的购买行为、市场参与者对价格的反应、各种资源在不同用途之间的最佳配置等各种经济问题。

2. **货币主义学派（Monetarist）** 货币主义学派是20世纪五六十年代在美国出现的一个经济学流派，也称货币主义，其创始人为美国芝加哥大学教授弗里德曼。货币学派在理论上和政策主张方面强调货币供应量的变动是引起经济活动和物价水平发生变动的根本和起支配作用的原因，布伦纳于1968年使用"货币主义"一词来表达这一流派的基本特点，此后被广泛沿用于西方经济学文献之中。

3. **凯恩斯主义（Keynesianism）** 凯恩斯主义经济学或凯恩斯主义是根据凯恩斯的著作《就业、利息和货币通论》的思想而形成的经济理论，主张国家采用扩张性的经济政策，通过增加需求促进经济增长。凯恩斯认为对商品总需求的减少是经济衰退的主要原因，所以维持整体经济活动数据平衡的措施可以在宏观上平衡供给和需求。因此，凯恩斯的理论及其他建立在凯恩斯理论基础上的经济学理论被称为宏观经济学。

4. **欧文·费雪（Irving Fisher）**（1867～1947年） 美国最早的新古典经济学家，由于他的经济理论现在被越来越多的学者接受传播，其现在名声远高于生前名声。以其名字命名的概念包括费雪方程、费雪假说、费雪分离定理。

5. **弥尔顿·弗里德曼（Milton Friedman）**（1912～2006年） 美国经济学家，诺贝尔经济学奖获得者。他最为著名的是其理论和实证研究，尤其是对消费函数理论和货币历史与理论的研究，以及对稳定政策的复杂说明。他反对政府干预，支持自由市场。作为芝加哥经济学派领导人，他影响了整个经济学的研究方向，被经济学家称为 "20世纪下半叶最有影响力的经济学家"。

Palai Central Bank

Unit 5

Palai Central Bank
帕莱中心银行

主题札记

　　帕莱中心银行是20世纪中叶的一家总部设立在印度南部喀拉拉邦的商业银行。从一个偏远小镇起家，帕莱银行不仅成为喀拉拉邦地区最大的银行，在政府时代之后还成为印度第十七大银行。然而在1960年，该银行却被政府（在印度储备银行的请求下）勒令停业清算。

Joseph Augusti Kayalackakom
约瑟夫·奥古斯蒂·卡亚拉卡科目

阅读长廊

Palai Central Bank

From the time of its founding in 1927 to its closure in 1960, the Bank had an eventful period. The history of the Bank gives an insight into a period of history preceding and immediately following India's independence, when Kerala——a small State in the far south——could exert only very little influence in the nation's capital. It was also a period when the need for protecting the interests of different segments of society was not a major consideration when policy decisions were taken by the Central Government.

The Bank was founded by Joseph Augusti Kayalackakom in Pala (Palai), a small town in the central part of the then native state of Travancore (which later became part of the Kerala State). Joseph Augusti had carried on some other businesses before going into banking. He had run textile business initially in Pala。

帕莱中心银行

从1927年建立到1960年关闭，帕莱银行与印度独立前后的历史相似也经历了辉煌的岁月。当中央政府还没有意识到保护社会各个阶层的利益时，帕莱银行以其超前的经营理念从一个小小的南方银行发展成为全印度知名的大银行。

帕莱银行由约瑟夫·奥古斯蒂·卡亚拉卡科目在川万克中心小镇帕莱建立。约瑟夫·奥古斯蒂在进入银行业之前最初在帕莱从事纺织业。

Some of the major Banks in India were formed during the beginning of last century. Between 1906 and 1913, Bank of India, Central Bank of India, Bank of Baroda, Canara Bank, Indian Bank, and Bank of Mysore were set up. In 1921 Imperial Bank of India was established through the amalgamation[26] of three Presidency Banks which were earlier set up by the English East India Company.

The Bank was on a growth track right from the beginning. Its style of functioning was quite different from the other banks of the day. It was more of "mass banking" than the "class banking" practised by other banks of those days. This was a welcome change for the people who, for their needs, had largely depended on small moneylenders, most of whom were from Kalladaikurichi in Tamil Nadu.

In 1929, when the Great Depression struck and Travancore's plantation sector was badly hit, the Bank gave liberal assistance to the plantations. The Bank, which later changed its name to "Palai Central Bank", started expanding its activities by opening branches at several places. When the Bank opened a branch in New Delhi, India's new capital city in 1932, it was the very first bank to do so, ahead of even

20世纪初期，印度的几家大银行相继成立，如印度国家银行、印度中央银行、巴罗达银行、卡纳拉银行、印度银行和麦索银行都是在1906年到1913年成立的。1921年，英国东印度公司将先前建立的三家管区银行合并为印度皇家银行。

帕莱银行正是在这种背景下成立的，它的经营理念与当时的其他大银行迥异。帕莱银行主要为大众服务而不受制于其他银行奉行的阶层观念的束缚。这使得帕莱银行受到喀拉拉邦（泰米尔地区）大众的欢迎，因为他们过去需要贷款时很大程度上依靠小额放贷者。而大多数放贷者即来自泰米尔的Kalladaikurichi。

1929年，经济大萧条严重地打击了喀拉拉邦的种植业，正是帕莱银行伸出了援助之手。随后，帕莱银行改名为帕莱中心银行，将分行延伸到印度其他地方。1932年，帕莱银行在新首都新德里开设分行，走在了其他北方大银行的前面。此外，帕莱银行还发现了阿鲁瓦的市场潜力，早在阿鲁瓦成为印度的工业重镇若干年前，该行就在那里开

---

[26] amalgamation: [ə,mælgə'meiʃən] n. 汞合，汞齐化，融合，合并

the established north-Indian banks. The Bank also discovered the potential of Aluva (Alwaye) by opening a branch there, years before Aluva became a major industrial town. Employees——both executives and staff——were trained to project the Bank's motto[27] of customer service. A young boy coming to deposit the scholarship amount he got received the same service that large depositors enjoyed. It was, therefore, natural that years later, when the bright youngster became District Collector, he still regarded the Bank as "his" bank. The Bank's branch managers followed an "open door" policy making them accessible to everyone. This was in sharp contrast with their counterparts of the Imperial Bank of India, who were totally unapproachable to the common man.

设了分行。帕莱银行上到经理下到员工，都奉行平等待人的原则。无论是对待一个存储奖学金的年轻人还是一个腰缠万贯的大户，一律热情相迎。多年后，当这名睿智的年青人荣任地区税务高官后，他仍把帕莱银行视为"他自己的"银行。这是很自然的。这种"敞开门"的政策，使得帕莱银行与客户建立了长期的良好关系，也使得帕莱银行的人气大升。而这种经营方式和理念与该行的竞争对手印度皇家银行大相径庭，后者从不与普通民众打交道。

财经宝库

　　印度储备银行（Reserve Bank of India，RBI）是印度的中央银行，按照1934年印度储备银行法案而成立于1935年4月1日。从开始起其总部一直设在孟买。起初该银行是

---

[27] motto: ['mɔtəu] *n.* 座右铭，箴言

私人拥有，在1949年国有化以后，完全归印度政府所有。

Reserve Bank of India Office
印度储备银行的办公室

1. How could the Palai Central Bank develop a life-long relationship with its customers?

2. What do you think is crucial to the Palai Central Bank's success during the 1930s?

3. Why do you think the Palai Central Bank could gain its popularity in Kerala area?

归类记忆卡片

商业银行 commercial bank | 资本 capital
中央银行 Central Bank | 放贷者 money lender

听力广场

Banking Crisis

In 1960 February, a new ministry assumed office in Kerala with Pattom Thanu Pillai as Chief Minister. In August that year, the Governor of RBI succeeded in persuading Desai for the closure of Palai Central Bank which, he told him, had too much of doubtful advances. That RBI gave false data to convince him is something which Desai himself would come to know only much later. After RBI moved the

银行业危机

1960年2月，新内阁就职喀拉拉邦，并任命巴登·皮来为首席部长。同年8月，印度储备银行总裁说服迪塞关闭帕莱银行，理由是帕莱银行有太多值得怀疑的超前做法。显然，印度储备银行向迪塞传递了错误的信息，迪塞后来过了好久才了解真相。尽管喀拉拉邦最高法院于8月8日接受印度储备银行关于关闭帕莱银行并进行停业清算的

petition for liquidation of the Bank, and it was finally ordered by the Kerala High Court on 8th August 1960, Desai vehemently defended his action in Parliament. He, however, had to admit later that the reasons earlier stated were not correct.

The liquidation of the Bank was followed by a banking crisis. Most of the Banks in the State faced "run" on their deposits. Even some of the Banks outside Kerala were affected. RBI had a tough time proving that all is well with its running of the country's banking system. Punjab National Bank, the worst affected among the northern Banks, received special support. But the affected Kerala banks were less lucky. They were amalgamated with other banks in the State or outside.

When the closure of the State's largest Bank also led to a crisis in the entire banking system, there was a hue and cry in all quarters, including the press. But out of sheer obstinacy, Desai refused to reconsider the matter. When a group of Kerala MPs met Nehru requesting that the Bank be revived, he told them that he would like to, but his insistence would lead to the resignation of Desai. He said there was a feeling that Finance Ministers did not thrive under him and so he did not want another resignation. In the larger interests of the nation, he asked the Kerala MPs to put up with the whole thing. With that, all doors for a revival from Government

建议,但是迪塞后来承认他在议会的言行是不正确的。

帕莱银行的停业清算造成了整个银行业的危机。大多数银行都出现存款挤提的情况,包括一些喀拉拉邦以外的银行。印度储备银行也出现了困难无法证实全国银行系统在它的经营下运行良好。北方银行中受影响最大的彭佳国民银行受到了特殊支持。而其他受影响的喀拉拉邦银行就没有那么幸运了,它们大多被邦内外的银行兼并。

全国最大的银行关闭也造成了整个银行系统的危机,也激起了社会各界包括媒体的不满。尽管如此,迪塞仍然拒绝重新考虑他所作出的决定。当喀拉拉邦的议会代表会见尼赫鲁时希望帕莱银行能够重整旗鼓,尼氏说他也希望如此,但如果这样做将导致迪塞的辞职。此外,尼赫鲁还认为财政部部长也没有按照他的指示行事,但为了顾全大局,他希望喀拉拉邦的议会代表能够容忍帕莱银行关闭一事,这也意味着帕莱银行的前途在政治层面上宣告结束。

side were closed.

A legal battle was then fought. But the delay of the legal process made a revival impossible. In the Supreme Court, the Bank's case was argued.The Court ruled in a 3-2 judgement that with the delay, a revival has been rendered infructuous[28].

此外，在法律层面，漫长的法律程序使帕莱银行重复新生的可能成为空谈。在最高法院,帕莱银行的重生计划最终以三比二通过，但司法的延误使得判决结果失去实际意义。

After the closure of the Bank the first impression of the public was that the Bank had gone bust. They assumed foul play. When the Finance Minister of the country states in Parliament that the Bank's deposits had hardly 15% asset backing, the people had no reason to disbelieve. They had to wait for years to know that even after bearing several years of liquidation expenses, the depositors got more than 90% of their money – but in petty installments[29].

帕莱银行的停业留给公众的第一印象就是帕莱银行由于违规操作而破产了。所以当财政部部长在议会宣布帕莱银行的储蓄只有不到15%的资产支持的时候，所有人都深信不疑。然而几年后帕莱银行被清算后，储户们还能得到90%以上的存款，（除去清算费用）尽管主要是分期付款。

The crisis that shook the banking sector of the country led to some changes in that sector. The demand for protecting the interests of depositors in the event of similar crises led to the passing of the Deposit Insurance Act by Parliament[30] in 1961 and the eventual formation of the Deposit Insurance & Credit Guarantee Corporation (DICGC). Another demand arose

这场危机在冲击着整个印度的银行业时也使该行业产生一些变化。在类似危机发生之际，保护储蓄者权益的呼声最终使得议会于1961年通过了储蓄保险法案，并推动了储蓄保险和信用担保公司的发展。此外，银行业还达成广泛共识，认为官僚机构在这场银行危机中无动于衷。因此，效仿美国建立

---

[28] infructuous: [in'frʌktjuəs] *a.* 无效果的，徒劳的

[29] installment: [in'stɔ:lmənt] *n.* 部分，分期付款（安装，一期）

[30] parliament: ['pɑ:ləmənt] *n.* 议会，国会

from the allegation[31] that RBI is a bureaucratic institution insensitive to the needs of the banking sector. Its advocates called for the formation of a Superintendent of Banking like that in the U.S. to carry out the function of supervision of banking in the country. This demand was partially met years later when Government introduced a policy to appoint a career banker as one of the Deputy Governors of RBI.

Political Fallout

When one looks now at the forced closure of an institution like Palai Central Bank, one sees it as a political failure too. Today, if the Central Government considers the closure of an institution (or even its shifting or merger or modification), all-party delegations of MPs and Ministers are seen rushing to Delhi to ensure that no such decision is taken. But way back in 1960, when the nation was barely 13 years into its independent status, the MPs and MLAs and even the Ministers were far less effective. When the largest institution of Kerala was being ordered to be closed by a Central Government agency, Kerala's politicians could not prevent it but had to meekly abide by the dictates of their national leadership. The people of central

全国范围内的银行监管体系的呼吁在几年后使得印度政府雇佣一名职业银行家做印度储备银行的副行长。

政治影响

当人们重新审视诸如帕莱银行的机构关闭案件时，人们发现这也暴露出制度上的缺陷。如果在今天，政府决定关闭（甚至转移，合并或修改）一家银行时，各地方的议会代表和部长一定会冲向新德里来确保政府不会作出这个决定。然而在1960年，当印度刚刚独立13年时，议会代表和立法机关成员甚至部员们手中的权力都不够。 当喀拉拉邦最大的银行被政府机关勒令停业时，喀拉拉邦的地方官员们甚至无法反抗只能屈从于国家领导的独裁。而喀拉拉邦的人民如果不服从，就会被国家放弃。

Flag of the Kerala Congress
喀拉拉邦议会的旗帜

---

[31] allegation: [ˌæliˈgeiʃ ən] *n.* 断言，主张，辩解

Kerala, however, felt abandoned, if not betrayed.

There was also another aspect. The Bank was considered to be an institution of the Christian community, although members of every religion and community were present among the Bank's innumerable account holders, employees, advisors and well-wishers. Today, if an institution of a minority community is touched by the Government, that community would create such a forre that anyone will think twice before taking a step forward. But minorities were much less aware of their rights way back in 1960. The Christian community, therefore, suffered in silence then.

另外，由于喀拉拉邦的大部分居民为基督教徒，尽管帕莱银行的庞大客户群、雇员、顾问以及祝福者包括各种宗教团体。如果在今天政府触动某个少数民族的利益时定会三思而后行，而在1960年，少数民族的维权意识尚不强烈，基督徒们也大都忍气吞声。

In 1964, barely 3 years after the closure of Palai Central Bank, a major upheaval occurred in the Congress Party in Kerala. Fifteen of its MLAs——mainly those from central Kerala——split and formed a new party by name Kerala Congress. It was the beginning of a change in the political equations in the State. The closure of Palai Central Bank is considered by many to be one of the root causes that led to the new chain of events.

1964年，仅在帕莱银行停业后不到三年，喀拉拉邦的国大党发生剧变，15位地区代表成立了新的政党——喀拉拉邦国大党。这也标志着整个印度政治平等运动的开始。许多人认为帕莱银行的关闭为之后一系列社会运动埋下了种子。

In the same year, the irrepressible Desai was removed from the Union Cabinet.

同年，不负责任的迪塞被联邦内阁弹劾。

非常点拨

　　喀拉拉邦，印度西南部的一个邦，濒临阿拉伯海，全邦面积为3.8万多平方公里，人口3,184万人。首府为特里凡得琅，官方语言为马拉雅拉姆语。喀拉拉邦河流纵横，遍布南北，江河湖泊里，商船、渔船和游船络绎不绝，给当地人民提供了便利的水路交通。漫长的海岸线为喀拉拉邦与海外各地联系提供了方便。该邦几乎四季如春。

Lion in Palai
帕莱的狮子

Unit 6

Barings Bank

Barings Bank
巴林银行

主题札记

巴林银行：地位显赫的英国老牌贵族银行，世界上最富有的女人——伊丽莎白女王也信赖它的理财水准，并是它的长期客户。

尼克·李森：国际金融界"天才交易员"，曾任巴林银行驻新加坡巴林期货公司总经理、首席交易员。以稳健、大胆著称。在日经225指数期货合约市场上，他被誉为"不可战胜的李森"。

1994年下半年，李森认为，日本经济已开始走出衰退，股市将会有大涨趋势。于是大量买进日经225指数期货合约和看涨期权。然而"人算不如天算"，事与愿违，1995年1月16日，日本关西大地震，股市暴跌，李森所持多头头寸遭受重创，损失高达2.1亿英镑。

这时的情况虽然糟糕，但还不至于能撼动巴林银行。只是对李森先生来说已经严重影响其光荣的地位。李森凭其天才的经验，为了反败为胜，再次大量补仓日经225指数期货合约和利率期货合约，头寸总量已达十多万手。

要知道这是以"杠杆效应"放大了几十倍的期货合约。当日经225指数跌至18,500点以下时，每跌一点，李森先生的头寸就要损失两百多万美元。

"事情往往朝着最糟糕的方向发展"，这是强势理论的总结。

2月24日，当日经225指数再次加速暴跌后，李森所在的巴林期货公司的头寸损失已接近整个巴林银行集团资本和储备之和。融资已无渠道，亏损已无法挽回，李森畏罪潜逃。

巴林银行面临覆灭之灾，银行董事长不得不求助于英格兰银行，希望挽回败局。然而这时的损失已达14亿美元，并且随着日经225指数的继续下挫，损失还将进一步扩大。因此，各方金融机构竟无人敢伸手救助巴林这位昔日的贵宾，巴林银行从此倒闭。

一个职员竟能短期内毁灭一家老牌银行，究其各种复杂原因，其中，不恰当的利用期货"杠杆效应"，并知错不改，以赌博的方式对待期货是造成这一"奇迹"的关键。

虽然最后很快抓住了逃跑的李森，但如果不能抓住期货风险控制的要害，更多的"巴林事件"还会发生，包括我们个人投资者中间的小"巴林事件"。

Nick Leeson (Right)
尼克·李森（右）

Barings Bank

Barings Bank (1762 to 1995) was the oldest merchant bank in London until its collapse in 1995 after one of the bank's employees, Nick Leeson, lost £ 827 million ($1.4 billion) speculating - primarily on futures contracts.

History

Barings Bank was founded in 1762 as the "John and Francis Baring Company" by Sir Francis Baring, the son of John Baring, originally from Bremen in Germany. The Baring family lives in both Germany and England.

In 1806, his son Alexander Baring joined the firm and they renamed it Baring Brothers & Co., merging[32] it with the London offices of Hope & Co., where Alexander worked with

巴林银行

巴林银行(1762年到1995年)是伦敦最古老的招商银行。然而在1995年，该银行的员工尼克·李森期货投资失败，损失高达8亿2千7百万英镑（14亿美元），使得该银行遭到灭顶之灾。

历史

巴林银行于1762年由法兰西·巴林先生（约翰·巴林的儿子）建立，起名约翰和法兰西巴林公司。巴林家族来自德国的布来梅，现居住在英格兰和德国。

1806年，法兰西的儿子亚历山大·巴林加入公司并改名为巴林兄弟公司，且和希望公司的伦敦部合并，亚历山大曾与亨

---

[32] merge: [mə:dʒ] v. 合并，消失，吞没

Henry Hope.

Barings had a long and storied history. In 1802, it helped finance the Louisiana Purchase, despite the fact that Britain was at war with France, and the sale had the effect of financing Napoleon's war effort. Technically the United States did not purchase Louisiana from Napoleon. Louisiana was purchased from the Baring brothers and Hope & Co..

Later daring efforts in underwriting[33] got the firm into serious trouble through overexposure to Argentine and Uruguayan debt, and the bank had to be rescued by a consortium[34] organized by the governor of the Bank of England, William Lidderdale, in the Panic of 1890. While recovery from this incident was swift, it destroyed the company's former bravado.

Its new, restrained manner made it a more appropriate representative of the British establishment, and the company established ties with King George V, beginning a close relationship with the British monarchy[35] that would endure until Barings' collapse. (Diana, Princess of Wales, was the great granddaughter of one of the Barings family. The descendants of the original five male branches of the Baring

利·霍普共事。

巴林银行有着很多故事。1802年，巴林兄弟公司资助了著名的路易斯安那购地案在金融上援助拿破仑。这在当时是非常有争议的，因为当时交战的双方是英国和法国。事实上，路易斯安那并非美国从拿破仑手中购得，而是从巴林兄弟公司和希望公司购得。

然而，随后对阿根廷和乌拉圭债务的过度风险暴露使巴林兄弟公司深陷泥潭。后经英格兰银行行长威廉·里德达尔组织银联救助，才摆脱了1890年的危机。尽管恢复迅速，但巴林兄弟公司再也没有往日的声势了。

此后，它谨慎的行事方式更能代表英国作风。此外，与英王乔志五世的紧密关系一直延续到它的倒闭。（戴安娜—威尔斯公主也是巴林家族的一员。 此外，巴林家族的五位男性成员也被封爵。分别授予巴仁力维斯特科诺斯布鲁克伯爵，授予巴仁阳市博物思和戈兰黛尔德巴仁霍韦克为克拉莫伯爵）尽管巴林银行没有在金融界的统治地

---

[33] underwrite: ['ʌndəraɪt] v. 签名，承诺支付，经营保险业
[34] consortium: [kən'sɔːtjəm] n. 联合，合伙，国际财团
[35] monarchy: ['mɔnəkɪ] n.君主政体，君主国，君主政治

family were all appointed to the peerage with the titles Baron Revelstoke, Earl of Northbrook, Baron Ashburton, Baron Howick of Glendale and Earl of Cromer.) The company's restraint during this period would cost it its pre-eminence in the world of finance, but would later pay dividends when its refusal to take a chance on financing Germany's recovery from World War I saved it the painful losses experienced by other British banks at the onset of the Great Depression.

During the Second World War, the British Government used Barings to liquidate assets in the United States and elsewhere to help finance the war effort. After the war Barings was overtaken in size and influence by other banking houses, but remained an important player in the market, until in 1995.

1995 Collapse

The Barings Bank collapse of 1995 is considered a pivotal turning point in the history of banking and has become a textbook example of accounting fraud. Over a period of three years, Nick Leeson, a Singapore-based management employee of London's Barings Bank, lost £827 million ($1.4 billion), primarily on futures contract speculation, and through manipulating the records, hid his actions until

位，但相比其他参与德国战后重建的英国银行，巴林银行还算幸运，因为它并没有在经济大萧条时遭受巨大的损失。

第二次世界大战期间，英国政府雇佣巴林银行来将它在美国和其他地方的资产变现。战后，巴林银行的部分资产被其他银行兼并，但仍是银行业的重要一员，直到1995年。

1995年倒闭事件

1995年的巴林银行倒闭案堪称银行业的一次重大转折，该案也因此成为财务欺诈的经典案例。在三年多的时间里，尼克·李森（新加坡分行的管理人员）通过瞒报谎报账目来达到他进行期货交易的目的。李森瞒天过海直到1995年2月。结果，期货交易的失败造成8亿2千7百万英镑（14亿美元）的损失，直接导致伦敦最古老的银行

February 1995. When the losses were revealed, Barings Bank — the oldest merchant bank in the City of London, the Queen's personal bank and the financier of the Napoleonic Wars — was forced to default on its accounts.

At the time of the massive trading loss, Leeson was supposed to be arbitraging, seeking to profit from differences in the prices of Nikkei-225 futures contracts listed on the Osaka Securities Exchange in Japan and the Singapore International Monetary Exchange. Such arbitrage involves buying futures contracts on one market and simultaneously selling them on another. Since the margins on this are small, the volumes traded by arbitrageurs tend to be large. However, because of the offsetting movements of the hedged position, the strategy is not very risky, and certainly would not have bankrupted the bank. Instead of hedging his positions, however, Leeson gambled on the future direction of the Japanese markets. According to Eddie George, the governor of the Bank of England, Mr. Leeson began doing this at the end of January 1995. Due to a series of internal and external events, his unhedged losses escalated rapidly.

（女王的私人银行和拿破仑战争的金库）被迫违约。

由于当时交易损失严重，李森利用日经225指数期货在日本大阪证券交易所和新加坡国际金融交易所的差价进行套利，也就是说在一个市场购买期货合同，同时在另一个市场卖出。因为差价很小，所以交易量必须很大才能盈利，并且采用套期保值可以降低风险。然而李森没有对冲其头寸，却赌博似的把赌注全部压在日本市场上的期货走势。根据英格兰银行行长艾迪·乔治介绍，李森从1995年1月末就开始了他的赌博，而结果是由于内部和外部原因，他那未经对冲的投资损失急剧扩大。

财经宝库

1. 套利，就是在某种金融资产拥有两个价格的情况下，以较低的价格买进，较高的价格卖出，从而获取收益。例如，某个股票同时在伦敦和纽约上市，同股同权，但是在纽约卖10美元，在伦敦却卖12美元，投资者就可以在纽约买进，到伦敦卖出。

2. 现实中的套利策略非常复杂，流行的分支有可转换债券套利（convertible arbitrage），股息套利（dividend arbitrage），兼并套利（merger arbitrage）等。在正统的金融学教材上，对套利行为有非常严格的数学定义，分为第一种套利机会和第二种套利机会。

3. 风险管理，又名危机管理，是一个管理过程，包括对风险的定义、测量、评估和发展应对风险的策略。目的是将可避免的风险、成本及损失最小化。理想的风险管理，事先已排定优先次序，可以优先处理引发最大损失及发生概率最高的事件，其次再处理风险相对较低的事件。实际状况中，因为风险与发生概率通常不一致，所以难以决定处理顺序。故须衡量两者比重，作出最合适的决定。因为牵涉机会成本(opportunity cost)，风险管理同时也要面对如何有效运用资源的难题。把资源用于风险管理可能会减少运用在其他具有潜在报酬活动的资源；理想的风险管理正是希望以最少的资源化解最大的危机。

DIY工作室

1. What role did Barings play in 1802 Louisianna Purchase?

2. What do you think are the most important for Baring's historical success?

3. Besides Leeson, what do you think accounts for Barings Bank's bancrupcy?

归类记忆卡片

套利 arbitrage
投机 speculate
债务 debt

对冲 hedge
保证金 margin

听力广场

Internal Auditing

内部审计

Barings Futures Singapore (BFS)'s management structure through 1995 enabled Leeson to operate without supervision from London headquarters. Leeson was not only

巴林银行新加坡期货公司的管理结构使得李森在整个1995年都未受到伦敦总部的监管。这是因为李森一人身兼二职，他不仅管理巴林

the floor manager for Barings' trading on the Singapore International Monetary Exchange, he was also the head of settlement operations, charged with ensuring accurate accounting for the unit. Normally the positions would have been held by two different employees. After the collapse, several observers, including Leeson himself, placed much of the blame on the bank's own deficient internal auditing and risk management practices.

People at the London end of Barings were all so know-all that nobody dared ask a stupid question in case they looked silly in front of everyone else.

—Nick Leeson, *Rogue Trader* (1996)

Some people did raise eyebrows about Leeson's activities but were ignored. Awaiting breakdown from my buddy Nick … (once they creatively allocate the numbers).

—Brenda Granger, Head of Futures and Options Settlements in London, January 1995 internal E-mail.

Corruption

Because of the absence of oversight, Leeson was able to make seemingly small gambles in the futures arbitrage market at Barings Futures Singapore (BFS) and cover for his shortfalls

银行在新加坡国际金融交易所的交易，还负责管理本单位的账目。而一般来讲，这两个职位应由两个不同的人担任。倒闭事件发生之后，几位观察家，包括李森自己都对巴林银行内部审计和风险管理实践上的漏洞提出批评。

伦敦总部的人也不会在其他人面前问一个似乎很愚蠢的问题。

——尼克·李森，《欺诈的交易员》(1996)

尽管有些人对李森的行为表示怀疑，但从未引起足够的重视。等待我的同事尼克垮台……(自从他们开始改变账目上的数字开始)

——布兰德·格兰泽，伦敦期货和期权高层，1995年1月内部电子邮件。

腐败问题

因为缺乏监管，李森能够将巴林期货新加坡分公司的短期亏损谎报成盈利给伦敦总部。具体地讲，李森改变了分行的错账账户（"五

by reporting losses as gains to Barings in London. Specifically, Leeson altered the branch's error account, subsequently known by its account number 88888 as the "five-eights account", to prevent the London office from receiving the standard daily reports on trading, price, and status.

By December 1994, Leeson had cost Barings £200 million. He reported to British tax authorities a £102 million profit. If the company had uncovered his true financial dealings then, collapse might have been avoided as Barings had capital of £350 million.

Kobe Earthquake

Using the hidden "five-eights account", Leeson began to aggressively trade in futures and options on SIMEX. His decisions routinely lost substantial sums, but he used money entrusted to the bank by subsidiaries for use in their own accounts. He falsified trading records in the bank's computer systems, and used money intended for margin payments on other trading. Barings Bank management in London at first congratulated and rewarded Leeson for what seemed to be his outstanding trading profits. However, his luck ran out when the Kobe earthquake sent the Asian financial markets into a tailspin. Leeson bet on a rapid recovery by the Nikkei Stock Average which failed to materialize.

个八账户"），来蒙蔽真实的日常交易信息，如股价等。

截至1994年12月，李森已经造成巴林银行损失高达两亿英镑，但他却向英国税务部门谎报银行盈利一亿零二百万英镑。事实上，如果李森的金融骗局能够被及时发现，巴林银行完全可以逃过灭顶之灾，因为巴林银行拥有三亿五千万英镑的资本。

神户地震

通过秘密的"五个八账户"，李森开始疯狂地在新加坡国际金融交易所进行期货和期权的交易。尽管他的交易经常遭受巨额损失，但他却把损失变成银行的内部补助。他还在银行的电脑系统上造假从而挪用银行其他交易的保证金。巴林银行伦敦总部起初还因为李森的业绩突出对他进行嘉奖。但是，李森的好运随着神户地震的来临而灰飞烟灭。李森打赌日经股指会在短期内回升，但他错了。

1.17 memorial in Kobe
1.17神户地震悼念

Discovery

On Thursday, 23 February 1995 Leeson left Singapore to fly to Kuala Lumpur. Barings Bank auditors finally discovered the fraud, around the same time that Barings' chairman, Peter Barings, received a confession note from Leeson, but it was too late. The Bank of England attempted a weekend bailout but it was unsuccessful. Barings was declared insolvent on Sunday, 26 February 1995 and appointed administrators began managing the finances of Barings Group and its subsidiaries. The same day, the Board of Banking Supervision of the Bank of England launched an investigation led by Britain's Chancellor of the Exchequer and their report was released on 18 July 1995. Lord Bruce of Donington, in the House of Lords' debate on the report, said:

"Even the provisional conclusions of the report are interesting. I should like to give them to the House so that we may be reminded what the supervisory body itself decided at the end of such investigation as it was able to make. It stated on page 250"

By 27 February 1995, Leeson's activities had generated losses totalling £827 million ($1.4 billion), twice the bank's available trading capital. The collapse (costing another £100 million) was dramatic; employees around the

违规败露

1995年2月23日星期四，李森离开新加坡飞往吉隆坡。巴林银行的审计人员发现了李森的欺骗，而此时，巴林银行的主席，皮特·巴林也收到了一封李森的忏悔信，无奈为时已晚。英格兰银行整个周末都在对巴林银行实行紧急援助，却未成功。2月26日星期日，巴林银行宣布资不抵债并聘请行政官员接管巴林集团及旗下的子公司。同一天，在英国财政大臣的带领下，英格兰银行的银行监管理事会开始调查巴林集团于1995年7月18日公布的报告。都宁顿的议员布鲁斯在上议院讨论报告时说：

"即使报告的部分结论很有意思，我还是应该把报告上交议会上级，由监管者在调查结束时作出他们的决定。这在250页有陈述。"

截至1995年2月27日，李森的行为已经造成8亿2千7百万英镑（14亿美元）的损失，相当于巴林银行交易资本的两倍。巴林银行的倒闭（造成另外1亿英镑的损失）

world did not receive their bonuses.

Aftermath

ING, a Dutch bank, purchased Barings Bank in 1995 for the nominal sum of £1and assumed all of Barings' liabilities, forming the subsidiary ING Barings. In 2001, ING sold the U.S. based operations to ABN Amro for $275 million, and folded the rest of ING Barings into its European banking division. This left only the asset management division, Baring Asset Management. In March 2005, BAM was then split and sold by ING to MassMutual. Barings Bank therefore no longer has a separate corporate existence, although the Barings name still lives on as the MassMutual subsidiary Baring Asset Management.

Nick Leeson fled Singapore but was arrested in Germany and extradited back to Singapore, where he was convicted of fraud and sentenced to six and a half years imprisonment. While in Changi prison he was diagnosed with cancer, recovered and was divorced by his wife. He wrote an autobiography, *Rogue Trader*, covering the events leading up to the collapse. Film-maker James Dearden later dramatized the book in the film *Rogue Trader*. In 2006, Leeson was appointed chief executive officer of Galway United, an association football club in Galway, Ireland.

使其全世界的员工都未能拿到分红。

破产清算

荷兰ING集团，于1995年以一英镑收购了巴林银行，承担其所有债务，并组建了ING集团巴林分公司。2001年，ING集团以2.75亿美元将巴林银行的美国营业部卖给荷兰银行并将巴林银行其他在欧洲的部门整合进入荷兰银行，仅仅留下巴林资产管理公司。2005年3月，巴林资产管理公司被拆分卖给麻省共同基金。从此，巴林银行再也不能作为独立公司出现，尽管巴林公司的名字保存下来作为麻省共同基金的附属公司：巴林资产管理公司。

尼克·李森在德国被捕并被遣送回新加坡。他被指控欺诈并处以六年半监禁。尽管在樟宜监狱中，他的妻子离他而去，而且他被查出患有癌症，然而他奇迹般地恢复，并且写下自传——《欺诈的交易员》，披露他在巴林银行的全部经历。詹姆斯·迪尔丹将其改编成电影。2006年，李森东山再起，他出任爱尔兰戈尔韦足球俱乐部的首席执行官。

Long Term Capital Management

Unit 7

1. **路易斯安那购地（Louisiana Purchase）**　是美国于1803年以大约每英亩三美分从法国购买超过529,911,680英亩（2,144,476平方公里）土地的交易案，该交易的总价为1,500万美元或相当于8,000万法郎（如以国内生产总值相对比例计算，此数在2004年相当于4,178亿美元）。

法国路易斯安那属地的版图超出今日美国路易斯安那州的实际范围很多；该属地包括了现今阿肯色州、密苏里州、爱达荷州、明尼苏达州密西西比河以西、南达科他州、北达科他州、内布拉斯加州、新墨西哥州、得克萨斯州北部、俄克拉何马州、堪萨斯州、蒙大拿州及怀俄明州部分地区、科罗拉多州落基山脉以东、加拿大缅尼托巴、沙士吉万、亚伯达各省南部之密苏里河流域地区，以及路易斯安那州密西西比河两岸（包括新奥尔良市）。

购地所涉土地面积是今日美国国土的22.3%，与当时美国原有国土面积大致相当。

2. **拿破仑战争**　是指拿破仑称帝统治法国期间（1804—1815年）爆发的各场战事，这些战争可说是自1789年法国大革命所引发的战争的延续。它促使了欧洲的军队和火炮发生重大变革，特别是军事制度。因为实施全民征兵使得战争规模庞大，史无前例。法国迅速崛起，雄霸欧洲，但是在侵俄战役惨败后一落千丈。拿破仑建立的帝国最终战败，让波旁王朝得以于1814年和1815年两度复辟。

拿破仑战争从那时开始，到了今天还没有共识。主要有以下三种说法：

1799年11月9日——拿破仑从政变中夺得了政权

1803年5月13日——英法两国结束了从1792年到1814年唯一一段短暂的和平

1804年12月2日——拿破仑称帝

随着拿破仑在滑铁卢被打败，各交战国签订巴黎条约后，拿破仑战争终于在1815年11月20日结束。

3. **英国税务与海关总署（Her Majesty's Revenue and Customs，直译为女皇陛下税务海关总署）**　是英国政府的非部长制政府部门之一，主要职责包括征收税款（直接税：所得税、公司税、资本增值税、遗产税；间接税：增值税、印花税等）、进口管制及部分形式的国家支援。

UK Revenue and Customs
英国税务与海关总署

Long Term Capital Management
长期资本管理公司

主题札记

投机市场中不存在百战百胜的法宝，任何分析方法与操作系统都有缺陷与误区。美国长期资本管理公司的故事是最新最有说服力的证据。

美国长期资本管理公司（以下简称LTCM）创立于1994年，主要活跃于国际债券和外汇市场，利用私人客户的巨额投资和金融机构的大量贷款专门从事金融市场炒作。它与量子基金、老虎基金、欧米伽基金一起被称为国际四大"对冲基金"。

LTCM掌门人是梅里韦瑟（Meriwehter)，被誉为能"点石成金"的华尔街债务套利之父。他聚集了华尔街一批证券交易的精英加盟：1997年诺贝尔经济学奖得主罗伯特·默顿（Robert Merton)和迈伦·舒尔茨（Myron Schols)，他们因期权定价公式荣膺桂冠；前财政部副部长及美联储副主席大卫·莫里斯（David Mullis)；前所罗门兄弟债券交易部主管罗森菲尔德（Rosenfeld)。这个精英团队内荟萃职业巨星、公关明星、学术巨人，真可称为"梦幻组合"。

在1994～1997年，LTCM业绩骄人。成立之初，资产净值为12.5亿美元，到1997年年末，上升为48亿美元，净增长2.84倍。每年的投资回报率分别为：1994年28.5%、1995年42.8%、1996年40.8%、1997年17%。

LTCM以"不同市场证券间不合理价差生灭自然性"为基础，制定了"通过电脑精密计算，发现不正常市场价格差，资金杠杆放大，入市图利"的投资策略。舒尔茨和默顿将金融市场历史交易资料，已有的市场理论、学术研究报告和市场信息有机结合在一起，形成了一套较完整的电脑数学自动投资模型。他们利用计算机处理大量历史数据，通过连续而精密的计算得到两种不同金融工具间的正常历史价格差，然后结合市场信息分析它们之间的最新价格差。如果两者出现偏差，并且该偏差正在放大，电脑立即建立起庞大的债券和衍生工具组合，大举套利入市投资；经过市场一段时间的调节，放大的偏差会自动恢复到正常轨迹上，此时电脑指令平仓离场，获取偏差的差值。

但是不能忽视的是，这套电脑数学自动投资模型中也有一些致命之处：

（1）模型假设前提和计算结果都是在历史统计基础上得出的，但历史统计永不可能完全涵盖未来现象；

（2）LTCM投资策略是建立在投资组合中两种证券的价格波动正相关的基础上。

Nassim Nicholas Taleb
纳西姆·尼古拉斯·塔利布

尽管它所持核心资产德国债券与意大利债券正相关性为大量历史统计数据所证明，但是历史数据的统计过程往往会忽略一些小概率事件，也即上述两种债券的负相关性。

LTCM万万没有料到，俄罗斯金融风暴引发了全球的金融动荡，结果它所估空的德国债券价格上涨，它所做多的意大利债券等证券价格下跌，它所期望的正相关变为负相关，结果两头亏损。它的电脑自动投

资系统面对这种原本忽略不计的小概率事件，错误地不断放大金融衍生产品的运作规模。LTCM利用投资者那儿筹来的 22亿美元做资本抵押，买入价值3,250亿美元的证券，杠杆比率高达60倍。由此造成该公司的巨额亏损。它从5月俄罗斯金融风暴到9月全面溃败，短短的150天资产净值下降90%，出现43亿美元巨额亏损，仅余5亿美元，已走到破产边缘。9月23日，美联储出面组织安排，以美林、摩根为首的15家国际性金融机构注资37.25亿美元购买了LTCM90%的股权，共同接管了该公司，从而避免了它倒闭的厄运。

阅读长廊

Long Term Capital Management (I)

长期资本管理公司（上）

Long Term Capital Management (LTCM) was a U.S. hedge fund which failed spectacularly in the late 1990s, leading to a massive bailout by other major banks and investment houses.

LTCM was founded in 1994 by John Meriwether (the former vice-chairman and head of bond trading at Salomon Brothers). Board of directors members included Myron Scholes and Robert C. Merton, who shared the 1997 Nobel Memorial Prize in Economics.

Initially enormously successful with annualized returns of over 40% in its first years, in 1998 it lost $4.6 billion in less than four months and became a prominent example of the risk potential in the hedge fund industry. The fund folded in early 2000.

The company had developed complex

　　长期资本管理公司(LTCM)是美国的一家对冲基金公司，在20世纪90年代后期倒闭，致使其他主要银行和投资机构对之进行大规模救援。

　　长期资本管理公司于1994年由约翰·梅里韦瑟（所罗门兄弟公司前副主席和债券交易部主管）建立，董事会成员包括迈伦·舒尔茨和罗伯特·默顿(1997年诺贝尔经济学奖得主)。

　　在建立之初（前5年），该公司可获得每年40%的惊人回报。直到1998年，公司在四个月内损失了46亿美元而成为对冲基金行业潜在风险的著名案例。2000年年初，该公司被重组。

　　公司运用复杂的数学模型来

mathematical models to take advantage of fixed income arbitrage deals (termed convergence trades) usually with U.S., Japanese, and European government bonds. The basic idea was that over time the value of long-dated bonds issued a short time apart would tend to become identical. However, the rate at which these bonds approached this price would be different, and more heavily traded bonds such as U.S. Treasury bonds would approach the long term price more quickly than less heavily traded and less liquid bonds.

Thus, by a series of financial transactions, it would be possible to make a profit as the difference in the value of the bonds narrowed.

As LTCM's capital base grew, they felt pressed to invest that capital somewhere and had run out of good bond-arbitrage bets. This led LTCM to undertake trading strategies outside their expertise. Although these trading strategies were non-market directional, i.e., they were not dependent on overall interest rates or stock prices going up (or down), they were not convergence trades as such. By 1998, LTCM had extremely large positions in areas such as merger arbitrage and S&P 500 options (net short long-term S&P volatility). In fact, some market participants believed that LTCM had been the primary supplier of S&P 500 vega[36], which had

从套利交易中获取固定收益（也称为收敛交易），通常进行美国、日本和欧洲的政府债券交易。这种套利基于一个基本原理，就是长期债券与其签发的短期部分价值将会趋于一致。但不同的债券趋向速度不同。经常交易的债券，如美国国库券，比起那些缺乏流动性的债券，趋向的速度会比较快一些。

这样，通过一系列的金融交易，两种债券的价差逐步缩小，从而可能获利。

这也使得长期资本管理公司拥有更多的资本向外扩张，将其触角延伸到它擅长的债券套利之外的地方。尽管这些交易策略并不受市场变化的左右（如利率和股价的波动），但也不是使长短期债券价格趋向一致的交易。到1998年，长期资本管理公司持有大量的合并套利和标准普尔500股票期权（长期标准普尔波动净空头）。事实上，有些市场参与者认为长期资本管理公司是标准普尔500精选的主要提供者，这也为美国保险公司两年前销售其股指年金产品提供需求。

---

[36] vega: ['veigə] *n.* 织女

been in demand by U.S. insurance companies selling equity indexed annuities products for the prior two years.

Because these differences in value were minute—especially for the convergence trades—the fund needed to take highly-leveraged[37] positions to make a significant profit. At the beginning of 1998, the firm had equity of $4.72 billion and had borrowed over $124.5 billion with assets of around $129 billion. It had off-balance sheet derivative positions with a notional value of approximately $1.25 trillion, most of which were in interest rate derivatives such as interest rate swaps. The fund also invested in other derivatives such as equity options.

Although success within the financial markets arises from immediate-short term turbulence[38], and the ability of fund managers to identify informational asymmetries, factors giving rise to the downfall of the fund were established prior to the 1997 East Asian financial crisis.

因为债券之间的差价很小（尤其对于趋势一致的交易来说），这些基金必须具有高杠杆头寸才能获得高额利润。1998年年初，公司拥有47.2亿美元的资产，但负债却高达1,245亿美元。而公司账面下的资产却达到1,290亿美元。表外衍生产品头寸的名义价值大约有1.25万亿美元，其中大多数为利率衍生产品，如利率互换。公司也对股票期权之类的其他衍生产品进行了投资。

尽管在中短期金融市场的波动中所取得的成功并不能代表基金管理者能够及时地发现信息不对称问题。这为公司后来在1997年东亚金融危机时的衰落埋下了伏笔。

---

[37] leverage: ['li:vəridʒ] *n.* 杠杆作用
[38] turbulence: ['tə:bjuləns] *n.* 喧嚣，狂暴，骚乱，动乱

财经宝库

1. **高盛（Goldman Sachs）** GS为跨国投资银行集团，属美国《财富》杂志评选的美国财富500强企业，总部位于美国纽约。高盛的业务涵盖投资银行、证券交易和投资管理；业务对象为企业、金融机构、(国家)政府及富人。

2. **美国国际集团（American International Group，AIG）** 是一家以美国为基地的国际性跨国保险及金融服务机构。于1919年在中国上海由史带先生创办。又在1931年在香港成立四海保险公司。

经多年发展，AIG业务已经遍布130多个国家及地区，也由保险业务扩展至其他金融服务类业务，包括退休金服务、非人寿保险类的财产保险、资产管理及相关投资等。美国国际集团成员公司通过保险业内最为庞大的全球化财产保险及人寿保险服务网络为各商户、机构和个人提供服务。美国国际集团成员公司是美国最大的工商保险机构，旗下的AIG American General更是全美最顶尖的人寿保险机构之一。

3. **标准普尔500指数** 英文简写为S&P 500，是记录美国500家上市公司的一个股票指数。这个股票指数由标准普尔公司创建并维护。

S&P 500覆盖的公司都是在美国主要交易所，如纽约证券交易所、NASDAQ交易所的上市公司。与道·琼斯指数相比，S&P 500指数包含的公司更多，因此风险更为分散，能够反映更广泛的市场变化。

4. **互换（Swap）** 是一种金融衍生产品（也称为金融衍生工具），指交易双方约定在未来某一期限相互交换各自持有的资产或现金流的交易形式。较为常见的是外汇互换和利率互换，多被用做避险和投机。

DIY工作室

1. What do you think contribute to LTCM's early success?

2. What do you think would be the potential risk for LTCM's operation?

归类记忆卡片

对冲基金 hedge fund
固定收益 fixed income
高杠杆头寸 highly-leveled position

紧急援助 bailout
股指年金 equity indexed annuity
利率互换 interest rate swap

听力广场

Long Term Capital Management(II)

长期资本管理公司
（下）

In May and June 1998 returns from the fund were -6.42% and -10.14% respectively, reducing LTCM's capital by \$461 million. This was further aggravated by the exit of Salomon Brothers from the arbitrage business in July 1998.

Such losses were accentuated[39] through the Russian Financial Crises in August and September of 1998, when the Russian Government defaulted[40] on their government bonds.

Panicked investors sold Japanese and European bonds to buy U.S. treasury bonds. The profits that were supposed to occur as the value of these bonds converged became huge losses

1998年5月和6月，长期资本管理公司的回报率分别为-6.42%和-10.14%，使得该公司亏损了4.61亿美元。7月，所罗门兄弟的撤资使得该公司雪上加霜。

8月和9月，由于俄罗期政府债券的违约导致的俄罗斯金融危机使得长期资本管理公司的损失加剧。

恐慌的投资者疯狂抛售日本和欧洲债券来购买美国国库券。8月底，不同债券利差的加大也给长期资本管理公司带来18.5亿美元的资

---

[39] accentuate: [æk'sentjueit] v. 以重音念，强调，重读
[40] default: [di'fɔ:lt] v. 默认，不履行义务，缺席，拖欠

as the value of the bonds diverged. By the end of August, the fund had lost $1.85 billion in capital.

As a result of these losses, LTCM had to liquidate a number of its positions at a highly unfavorable moment and suffer further losses.

The company, which was providing annual[41] returns of almost 40% up to this point, experienced a Flight-to-Liquidity. In the first three weeks of September, LTCM's equity tumbled from $2.3 billion to $600 million without shrinking the portfolio, leading to a significant elevation of the already high leverage.

Goldman Sachs, AIG and Berkshire Hathaway offered then to buy out the fund's partners for $250 million, to inject $3.75 billion and to operate LTCM within Goldman Sachs's own trading. The offer was rejected and the same day the Federal Reserve Bank of New York organized a bail out of $3.625 billion by the major creditors to avoid a wider collapse in the financial markets.

The fear was that there would be a chain reaction as the company liquidated its securities to cover its debt, leading to a drop in prices,

本损失，而并非不同债券利差的减小所带来的盈利。

正因为这些损失，长期资本管理公司不得不将其部分资产变现来渡过难关。

这个曾经年回报率高达40%的公司经历了"流动性迁徙"。9月的前三周里，长期资本管理公司的股份从23亿美元跌至6亿美元（缩水），使公司本已很高的杠杆率显著上升。

高盛集团，美国国际集团和伯克式尔·哈萨维集团出资2亿5千万美元收购长期资本管理公司，另外注资37.5亿美元将其纳入高盛集团旗下。然而，该提议被拒绝。同一天，纽约联邦储备银行为了避免金融市场的大面积崩盘，由主要债权人出资36.25亿美元对长期资本管理公司进行了援助。

随着长期资本管理公司将其持有的证券变现来偿还债务，一系列连锁反应也相伴而生，这将导致对

---

[41] annual: ['ænjuəl] *a.* 每年的，年度的

which would force other companies to liquidate their own debt creating a vicious cycle.

The total losses were found to be $4.6 billion. Long Term Capital was audited by Price Waterhouse LLP.Unsurprisingly, after the bail-out by the other investors, the panic abated.

Some industry officials said that Federal Reserve Bank of New York involvement in the rescue, however benign, would encourage large financial institutions to assume more risk, in the belief that the Federal Reserve would intervene on their behalf in the event of trouble. Federal Reserve Bank of New York actions raised concerns among some market observers that it could create moral hazard.

The profits from LTCM's trading strategies were generally not correlated with each other and thus normally LTCM's highly leveraged portfolio benefited from diversification. However, the general flight to liquidity in the late summer of 1998 led to a marketwide repricing of all risk leading these positions to all move in the same direction. As the correlation of LTCM's positions increased, the diversified aspect of LTCM's portfolio vanished and large losses to its equity value occurred. Thus the primary lesson of 1998 and the collapse of LTCM for Value at Risk

证券价格下跌的担忧。这也会迫使其他公司竞相变现手中的证券来偿还债务，从而导致恶性循环。

这场危机总计损失46亿美元。长期资本管理公司的账目也由普华永道负责审计调查。经过其他银行的紧急救援，这场危机带来的恐慌也毫无悬念的停止了。

然而，纽约联邦储备银行参与救援行动却遭到许多行业管理者的质疑。他们认为政府在危机中介入的做法可能会使更多的投资银行铤而走险，甚至会产生道德风险。

长期资本管理公司的交易策略是多样化的，各投资项目的利润通常都不相关。然而，1998年夏末的"流动性迁徙"导致金融市场上出现了对风险重新定价的风潮，使各投资项目利润的相关性增大，长期资本管理公司资产组合的多样性荡然无存，股票价值大幅亏损。长期资本管理公司的倒塌给风险价值模型的使用者上了很重要的一课，因为长期资本管理公司的倒塌不是流动性的原因。最根本的原因在于风险价值模型中的协方差矩阵也应随着时间而变化，而不是静止的。

(VaR) users is not a liquidity one, but more fundamentally that the underlying Covariance matrix used in VaR analysis is not static but changes over time.

Also, if the fund had been less leveraged, it would have weathered the spike in volatility and credit risk: In the end, the idea of LTCM's directional bets was correct, in that the values of government bonds did eventually converge. Due to the high leverage, however, this only happened after the firm's capital was wiped out.

Thus, the incident confirms an insight often (though perhaps apocryphally) attributed to the economist John Maynard Keynes, who is said to have warned investors that although markets do tend toward rational positions in the long run, "the market can stay irrational longer than you can stay solvent[42]".

Nassim Taleb compared LTCM's strategies to "picking up pennies in front of a steamroller" — a likely small gain balanced against a small chance of a large loss, like the payouts from selling an out-of-the-money option. These strategies would have operated as sort of a reverse St. Petersburg lottery. Even in the particular conditions which resulted in

事实上，如果公司的杠杆率低一些，便能减弱信用风险和剧烈波动。最终，长期资本管理公司在方向上的预测是正确的，因为政府债券确实有这样的趋势。然而，由于公司的杠杆率太高，这样的趋势只有在公司将其资本削减后才会出现。

这起事件更加证明了约翰·梅纳德·凯恩斯对投资者的告诫：长期来讲，市场会趋于理性，然而，"市场也会经常变得盲目而使你破产"。

纳西姆·塔雷伯将长期资本管理公司的战略比做"在压路机前面捡硬币"，形容在巨大的风险面前去争取一点小利润。长期管理资本公司的战略相当于圣彼得堡悖论的反例。即使公司的利润有所下滑，如果公司持有的头寸到期，也不会蒙受巨大损失。然而1998年的事件加大了巨大损失的可能，主要是长

---

[42] solvent: ['sɔlvənt] a. 有偿付能力的

the fund's downfall, these large losses would not, if the positions were held to maturity, have come to pass. However, the events of 1998 increased the perceived probability of large losses, to the point where LTCM's portfolio had negative value.

期资本管理公司的资产组合出现了负值。

非常点拨

1. **协方差矩阵**（Covariance matrix） 在统计学与概率论中，协方差矩阵(或称共变异矩阵) 是一个矩阵，其每个元素是各个向量元素之间的方差。

2. **风险价值**（Value at Risk,VaR） 资产组合在持有期间内在特定的置信区间内由于市场价格变动所导致的最大预期损失的数值。由此衍生出来的"风险价值"方法是风险管理中应用广泛、研究活跃的风险定量分析方法之一。

3. **彼得堡悖论** 是决策论中的一个悖论。18世纪30年代，数学家丹尼尔·伯努利（Daniel Bernoulli）的表兄尼古拉·伯努利提出一个谜题：掷硬币，若第一次掷出正面，你就赚1元。若第一次掷出反面，那就要再掷一次，若第二次掷的是正面，你便赚2元。若第二次掷出反面，那就要掷第三次，若第三次掷的是正面，你便赚2×2元……依此类推，即可能掷一次游戏便结束，也可能反复掷却没完没了。

Bank of Credit and
Commerce International

Unit 8

Bank of Credit and Commerce International
国际信贷商业银行

主题札记

国际商业信贷银行(Bank of Credit and Commerce International，BCCI)是一家于卢森堡注册，于1991年7月5日倒闭的银行。当时，在全球65个国家和地区设有超过350个办事处。

BCCI由巴基斯坦人阿甘·哈桑·阿贝迪创立，于1972年在英国伦敦开业。1988年，因美国佛罗里达分行涉嫌为贩毒集团处理赃款而声誉受损。

1991年，英伦银行在例行调查时发现，BCCI于1990年严重亏损，但没有对外公布。其后英格兰银行认为事态严重，在与卢森堡和开曼群岛的金融机构讨论后，三方一致同意接管该行。

1991年7月5日，英伦银行正式宣布接管后，全球各地的金融管理机构均勒令该行在当地停业。几日后，全球的业务均相继停止。经调查，该行被发现涉及一连串诸如洗钱、替恐怖分子输送资金等违法行为，同时其贷款部门未作有效审查导致无法收回贷款，为吸取资金补偿坏账又以高息存款吸引储户及向其他银行借贷，均是倒闭原因。

同月29日及8月10日，两位调查有关事件的记

Agha Hasan Abedi
阿甘·哈桑·阿贝迪

103

者突然"猝死",但死因未明。其中,死于危地马拉的是一位原籍马来西亚的华裔吴姓记者,据说他当时正在追查BCCI在当地的一大新闻;另一位在西弗吉尼亚州出事的美国记者卡索拉若,据说也正在追查BCCI内幕。

BCCI的倒闭,是20世纪末在国际金融界引起极大反应的事件,被视为"世界金融史上最大的丑闻"。值得一提的是,BCCI五度有意进军新加坡,但监管当局均拒绝有关申请,认为其作风不稳健。

Abu Nidal
阿布尼达

Introduction of BCCI

The Bank of Credit and Commerce International (BCCI) was a major international bank founded in London, United Kingdom in 1972 by Agha Hasan Abedi, a leading Pakistani financier. The company was registered in Luxembourg. At its peak, it operated in 78 countries, had over 400 branches, and had assets in excess of $ 20 billion making it the 7th largest bank in the world by assets.

BCCI became the focus in 1991 of the world's worst financial scandal and what was called a "$20-billion-plus heist[43]".Regulators in the United States and the United Kingdom found it to be involved in money laundering, bribery[44], support of terrorism, arms trafficking[45], the sale

国际信贷商业银行简介

国际信贷商业银行（BCCI）是巴基斯坦金融家阿甘·哈桑·阿贝迪于1972年在英国伦敦建立的一家主营国际业务的银行。该银行在卢森堡注册，在巅峰时期，曾在78个国家拥有400多家分行，并拥有超过200亿美元的资产，若按资产论，曾经是世界第七大银行。

BCCI在1991年因为金融界最大丑闻"200亿美元加抢劫"成为世界焦点。英国和美国的检察官发现BCCI与洗钱、行贿、支持恐怖分子、贩卖军火、出售核技术、偷税漏税、走私、非法移民、非法购置房地产和非法收购银行等多项罪

---

[43] heist: [haist] *n.* 强夺，拦劫，抢劫
[44] bribery: ['braibəri] *n.* 贿赂行为，行贿，受贿
[45] traffick: ['træfik] *vi.* 交易，买卖，运输，贸易

of nuclear technologies, the commission and facilitation of tax evasion, smuggling[46], illegal immigration, and the illicit purchases of banks and real estate. The bank was found to have at least $13 billion unaccounted for. The bank was dubbed satirically the "Bank of Crooks[47] and Criminals International".

名有关。此外，该银行还被指控拥有至少130亿美元的不明资产，因此被冠以"国际犯罪和诈骗银行"的绰号。

Investigators in the U.S. and the UK revealed that BCCI had been "set up deliberately to avoid centralized regulatory review, and operated extensively in bank secrecy jurisdictions[48]. Its affairs were extraordinarily complex. Its officers were sophisticated international bankers whose apparent objective was to keep their affairs secret, to commit fraud[49] on a massive scale, and to avoid detection"; BCCI organized its own intelligence network, diplomatic corps and shipping & trading companies.

美国和英国的检察官还披露BCCI在逃避中央的监管并且越权经营。它所经营的业务极其复杂。它的职员大都是具有复杂的国际背景的国际银行家，并且明显隐瞒其经营业务，涉嫌大规模诈骗和逃避调查。BCCI还组织自己的信息网，外交团队和运输贸易公司。

It is widely held amongst stakeholders[50] in many Islamic countries that the Bank's closure was due to its perceived threat to Western interests. The perception of threat derived from the Bank's predominantly Islamic client base, and its loans to the Government of Pakistan at

许多伊斯兰国家的利益相关方认为该银行的停业是因为它的存在潜在地威胁了西方国家的利益。这主要是因为该银行的绝大多数客户来自穆斯林国家，同时该银行在美国对巴基斯坦实行封锁时（因为

---

[46] smuggling: ['smʌɡliŋ] *v.* 走私
[47] crook: [kruk] *n.* 钩，弯曲部分，恶棍
[48] jurisdiction: [,dʒuəris'dikʃən] *n.* 司法权，审判权，管辖权
[49] fraud: [frɔd] *n.* 骗子，欺骗，诈欺
[50] stakeholder: ['steikhəuldə(r)] *n.* 保管赌注的人，利益相关者

a time when the U.S. had imposed sanctions[51] against Pakistan, citing that government's pursuit of nuclear technology.

Corrupt and Questionable Practices

BCCI's rapid growth alarmed the financial community, as well as regulators. When a bank grows rapidly, it is lending more and more money each year. BCCI contended that its growth was fueled[52] by the large number of deposits by the wealthy oil barons[53] who owned stock in the bank. However, this wasn't enough to mollify[54] the regulators. For example, the Bank of England ordered BCCI to cap its branch network in the United Kingdom at 45 branches.

There was particular concern over BCCI's loan portfolio because of its roots in an area where modern banking was still an alien[55] concept. In Abedi's native Pakistan, the borrower's status in the community and relationship with his banker were more important than the ability to pay. One particularly notable example is the Gokal family,

巴基斯坦政府研发核技术），向巴基斯坦提供了贷款。

腐败和可疑操作

BCCI的迅速扩大不仅震动了金融界，并且也警示了监管者。当一家银行迅速扩大的时候，也就意味着它每年的贷款数额也在增大。BCCI承认它迅速的成长得益于石油大亨的资金注入（通过持有该银行的股票）。但是，这并不能打消监管者的疑虑。例如，英格兰银行限制BCCI在英国开设分行不得超过45家。

此外，BCCI的贷款组合也让人疑虑，因为它的根基是在现代银行概念还未形成的地区。在阿贝迪的家乡，借款者的地位及其与银行的关系比其偿还能力更重要。例如，高卡家族，当地的运输巨头，他们和阿贝迪的关系要追溯到联合银行时期。阿贝迪向他们提供

---

[51] sanction: ['sæŋkʃən] n. 核准，处罚，约束力
[52] fuel: [fjuəl] v. 加燃料，供以燃料
[53] baron: ['bærən] n. 男爵（英国世袭的最低级的贵族爵位）
[54] mollify: ['mɔlifai] v. 安慰，安抚
[55] alien: ['eiljən] a. 外国的，相异的

a prominent[56] family of shipping magnates[57]. They had a relationship with Abedi dating back to his days at United Bank. Abedi personally handled their loans, with little regard for details such as loan documents or creditworthiness. At one point, BCCI's loans to the Gokal companies were equivalent[58] to three times the bank's capital. Standard banking practices dictate that a bank should not lend more than 10 percent of its capital to a single customer. As early as 1977, BCCI began concealing[59] its shakier loans from regulators and auditors by transferring some of them to the Caymans, using a network of dummy companies to make it appear that they were being kept current.

Management moved money between BCCI, ICIC and other parts of the network to manufacture equity[60] capital and manipulate the stock price. Most of the bank's stockholders, as it turned out, didn't put actual capital into the bank. Rather, they borrowed money from BCCI and used it to buy BCCI stock. In exchange for not having to repay the loans, they were promised guaranteed rates of return on their stock. This made it appear that the bank was sounder than it actually was.

贷款时从不作信用调查，完全凭借其私人关系，以至于BCCI向高卡家族的贷款数量曾达到BCCI资产的三倍。而标准的银行业准则要求一家银行向一个客户贷款不应超过它全部资产的10%。早在1977年，BCCI就试图向监管者和审计委员会隐瞒其不良贷款，通过将其贷款转移到开曼群岛公司，再转移到其他虚拟公司，使这些公司看上去仍在经营。

此外，BCCI的管理层还通过与ICIC和其他公司之间转移股本的方式来操纵其股票价格。事实上，大多数BCCI的股东并没有注入资金，而是通过BCCI向他们提供的贷款购买了BCCI的股票。BCCI不仅不需要他们偿还贷款，还向他们保证股票的回报。这使得BCCI的股票价格远远超过其实际价值。

---

[56] prominent: ['prɔminənt] *a.* 杰出的，显著的，突出的

[57] magnate: ['mægneit] *n.* 富豪；巨头

[58] equivalent: [i'kwivələnt] *a.* 相同的，相等的

[59] conceal: [kən'si:l] *v.* 隐藏

[60] equity: ['ekwiti] *n.* 权益，产权，股本，证券

BCCI was also not shy about dealing with criminal elements. It frequently handled laundered money for various purposes, and was the banker for such dictators as Saddam Hussein, Manuel Noriega, Hussain Mohammad Ershad and Samuel Doe. In some cases, it actively took part in criminal activity. This led some to nickname the bank "the Bank of Crooks and Criminals International".

同时，BCCI在犯罪方面也不甘寂寞。它不仅经常因各种目的而洗钱，还为众多独裁者（如萨达姆·侯赛因、曼纽尔·诺利加、侯赛因·穆罕默德·艾沙德和塞缪尔·多伊）提供服务。难怪会被冠以"国际诈骗和犯罪银行"的绰号。

财经宝库

1. Money Laundary 洗钱　是指犯罪分子通过一系列金融账户转移非法资金，以便掩盖资金的来源、拥有者的身份，或是使用资金的最终目的。需要"清洗"的非法钱财一般都可能与恐怖主义、毒品交易或是集团犯罪有关。

2. Bank of England　英格兰银行　是英国政府的中央银行，于1694年成立，但从1946年才归国有。它负责货币供给、印发钞票和铸造硬币，向政府和其他银行提供货币，管理黄金和通货储币。该银行因设在伦敦城的位置而被人称为"针线街的老管家婆"（the old lady in thread needle street）。银行的首脑为总裁，由政府任命。

3. Saddam Hussein 萨达姆·侯赛因　1979年至2003年任伊拉克总统、伊拉克总理、伊拉克最高军事将领、伊拉克革命指挥委员会主席与伊拉克复兴党总书记等职。

在2003年伊拉克战争中，其政权被美国推翻，萨达姆逃亡半年后被美军俘获。经伊拉克法庭审判，于2006年11月5日被判绞刑，并于12月30日当地时间清晨6时5分执行，享年69岁。

4. Manuel Noriega 曼纽尔·诺利加　前巴拿马军事强人。出生于巴拿马市。1983年8月至1990年1月3日曾是巴拿马的实际领导人。

1. What criminal elements did BCCI get involved into?

2. What made BCCI so large?

3. Why is BCCI's shut down controversial?

洗钱 money laundary
制裁 sanction
信用 credit

偷税 tax evasion
贷款组合 loan portfolio
利益相关方 stakeholder

Shut down of BCCI-Sandstorm Report

BCCI的关闭——沙漠风暴报告

In March 1991, the Bank of England asked Price Waterhouse to carry out an inquiry. On June 24, 1991, using the codename "Sandstorm" for BCCI, Price Waterhouse submitted the Sandstorm report showing that BCCI had engaged in "widespread fraud and manipulation" that made it difficult, if not impossible, to reconstruct BCCI's financial history.

The Sandstorm report, parts of which were leaked to The Sunday Times, included details of how the Abu Nidal terrorist group had held accounts at BCCI's Sloane Street branch, near Harrods in London. Britain's internal security service, MI5, had signed up two sources inside the branch to hand over copies of all documents relating to Abu Nidal's accounts.

1991年3月，英格兰银行聘请普华永道会计公司对BCCI进行全面调查。1991年6月24日，普华永道公司秘密地递交了一份名为沙漠风暴的报告，指出BCCI广泛地参与了欺诈和操控，使得重铸其金融辉煌即使有一线希望，也是困难重重。

该报告指出阿布尼达恐怖集团在BCCI在Sloane大街的分行开设账户。同时，英国的国家内部安全机构（军情五处），派驻2名特工进入BCCI收集有关阿布尼达账户的资料。

Closure of the Bank

关闭银行

BCCI was awaiting final approval for a restructuring plan in which it would have reemerged as the "Oasis Banks". However, after the Sandstorm report, a consortium of regulators decided that BCCI was so riddled with fraud that it would have to be seized. It had already been ordered to shut down its American operations in March for its illegal control of First American.

当BCCI在等待重振旗鼓的时候（改名绿洲银行），沙漠风暴报告促使检察官决定将BCCI捉拿归案。事实上，3月时，BCCI因为它对第一美国银行的非法操纵已经被勒令停止它在美国的业务。

On July 5, 1991, the regulators persuaded a court in Luxembourg to order BCCI liquidated because it was hopelessly insolvent and had lost more than its entire capital and reserves in 1990. At 1 p.m. London time that day, regulators in five countries marched into BCCI's offices and shut them down. Within a few days, BCCI was no more.

1991年7月5日，监管当局说服卢森堡法院命令BCCI停业清算，因为1990年BCCI的亏损已远超过了其资本和储备之和而无力回天。伦敦时间当天下午1点，BCCI在五个国家的办事处被停业。几天以后，BCCI成为了历史。

Around a million depositors[61] were affected. Court-appointed liquidators for BCCI later found that its balance sheet was a total fabrication[62]; some of its liabilities and most of its assets didn't even exist. Moreover, $9.5 billion had been lost or stolen.

大约100万储户受到了影响。清算组发现，BCCI的资产负债表可以说是完全捏造，因为上面的部分负债和绝大多数资产都不存在，并且，有95亿美元不知去向。

On July 17, officials in the United

7月17日，英国官员披露BCCI

---

[61] depositor: [di'pɔzitə] *n.* 寄托者，存款人
[62] fabrication: [ˌfæbri'keiʃ ən] *n.* 制造，建造，虚构的谎言

Kingdom revealed that BCCI had used First American's stock as collateral[63] for loans used to cover up fraud at BCCI. They also revealed BCCI had probably never turned a profit during its existence.

On July 29, Manhattan District Attorney Robert Morgenthau said that all of BCCI's deposits had been fraudulently[64] collected because the bank misled depositors about its ownership structure and financial condition. He described BCCI as "the largest bank fraud in world financial history".

On November 15, BCCI, Abedi and Naqvi were indicted on federal charges that it had illegally bought control of another American bank, Independence Bank of Los Angeles.

However, many of the major players in the scandal have never been brought to trial in American or UK courts. Pharaon, for example, is still a fugitive[65] as of 2008.

In 1992, United States Senators John Kerry and Hank Brown co-authored a report on BCCI, which was delivered to the Committee on Foreign Relations. The report found that Clifford and his legal/business partner Robert A. Altman had been closely involved with the

用第一美国银行的股票做抵押来掩盖它的欺诈行为。他们还透露BCCI可能在存在期间从未盈利过。

7月29日，曼哈顿地区律师罗伯特·摩根索认为BCCI所有的存款均不合法，因为它欺骗了储蓄者，隐瞒了它真正的产权结构和财务状况。他认为BCCI是世界金融史上最大的银行诈骗案。

11月15日，BCCI的阿贝迪和那可威被联邦法院指控非法收购并操纵另一家美国银行，洛杉矶独立银行。

然而，本次事件的主要人物并没有收到美国和英国法院的传票。例如，法拉让，直到2008年仍逍遥法外。

1992年，美国参议员约翰·克里和汉克·布朗联名上书对外关系委员会。该报告指出克里佛德和他的法律/商业伙伴罗伯特·A.奥特曼从1978年开始便与BCCI有过亲密的接触，并且应该了解BCCI操控第一美国银行的行为。

---

[63] collateral: [kəˈlætərəl] *n.* 旁系亲属，担保品，附属担保物
[64] fraudulently: [ˈfrɔːdjuləntli] *ad.* 欺诈地，不正地
[65] fugitive: [ˈfjuːdʒitiv] *a.* 逃亡的，易变的，无常的

bank from 1978, and should have known BCCI control First American Bank.

The British government also set up an independent inquiry, chaired by Lord Justice Bingham, in 1992. Its House of Commons Paper, Inquiry into *the Supervision*[66] *of the Bank of Credit and Commerce International*, was published in October of that year. Following the report, the bank's liquidators launched[67] the Three Rivers vs. Bank of England case, on behalf of thousands of BCCI creditors[68] who are suing the Bank of England for its failure to properly oversee the bank. The BCCI creditors sought £850million in damages, claiming that the Bank of England was guilty of misfeasance[69] in public office.

The case collapsed in November 2005, with the Bank of England seeking to re-claim legal bills. The cost of the case to the creditors could be as high as £100million.

英国政府也在1992年由宾汉大法官领导对BCCI进行了独立的调查并于同年10月出版了《国际信贷商业银行调查报告》。此外，BCCI的清算组发动了三河对英格兰银行案，代表数千名BCCI的债权人起诉英格兰银行，理由是英格兰对BCCI缺乏适当地监管。同时，BCCI的债权人寻求8亿5千万英镑的损失，并声称英格兰银行在公共事务上滥用职权。

直到2005年11月，该案才以英格兰银行胜诉而告终。而对那些债权人来说，本案的成本高达1亿英镑。

---

[66] supervision: [ˌsjuːpəˈviʒən] *n.* 监督，管理
[67] launch: [lɔːntʃ, laːntʃ] *n.&v.* 下水，发射，开始，升天，汽艇
[68] creditor: [ˈkreditə] *n.* 债权人
[69] misfeasance: [misˈfiːzəns] *n.* 不当行为，行为失检，过失

非常点拨

1. **普华永道会计师事务所** 1998年合并组建而成。普华永道和毕马威（KPMG）、安永（Ernst&Young）以及德勤（Deloitte Touche Tohmatsu）合称为四大会计师事务所。

2. **军情五处（MI5）** 是英国国内的反情报及国家安全部门（The Security Service），隶属于英国内政部，负责打击国内的严重罪案、军事分离主义、恐怖主义及间谍活动，而对外的国安职务则由军情六处负责。

3. **资产负债表（Balance Sheet）** 为会计、商业会计或簿记实务上的财务报表之一，与购销损益账、现金流量表、股东权益变动表并列为企业四大常用财务报表。资产负债表利用会计平衡原则，将合乎会计原则的资产、负债、股东权益交易科目分为"资产"和"负债及股东权益"两大区块，在经过分录、转账、分类账、试算、调整等会计程序后，以特定日期的静态企业情况为基准，浓缩成一张报表。其报表功用除了企业内部除错、防止弊端外，也可让所有阅读者于最短时间内了解企业经营状况。

4. **抵押（Collaterlization）** 是指债务人或第三人不转移财产的占有权，而将财产抵押作为债权的担保，当债务人不履行债务时，债权人有权依法以抵押财产折价或以拍卖、变卖抵押财产的价款优先受偿。

Japan's Asset Bubble

Unit 9

Japan's Asset Bubble
日本资产泡沫

主题札记

1985年，随着利率的降低，日本经济出现流动性过剩的萌芽。

1987年美国股市暴跌之后，日本股市率先恢复，并且带动了全球股市的回升。此后，日本股市一直呈上升态势。1987年1月，东京证券交易所证券市价总额突破300万亿日元，日经股价指数1月突破2万亿日元，6月突破2.5万亿日元大关。1988年年初，大藏省打出"以特定金钱信托强化基金托拉斯弹性"的方针，给法人投资者注入了强心剂，鼓励法人投资者，股票市场创出新高。8月，为了防止内部交易，颁布的《日本证券交易法》新增了"防火墙"的规定，要求各公司内部把交易部门和投资咨询部门分开。1989年，日本银行逐步调高利率。1989年12月，东京证券交易所开市的日经平均股指高达38,915点，这也是投资者们最后一次赚取暴利的机会。

进入20世纪90年代，股市价格旋即暴跌。到1990年10月，日经平均股指跌破20,000点。1991年上半年略有回升，但下半年跌势更猛。 1992年4月1日，东京证券市场的日经平均股指跌破了17,000点，日本股市陷入恐慌。8月18日降至14,309点，基本上回到了1985年的水平。到此为止，股指比最高峰时期下降了63%，上市股票市价总额由1989年年底的630万亿日元降至299万亿日元，三年减少了331万亿日元，日本股市的泡沫彻底破裂。

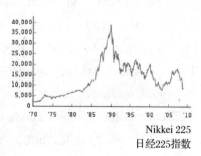

Nikkei 225
日经225指数

阅读长廊

Japanese Asset Price Bubble

The Japanese asset price bubble was a time of skyrocketing land and stock prices in the Japanese economy, that peaked from 1986 to 1990 and hit bottom in its valuation of the Nikkei index in 2003. It is one of the more famous speculative bubbles in economic history.

In the decades following World War Ⅱ, Japan implemented stringent tariffs[70] and policies to encourage the people to save their income. With more money in banks, loans and credit became easier to obtain, and with Japan running large trade surpluses, the yen was able to appreciate against foreign currencies. This allowed Japanese companies to invest in capital resources much more easily than their competitors making goods cheaper and widening the trade surplus further. And, with the

日本资产价格泡沫

日本资产价格泡沫是指1986年到1990年日本国内土地和股票价格飞涨，日经平均股指于2003年触底，这是经济史上最著名的投机泡沫之一。

第二次世界大战后的几十年间，日本政府采取严厉的关税政策并鼓励人们储蓄。随着更多银行储蓄的增加，贷款变得越来越容易，同时贸易顺差的加大使得日元升值成为可能，这也使得日本公司比它们的竞争对手更有投资能力，进一步降低产品价格，使贸易顺差进一步加大，日元升值也使投资金融资产更加有利可图。

---

[70] tariff: ['tærif] *n.* 关税

yen appreciating, financial assets became very lucrative[71].

Unfortunately, with so much money readily available for investment, speculation was inevitable, particularly in the Tokyo Stock Exchange and the real estate market. The Nikkei stock index hit its all-time high on December 29, 1989 when it reached an intra-day high of 38,957.44 before closing at 38,915.87. The rates for housing, stocks, and bonds rose so much that at one point the government issued 100-year bonds. Additionally, banks granted increasingly risky loans.

At the height of the bubble, a commonly-quoted claim was that the land beneath[72] the Imperial Palace in Tokyo was worth more than the entire state of California. Japan regained a sense of national pride and assertiveness as a result of its new power, which manifested[73] itself in works such as *The Japan That Can Say No* by Shintaro Ishihara and SONY founder Akio Morita. Many outside Japan were alarmed by this resurgence, leading to criticism from foreign observers. Michael Crichton, for example, wrote *Rising Sun* at this time, which highlighted U.S. concerns with the growing Japanese economic

不幸的是，随着资金面的日益充足，股票市场（东京股票交易所）和房地产市场上的投机也不可避免。日经平均股指于1989年12月29日达到前所未有的最高点38,957.44点，收于38,915.87点。住房、股票和债券价格飙升的背后是日本政府发行了百年债券，此外，银行也发放了大量高风险贷款。

在这场泡沫中，最出名的引用就是东京皇居下面的土地比整个美国加利福尼亚州的土地都值钱。随着日本经济的崛起，日本民族的自豪感也在膨胀，这也表现在索尼公司的创始人盛田昭夫和右翼政客石原慎太郎的书《日本可以说不》中。同时也引起了许多国外观察家的注意，例如在迈克尔·克莱顿的《升起的太阳》中，表达了美国对日本经济实力增长的担忧。

---

[71] lucrative: ['lu:krətiv,lju:-] *a.* 有利益的，获利的，合算的

[72] beneath: [bi'ni:θ] *prep.* 在……之下

[73] manifest: ['mænifest] *v.* 显示，出现，证明

power.

Prices were highest in Tokyo's Ginza district in 1989, with some fetching over $1.5 million per square meter, and only slightly less in other areas of Tokyo. By 2004, prime "A" property in Tokyo's financial districts were less than 1/100th of their peak, and Tokyo's residential homes were 1/10th of their peak, but still managed to be listed as the most expensive real estate in the world. Some $20 trillion was wiped out with the combined collapse of the real estate market and the Tokyo stock market.

With Japan's economy driven by its high rates of reinvestment, this crash hit particularly hard. Investments were increasingly directed out of the country, and Japanese manufacturing firms lost some degree of their technological edge. As Japanese products became less competitive overseas, the low consumption rate began to bear on the economy, causing a deflationary[74] spiral.

The easily obtainable credit that had helped create and engorge the real estate bubble continued to be a problem for several years to come, and as late as 1997, banks were still making loans that had a low guarantee of being repaid. Correcting the credit problem became

1989年，东京银座地区的房价达到高峰，超过150万美元/平方米，然而这仅比东京其他地区的房价略高。2004年，东京金融区的优质房价格跌到高峰时的百分之一，东京居民住房的价格也仅为高峰时的十分之一，尽管如此，东京地区的房产仍被认为是世界上最贵的。当东京股价和房价大跌时，缩水近20万亿美元。

因为日本经济增长主要来自其再投资的高回报率，资产泡沫的破裂对日本经济打击尤为严重。随着大量投资从日本撤出，日本从事制造业的公司失去了以往的技术优势，日本产品在海外市场的竞争力减弱，消费的减弱引起了通货紧缩的加剧。

贷款发放的过度宽松成了房地产泡沫的罪魁祸首。直到1997年，银行仍然向偿还率很低的企业发放贷款。因为政府对经营失败的企业和银行的大量补助使得修正银行坏账问题变得更加困难，这些企业也被称为"僵尸企业"。

---

[74] deflation: [diˈfleiʃ(ə)n] *n.* 通货紧缩

even more difficult as the government began to subsidize[75] failing banks and businesses, creating many so-called "zombie businesses".

The time after the bubble's collapse, which occurred gradually rather than catastrophically, is known as the "lost decade or end of the century" in Japan. The Nikkei 225 stock index eventually bottomed out at 7,603.76 in April 2003 before resuming an upward climb.

20世纪的最后十年对日本来说可谓是"失去的十年"，资产泡沫的破裂并不是突然性的而是渐渐的。日经225股指直到2003年4月触底后（7,603.76点）才开始进入上行通道。

财经宝库

1. **日经平均指数**（Nikkei225，又名日经225，另译做日经平均股票价格、日经225指数） 全名为日本经济平均指数，是由日本经济新闻推出的东京证券交易所的225个品种的股价指数，1971年第一次发布。

日经指数的最高点是1989年12月29日一度升至的38,957.44点，当日日经指数收盘于38,915.87点。东京证券交易所（TSE）的另外一个主要指数是Topix。

2. **净出口**（net exports）或称**贸易余额**（balance of trade） 是指一国在一定时期内的出口总值（exports）和进口总值（imports）的差额，经济学上为了方便，常以NX符号代替。

净出口为正值时，称为贸易盈余、贸易顺差或出超（trade surplus）；净出口为负值

---

[75] subsidize ['sʌbsidaiz] v. 资助，给……补助金

121

时，则称为贸易赤字、贸易逆差或入超（trade deficit）。

实务上，净出口（贸易余额）有时又细分成有形商品和无形服务两个部分。如美国商务部的 *Survey of Current Business* 报告书中，有着 "商品贸易余额"（Merchandise Trade Balance）和 "服务贸易余额"（Balance on Services）的项目；在英国则使用 "有形贸易余额"（visible balance）和 "无形贸易余额"（invisible balance）的称呼。

3. 东京证券交易所（日文：东京证券取引所；英文：Tokyo Stock Exchange） 是日本的证券交易所之一，简称 "东证"（東証），总部位于东京都中央区日本桥兜町。其事业体分为 "株式会社东京证券交易所" 及 "东京证券交易所自主规制法人" 两个法人。

4. 皇居 是指日本天皇居住的宫殿，古代因为没有定都的想法，所以古代的皇居经常变更，几乎都是以该天皇的即位地为国都，并以该天皇原本居住的宫室为皇居。

Tokyo Stock Exchange
东京证券交易所

Tokyo Stock Exchange
东京证券交易所

DIY工作室

1. What makes Japan so proud during 1960s and 1970s?

2. What do you think is the foundamental reason of Japan Asset Bubble?

归类记忆卡片

贸易盈余 trade surplus
放贷 make loan
投机泡沫 speculative bubble

再投资 reinvestment
通货紧缩 deflation

听力广场

Japan — The Lost Decade: Bubble Economics

Japan is the second biggest industrial economy in the world. In the 1980s it experienced a huge speculative bubble, just like the housing bubble that has burst in the USA and is on the point of bursting in Britain now. When the bubble burst, the Japanese people,

日本——失去的十年：泡沫经济

日本是全球第二大经济体，20世纪80年代，日本经济经历了巨大的投机泡沫，正如时下美国和英国的房地产泡沫一样。当这个泡沫破裂的时候，日本人结束了被他们称为"经济奇迹"的时期，而是经历了十年的衰退——"失去的十年"。

123

who up till then were regarded as living in a "miracle economy", experienced a decade of recession-a "lost decade".

After the Second World War Japanese capitalism was a smoking ruin. But within a few years it had reconstructed itself and by the 1950s was growing at an annual rate of 10%, a speed which no other capitalist nation had achieved till then. This growth was export-led. Japan was widely recognised as an economic miracle. Rivals muttered bitterly about the "yellow peril[76]", sensing that a great capitalist nation was emerging.

Japan was a different type of capitalism from the Anglo-Saxon model. Firms were organised in groups called keiretsu, held together by an interventionist bank or banks. The banks provided the funds for long term investment, under the direction of MITI, the Ministry of International Trade and Industry. By contrast British and American banks were historically unconcerned with industry and reluctant to lend long-term to manufacturers.

After 1945, world trade was conducted by means of fixed exchange rates against the dollar, which was the world's reserve currency.

第二次世界大战刚结束时，日本还是一片焦土。然而几年之后，日本不仅完成了战后重建，日本经济在整个50年代都保持了10%的增长，这种速度是其他资本主义国家所不及的。由出口带动的日本经济的高速增长被广泛称为经济奇迹。尽管被竞争对手称为黄色恐慌，但这恰恰证明了日本的崛起。

日本经济与盎格鲁—萨克逊经济（英美）模式最大的不同在于公司组合在一起形成大的财阀，同时银行在其中起到穿针引线的作用。银行在国际和贸易工业部门的领导下对公司提供融资或进行长期投资。而英美银行由于历史原因往往不愿意向制造型企业发放长期贷款。

自1945年后，大多数国家都通过各种方式对美元这一世界储备货币采用固定汇率政策来进行国际

---

[76] peril: ['peril] *n.* 危险，冒险

For much of this early post-War period there were 360 yen to the dollar. This proved to be a very competitive rate, central to Japan's export success.

It was for a time the most competitive capitalist nation in the world and built up huge surpluses with other countries, particularly the USA. The emergence of dynamic capitalist powers such Japan and Germany challenge the U.S. hegemony[77]. Eventually the edifice[78] created at Bretton Woods cracked, as the international balance of forces changed in the course of the post-War economic boom. The USA, no longer able to pay its bills, floated the dollar in 1971.

The world moved to a floating exchange rate system. The yen appreciated and exports became dearer and less competitive. By the mid-1970s the dollar would only buy 210 yen, not 360. By 1988 it bought just 120 yen. Japan was still able to achieve 5% growth rates throughout the 1970s, and 4% in the 1980s, but the rising yen was hurting.

Under Reagan, the American economy was in a worse and worse state. At the *Plaza Accord* in 1985 the Americans decided to pistol[79] whip[80]

贸易。 第二次世界大战初期的很长一段时间，日元兑美元汇率都在360日元兑1美元左右。这样低的汇率也为日本出口的成功起到重要作用。

这个当时最有竞争力的资本主义国家积累起巨额的贸易顺差，尤其是与美国。日本和德国经济的崛起挑战着美国的经济霸权，布雷顿森林体系建立起来的秩序开始垮台。1971年，美国由于无力支付其巨额开支，美元开始实行浮动汇率政策。

浮动汇率使得日元升值，到70年代中期，1美元只能兑换210日元而不是360日元，而到1988年，1美元只能兑换120日元。日元升值给日本的出口带来巨大压力，尽管如此，日本还是在整个70年代保持了5%的增长率，80年代保持了4%的增长率。

在里根时代，美国经济每况愈下，在1985年的《广场协议》中，美国为了修正其巨大的贸易逆差，

---

[77] hegemony: [hi(:)'gemeni] *n.* 霸权，领导权
[78] edifice: ['edifis] *n.* 大厦，大建筑物
[79] pistol: ['pistl] *vt.* 用手枪射击
[80] whip: [(h)wip] *n.* 鞭打，鞭，执鞭者

their "trading partners" and rivals into letting the dollar slide and pushing up their own currencies in order to correct the U.S. deficit. This meant putting the yen sky high.

Japanese banks had their arms twisted to liberalise, to lend more money. The loans were often secured by land as collateral. This was the prime cause of the land price bubble after 1985. More lending increased the demand for land, so its price went up. So people borrowed still more money to buy land, in order to borrow even more. Interest rates in Japan were slashed from 5% to 2.5%. The Japanese government supported this as they felt it would stimulate growth at home now the export market was under threat.

Borrowing drove prices up for land and for shares. From 1985 to 1990 land prices soared. By the end of this period the land beneath the emperor's palace was "worth" more than the whole of California. Land in Japan was "worth" more than all the land in the rest of the world put together. Sky high land prices are not good for business. "At the height of the land price explosion the market value of the land owned by the non-financial corporations (NFCs) exceeded the value of the machinery, buildings and inventories, thus halving the profit rate and bringing it to a very low level by the end of the boom."

敦促其主要贸易伙伴和竞争对手提高对美元的汇率，这也就意味着日元将被推向天价。

日本银行也开始大量放贷。由于这些贷款将土地作为抵押物，这为1985年之后的土地价格泡沫埋下了伏笔。借贷需求的增大也使得土地需求增大和价格升高，这是因为许多人用借来的钱买地后又将土地抵押给银行以获得新的贷款。同时，为了刺激国内经济增长，日本政府将利率从5%骤降到2.5%，然而这给出口企业带来了威胁。

大量的贷款也使土地和股票的价格大幅升高。1985年到1990年，土地价格飙升。最终的结果是皇居下的土地比整个美国加利福尼亚州的土地都值钱，日本的土地价值超过世界所有其他国家土地价值的总和。然而，如此高的地价对工商企业不利。非金融企业所持有的土地价值超过机器、建筑物和库存的价值，也使得这些企业的利润率在泡沫高峰阶段末降到很低的水平。

At the same time the Nikkei share index soared to 40,000. We can see now that all this was madness. The bubble in Japan did stimulate economic activity for a time. In the late 1980s Japan was regarded as a world leader in cars, in consumer electronics and in robotics. Commentators began to talk about a "new paradigm[81]". The next time the phrase was used was during the IT share price bubble that burst in 2001. When the sages speak of a "new paradigm" it's time to sell the shares!

Source: Socialist Appeal UK.

同时，日经平均股指也冲到了4万点。现在我们可以看到这简直是疯狂。经济泡沫也在一定程度上刺激了日本经济的发展。20世纪80年代末期，日本已成为世界汽车、家电和机器人技术的"领头羊"。这时评论家们开始谈论"新范式"，而当2001年IT泡沫破裂时，这个词同样被提起。看来当下次智者们使用这个词时，就是抛售手中股票的时候了。

摘自　英国Socialist Appeal UK。

非常点拨

1. 1988～1989年，公司投资急剧膨胀。伴随高股价，新股票快速升值，当银行在不动产方面寻找资金投向时，股票发行便成为公司融资的一个重要来源。反过来，公司利用它们持有的不动产进行间接的股市投机，从而形成了不动产与股市双重泡沫——房地产价格持续暴涨及日经225股票指数持续暴涨。

---

[81] paradigm: ['pærədaim,-dim] *n.* 示例，模范

2. 1985年年底，日经225股票指数收于13,083点，1989年年底收于38,916点，四年间日经225指数累计上涨197.45%。1987年年底，日本股票市值竟然占到全球股票总市值的41.7%，并赶超了美国，成为世界第一。1989年年底股票总市值继续膨胀至896万亿日元，占当年国民生产总值的60%。

股市泡沫与房地产泡沫是日本泡沫经济的两大根本"支柱"。当日本股市一路凯歌高奏之时，日本房地产价格也正在疯狂上涨。据日本不动产研究所的调查，日本六大主要城市的商业区地价指数，若1955年为100，到1965年，则上涨超过了1,000，到1988年则超过了10,000，也就是说，日本城市房地产价格在33年间上涨了100倍，而同期名义国民生产总值上涨却不足40倍，制造业工人的平均工资上涨不到20倍。1990年高峰期时，东京商业区的地价涨至1985年的2.7倍，住宅区地价则涨至1985年的2.3倍。与此同时，由于日元大幅升值，也严重刺激了日本人海外收购与海外投资热情。

1990年，随着日本股市泡沫的率先破裂，日本房地产泡沫也随之破裂。

1989年5月，政府紧缩其货币政策以抑制诸如房地产等资产价格的上涨。然而，更高的利率使股市螺旋向下。1990年年底，东京股票市值已下跌了38%，300万亿日元（折合2.07万亿美元）的股票市值瞬间消失，房地产价格从投机巅峰陡降下来，从而使日本经济陷入了"泡沫经济"破灭后的萧条之中。

3. 银行业受到严重打击。在日本股市泡沫与房地产泡沫形成过程中，银行始终是充满激情，并推波助澜，且从中大为受益。然而，双泡沫破裂的同时，日本银行业也遭受了灭顶之灾的报复与打击。股市暴跌，上市银行再融资受阻；房地产泡沫破裂，不动产贷款成为呆账；企业效益陡降，银行不良资产剧增。20世纪80年代的泡沫经济直接为90年代中期日本银行赤字风暴与金融危机埋下了隐患。

4. 证券业出现空前萧条。随着股市泡沫的破裂，日经225指数一路直线下跌，几乎毫无反抗之力。直到2000年年底，当欧美股市及新兴股市均纷纷上涨至历史新高时，日经225指数却低收至13,785点。与此同时，日本经济也经历了长达10年的持续萧条。2003年4月28日，日本股市更是跌至近20年来的最低点7,607点。2006年年底，当大多数欧美及新兴股市再次刷新历史新高时，日经股市才终于缓过气来，勉强收在了近五年来的新高17,225点，与历史最高点38,916点相比却相去甚远，大致相差约21,700点。

5. 对企业与消费者的猛烈冲击。虚假的繁荣背后的苦果，其实是由企业和消费者来承受的。日本经济泡沫的破裂直接打击了本国企业和居民的信心，投资信心严重受挫，企业不良资产增加，银行不良贷款剧增，个人消费萎缩，经济增长停滞甚至出现负增长，失业增加，居民生活水平下降。

6. 20世纪90年代，日本国内生产总值（GDP）的实际年均增长率为1.1%，而且就连这1.1%的增长也是日本政府累计10次动用财政手段刺激景气（"景气对策"总规模高达136万亿日元，接近日本GDP的三分之一）才勉强获得的。由此可见，日本人要想再次见到80年代中后期平均5%的经济增长已是十分困难的了。

Asian Financial Crisis

Unit 10

Asian Financial Crisis
亚洲金融危机

主题札记

发生在1997~1998年的亚洲金融危机，是继20世纪30年代世界经济大危机之后，对世界经济有深远影响的又一重大事件。这次金融危机反映了世界和各国的金融体系存在着严重缺陷，包括许多被人们认为是经过历史发展选择的比较成熟的金融体制和经济运行方式，在这次金融危机中都暴露出许许多多的问题，需要进行反思。这次金融危机给我们提出了许多新的课题，提出了要建立新的金融法规和组织形式的问题。本文研究的中心问题是如何解决21世纪初货币制度改革之后在不兑现的纸币本位制条件下各国形成的货币供应体制和企业之间在新形势下形成的债务衍生机制带来的几个世纪性的经济难题，包括：

（1）企业债务重负，银行坏账丛生，金融和债务危机频繁；

（2）社会货币供应过多，银行业务过重，宏观调控难度加大；

（3）政府税收困难，财政危机与金融危机相伴；

（4）通货膨胀缠绕着社会经济，泡沫经济时有发生，经济波动频繁，经济增长经常受阻；

（5）企业资金不足带来经营困难，提高了破产和倒闭率，企业兼并活动频繁，降低了企业的稳定性，增加了失业，不利于经济增长和社会的稳定；

（6）不平等的国际货币关系给世界大多数国家带来重负并造成许多国际经济问题。

　　以上问题最深层的原因，是货币制度的不完善和在社会化大生产条件下企业之间交易活动产生的新机制未被人们充分认识。本文的思路是建立一种权威性的企业交易结算的中介系统——国家企业交易中介结算系统，解脱企业之间的债务链，消除企业和银行坏账产生的基础，以避免债务和金融危机的发生，并减少通货膨胀和泡沫经济的危害，促进经济的稳定增长。在这个创新过程中，还会加速国家税收和财政支出方式的创新，减少财政赤字的发生。同时，还会产生企业制度的创新，减少企业的破产倒闭和兼并现象，增强企业的稳定性。并且，还将对国际结算方式进行创新，对国际货币的使用进行改革。这个过程不是一个简单的经济问题的治理，而是对纸币制度所存在的严重缺陷的修正，是对货币供应和流通体制的创新，是金融体制的重大变革和这种变革带来经济运行机制的诸多方面的调整。

阅读长廊

1997 Asian Financial Crisis(I)

1997年亚洲金融危机（上）

The Asian Financial Crisis was a period of financial crisis that gripped much of Asia beginning in July 1997, and raised fears of a worldwide economic meltdown. It is also commonly referred to as the IMF crisis.

The crisis started in Thailand with the financial collapse of the Thai baht caused by the decision of the Thai government to float the baht, cutting its peg to the USD, after exhaustive efforts to support it in the face of a severe financial overextension that was in part real estate driven. At the time, Thailand had acquired a burden of foreign debt that made the country effectively bankrupt even before the collapse of its currency. As the crisis spread, most of Southeast Asia and Japan saw slumping currencies, devalued stock markets and other asset prices, and a precipitous rise in private

　　1997年的亚洲金融危机（也称国际货币基金组织危机）不仅席卷了亚洲大多数国家，还造成了全世界范围内关于经济衰退的恐慌。

　　这场危机起始于泰铢的贬值。由于泰国政府放弃泰铢钉住美元的固定汇率政策，再加上之前泰国政府为了阻挡房地产业的过热而带来沉重的外债负担，使得泰国经济濒临崩溃。此外，东南亚地区以及日本都出现了货币贬值，股价和其他资产价格狂跌，私人债务增加。

debt.

Though there has been general agreement on the existence of a crisis and its consequences, what is less clear were the causes of the crisis, as well as its scope and resolution[82]. Indonesia, South Korea and Thailand were the countries most affected by the crisis. Hong Kong China, Malaysia, Laos and the Philippines were also hurt by the slump. The Mainland China, India, Taiwan China, Singapore and Vietnam were less affected, although all suffered from a loss of demand and confidence throughout the region.

Foreign debt-to-GDP ratios rose from 100% to 167% in the four large ASEAN economies in 1993–1996, then shot up beyond 180% during the worst of the crisis. In Korea, the ratios rose from 13%–21% and then as high as 40%.

Although most of the governments of Asia had seemingly sound fiscal policies, the International Monetary Fund (IMF) stepped in to initiate a $40 billion program to stabilize the currencies of South Korea, Thailand, and Indonesia, economies particularly hard hit by the crisis. The efforts to stem a global economic crisis did little to stabilize the domestic situation in Indonesia, however. After 30 years in power, President Suharto was forced to step down in May 1998 in the wake of widespread rioting

尽管各国专家学者对关于这场金融危机的出现和影响达成广泛共识，但对金融危机产生的原因、范围和解决方式有着较大分歧和争议。印度尼西亚、韩国和泰国是受这次危机影响最为严重的国家；中国香港、马来西亚、老挝和菲律宾出现了股市和房市的衰落；中国大陆、印度、中国台湾、新加坡和越南尽管出现了地区性的需求和投资减退，但影响不大。

从1993年到1996年，外债对GDP的比率从100%升到了167%，在金融危机最严重时升到了180%。在韩国，该比值从13%上升到21%，在金融危机中上升到40%。

尽管亚洲大多数国家的政府都采取了看似稳健的财政政策，但是国际货币基金组织还是出资400亿美元来稳定韩国、泰国和印度尼西亚的货币，但是收效甚微。1998年5月，印度尼西亚总统苏哈托由于印尼盾大幅贬值导致物价飞涨结束了30年的任期被迫辞职。危机持续了整整一年。菲律宾在1998年的经济增长为零。新加坡和中国台湾没怎么受到冲击，尤其是新加坡由于其规模和地理位置（在马来西亚和

---

[82] resolution: [ˌrezəˈljuːʃən] *n.*坚定，决心，决议

that followed sharp price increases caused by a drastic devaluation of the rupiah. The effects of the crisis lingered through 1998. In the Philippines growth dropped to virtually zero in 1998. Only Singapore and Taiwan China proved relatively insulated from the shock, but both suffered serious hits in passing, the former more so due to its size and geographical location between Malaysia and Indonesia. By 1999, however, analysts saw signs that the economies of Asia were beginning to recover.

IMF Role

Such was the scope and the severity of the collapses involved that outside intervention, considered by many as a new kind of colonialism, became urgently needed. Since the countries melting down were among not only the richest in their region, but in the world, and since hundreds of billions of dollars were at stake, any response to the crisis had to be cooperative and international, in this case through the International Monetary Fund (IMF). The IMF created a series of bailouts ("rescue") packages for the most affected economies to enable affected nations to avoid default, tying the packages to reforms that were intended to make the restored Asian currency, banking, and financial systems as much like those of the United States and Europe as possible.

印度尼西亚之间）的原因损失更为严重。直到1999年，亚洲经济才出现恢复的迹象。

国际货币基金组织的角色

由于金融危机的范围广、影响深，外部的救援就显得极为迫切（尽管很多人认为这是新殖民主义）。因为这场金融危机已不是一个地区最富裕人口的问题，全世界几千亿美元的资产都处在十分危险的境地，解决这场金融危机必须通过各国在国际货币基金组织领导下的协调与合作。国际货币基金组织通过一揽子紧急援助（"救援"）方案，试图帮助这些国家货币复值，并使其银行与金融系统更加接近美国和欧洲。

In other words, the IMF's support was conditional on a series of drastic[83] economic reforms influenced by neoliberal economic principles called a "structural adjustment package" (SAP). The SAPs called on crisis-struck nations to cut back on government spending to reduce deficits, allow insolvent banks and financial institutions to fail, and aggressively raise interest rates. The reasoning was that these steps would restore confidence in the nations' fiscal solvency, penalize insolvent companies, and protect currency values.

Above all, it was stipulated that IMF-funded capital had to be administered[84] rationally in the future, with no favored parties receiving funds by preference. There were to be adequate government controls set up to supervise all financial activities, ones that were to be independent, in theory, of private interest. Insolvent institutions had to be closed, and insolvency itself had to be clearly defined. In short, exactly the same kinds of financial institutions found in the United States and Europe had to be created in Asia, as a condition for IMF support. In addition, financial systems had to become "transparent", that is, provide the kind of reliable financial information used in the West to make sound financial decisions.

换句话说，国际货币基金组织的支持是建立在这些国家内部一系列新自由主义经济政策（"一揽子结构性调整方案"）的基础上的。具体措施包括削减政府开支减少赤字，允许资不抵债的银行和金融机构倒闭，大幅提高利率。这样做不仅可以保护国家财政，惩罚破产企业，而且可以保护本国货币价值。

关键是，国际货币基金组织的注资必须合理、公平，不能倾向于任何金融集团。同时政府要对金融活动进行必要的监管，尽管在理论上，金融活动应自由独立。破产的机构必须停业。同时，破产的概念也应清晰界定。简而言之，就是在亚洲建立与欧美一样的金融机构，正如国际货币基金组织救援的条件一样。此外，还应增强金融体系的透明度，像西方国家一样通过可靠的财务信息作出稳健的财务决策。

---

[83] drastic: ['dræstik] *a.* 激烈的，猛烈的
[84] administer: [əd'ministə] *vt.* 给予，投药，管理，实施，料理，支配

However, the greatest criticism of the IMF's role in the crisis was targeted towards its response. As country after country fell into crisis, many local businesses and governments that had taken out loans in US dollars, which suddenly became much more expensive relative to the local currency which formed their earned income, found themselves unable to pay their creditors. The dynamics of the situation were closely similar to that of the Latin American debt crisis. The effects of the SAPs were mixed and their impact controversial.

Critics, however, noted the contractionary nature of these policies, arguing that in a recession, the traditional Keynesian[85] response was to increase government spending, prop up major companies, and lower interest rates. The reasoning was that by stimulating the economy and staving off recession, governments could restore confidence while preventing economic pain. They pointed out that the U.S. government had pursued expansionary policies, such as lowering interest rates, increasing government spending, and cutting taxes, when the United States itself entered a recession in 2001.

Although such reforms were, in most cases, long needed, the countries most involved had ended up undergoing an almost complete

然而，对国际货币基金组织的批评也接踵而至。由于向这些国家提供的贷款是美元贷款，随着这些国家货币的贬值，外债的负担也就越来越重，这些国家相继陷入危机。这与拉丁美洲的债务危机极为相似。结构性调整政策的影响很广泛，但也充满争议。

争议主要集中在这些政策自相矛盾的本质上，因为根据凯恩斯的理论，当经济进入萧条期时，应该通过加大政府支出和降低利率来刺激经济的主要部门。而这样不仅可以减少经济衰退带来的阵痛，而且还可以重振公众的信心。此外，批评还指出美国政府在2001年经济衰退时也采取了扩张性的政策，如降息、减税、增加政府支出。

尽管这些措施从长期来看大多数都是有效的，但这些国家此时正在经历彻底的政治和金融体系的改

---

[85] Keynesian: ['keinziən] a. 凯恩斯的，凯恩斯主义的

political and financial restructuring. They suffered permanent currency devaluations, massive numbers of bankruptcies, collapses of whole sectors of once-booming economies, real estate busts, high unemployment, and social unrest. For most of the countries involved, IMF intervention had been roundly criticized.

The role of the International Monetary Fund was so controversial during the crisis, that many locals called the financial crisis the "IMF crisis". To begin with, many commentators in retrospect criticized the IMF for encouraging the developing economies of Asia down the path of "fast track capitalism", meaning liberalization of the financial sector (elimination of restrictions on capital flows); maintenance of high domestic interest rates in order to suck in portfolio investment and bank capital; and pegging of the national currency to the dollar to reassure foreign investors against currency risk. In other words, that the IMF itself was the cause.

革。如货币的永久性贬值,企业的破产潮,曾经的支柱产业房地产泡沫的破裂,高的失业率和社会动荡。正因为这些,国际货币基金组织备受指责。

国际货币基金组织在这场危机中的角色也受到了许多批评,有人干脆把这场危机称做"国际货币基金组织危机"。因为国际货币基金组织鼓励亚洲发展中国家进入"快速资本主义",这也就意味着加快这些国家的金融自由化改革(取消对资本流动的限制),保持国内的高利率来吸引投资和银行资本,同时实行钉住美元的固定汇率政策从而打消外国投资者对货币风险的担忧。换句话说,国际货币基金组织本身就是产生这场金融危机的原因。

财经宝库

1. 国际货币基金组织(International Monetary Fund, IMF) 于1945年12月27日成

立，为世界两大金融机构之一，职责是监察货币汇率和各国贸易情况、提供技术和资金协助，确保全球金融制度正常运作，其总部设在华盛顿。

Headquarters in Washington D.C.
IMF在华盛顿的总部

2. 殖民主义是指一个比较强大的国家越过自身的边界而建立移民殖民地或行政附庸机构，借以对外延伸其主权。而该地区的原住民会受到直接统治，或被迁徙至其他地区。

3. 财政政策指政府为稳定和发展经济、实现公共政策目标在公共财政领域的政策和决策。财政政策和货币政策是政府控制与管理经济的最重要的两个宏观经济调控工具：财政政策借助政府财政开支、税收、债务融资方面的变化来刺激或减缓经济增长；货币政策则侧重对经济体中货币发行量的调节。

DIY工作室

1. What role did IMF play in 1997 Asian Financial Crisis?

2. What do you think is the fundamental reason for this crisis?

归类记忆卡片

财政政策 fisical policy | 货币政策 monetary policy

政府支出 government spending
结构性调整 structual adjustment

减税 cutting tax
资本流动 capital flow

听力广场

1997 Asian Financial Crisis（Ⅱ）
Consequence
Asia

1997年亚洲金融危机（下）影响
亚洲以内

The crisis had significant macro-level effects, including sharp reductions in values of currencies, stock markets, and other asset prices of several Asian countries. The nominal U.S. dollar GDP of ASEAN fell by $9.2 billion in 1997 and $218.2 billion (31.7%) in 1998. In Korea, the $170.9 billion fall in 1998 was equal to 33.1% of the 1997 GDP. Many businesses collapsed, and as a consequence, millions of people fell below the poverty line in 1997–1998. Indonesia, South Korea and Thailand were the countries most affected by the crisis.

The economic crisis also led to political

从宏观上看,这场金融危机带来了深远的影响,亚洲各国的货币急剧贬值,股票和其他资产价格骤降。1997年东盟的GDP下降了92亿美元,1998年更是下降了2,182亿美元（占当年GDP的31.7%）。韩国1998年GDP减少了1,709亿美元（占当年GDP的33.1%）。1997年到1998年由于许多企业倒闭,上百万的人口进入贫困线以下。其中印度尼西亚,韩国和泰国是这场危机中最大的受害者。

经济危机也带来了政治的剧

upheaval[86], most notably culminating in the resignations of President Suharto in Indonesia and Prime Minister General Chavalit Yongchaiyudh in Thailand. There was a general rise in anti-Western sentiment[87], with George Soros and the IMF in particular singled out as targets of criticisms. Heavy U.S. investment in Thailand ended, replaced by mostly European investment, though Japanese investment was sustained. Islamic and other separatist movements intensified[88] in Southeast Asia as central authorities weakened.

More long-term consequences included reversal of the relative gains made in the boom years just preceding the crisis. Nominal U.S. dollar GDP per capital fell 42.3% in Indonesia in 1997, 21.2% in Thailand, 19% in Malaysia, 18.5% in Korea and 12.5% in the Philippines. The CIA *World Factbook* reported that the per capita income (measured by purchasing power parity) in Thailand declined from $8,800 to $8,300 between 1997 and 2005; in Indonesia it declined from $4,600 to $3,700; in Malaysia it declined from $11,100 to $10,400. Over the same period, world per capita income rose from $6,500 to $9,300. Indeed, the CIA's analysis

变，其中，最为引人注目的就是印度尼西亚总统苏哈托和泰国总理差瓦利·永猜裕的辞职。同时乔治·索罗斯和国际货币基金组织也成为反对西方情绪和批评家攻击的目标。美国在泰国大量的投资被欧洲的投资所代替，尽管日本在泰国的投资仍在继续。伊斯兰和其他分裂活动的加剧也弱化了东南亚国家的中央集权。

这场金融危机使得这些国家在危机前所积累的盈利被抵消。1997年，印度尼西亚的名义人均GDP下降了42.3%，泰国下降了21.2%，马来西亚下降了19%，韩国下降了18.5%，菲律宾下降了12.5%。中情局的《世界概况》报告，从1997年到2005年，泰国人均GDP(以购买力平价衡量)，从8,800美元降到8,300美元，印度尼西亚从4,600美元下降到3,700美元，马来西亚从11,100美元下降到10,400美元。而在这一时期，世界人均GDP从6,500美元上升到9,300美元。同时，该报告还指出，2005年印度尼

---

[86] upheaval: [ʌpˈhiːvəl] *n.* 举起，隆起，大变动
[87] sentiment: [ˈsentimənt] *v.* 感情，情绪；意见，观点
[88] intensify: [inˈtensifai] *vt.* 使强烈，加强，增强（强化，加剧，加厚）

asserted that the economy of Indonesia was still smaller in 2005 than it had been in 1997, suggesting an impact on that country similar to that of the Great Depression. Within East Asia, the bulk of investment and a significant amount of economic weight shifted from Japan and ASEAN to China and India.

The crisis has been intensively analyzed by economists for its breadth, speed, and dynamism; it affected dozens of countries, had a direct impact on the livelihood of millions, happened within the course of a mere few months, and at each stage of the crisis leading economists, in particular the international institutions, seemed a step behind. Perhaps more interesting to economists was the speed with which it ended, leaving most of the developed economies unharmed. These curiosities have prompted an explosion of literature about financial economics and a litany of explanations why the crisis occurred.

A number of critiques have been leveled against the conduct of the IMF in the crisis, one by former World Bank economist Joseph Stiglitz. Politically there were some benefits. In several countries, particularly South Korea and Indonesia, there was renewed push for improved corporate governance. Rampaging inflation weakened the authority of the Suharto regime and led to its toppling in 1998, as well as accelerating East Timor's independence.

西亚的经济仍然比1997年时规模小，这个国家与大萧条时十分类似。同时有相当大部分的投资从东盟和日本转移到了中国和印度。

这场金融危机的广度，深度和动向也成为经济学家研究的热点，因为它不仅在很短的时间里（仅几个月）影响了很多国家，同时影响了数百万人的生活，而当金融危机发生到每个阶段时，世界领先的经济学家，特别是一些国际机构，反应似乎都滞后了一步。也许最有意思的是这场金融危机结束的速度之快使主要先进经济体毫发未损。这也激发出大量的文献对这场金融危机产生的原因以及金融经济学的研究。

在一些针对国际货币基金组织的批评声中，最著名的莫数世界银行的经济学家约瑟夫·斯蒂格利茨了。而在这场金融危机中，政客成为唯一的受益者，尤其是印度尼西亚和韩国，因为在这些国家加强了对公司的治理。通货膨胀的肆虐削弱了苏哈托当局的政权，使之在1998年被推翻，同时也加速了东帝汶的独立。

Outside Asia

After the Asian crisis, international investors were reluctant to lend to developing countries, leading to economic slowdowns in developing countries in many parts of the world. The powerful negative shock also sharply reduced the price of oil, which reached a low of $8 per barrel towards the end of 1998, causing a financial pinch in OPEC[89]nations and other oil exporters. This reduction in oil revenue contributed to the Russian financial crisis in 1998, which in turn caused Long-Term Capital Management in the United States to collapse after losing $4.6 billion in 4 months. A wider collapse in the financial markets was avoided when Alan Greenspan and the Federal Reserve Bank of New York organized a $3.625 billion bail-out. Major emerging economies Brazil and Argentina also fell into crisis in the late 1990s.

The crisis in general was part of a global backlash against the Washington Consensus and institutions such as the IMF and World Bank, which simultaneously became unpopular in developed countries following the rise of the anti-globalization movement in 1999. Four major rounds of world trade talks since the crisis, in Seattle, Doha, Cancún, and Hong

亚洲以外

亚洲金融危机后，国际投资者变得不情愿借款给发展中国家，这也是许多发展中国家经济发展放缓的主要原因。强有力的经济衰退也使得石油价格下降到1998年年底时的8美元/桶，这使得欧佩克国家和其他石油出口国家财政吃紧。石油收益的减少也造成了1998年的俄罗斯金融危机，这也使得美国的长期资本管理公司在4个月内损失了46亿美元。阿伦·格林斯潘和纽约联邦储备银行筹集了一笔36.25亿美元的紧急援助，金融危机才没有进一步扩展。巴西和阿根廷等主要新兴经济体都在90年代后期陷入金融危机。

这场金融危机总体上也可以看成是全球反对华盛顿共识和对世界银行和国际货币基金组织的抵抗，这几乎与1999年兴起的反对全球化运动一样不受发达国家的欢迎。四轮（分别在西雅图、多哈、坎昆和香港）关于国际贸易的对话也没有达成显著的共识。随着发展中国家变得越来越果断，国家更倾向于

---

[89] OPEC: ['əʊpek] *n.* 欧佩克（石油输出国家组织）

Kong, have failed to produce a significant agreement as developing countries have become more assertive, and nations are increasingly turning toward regional or bilateral FTAs (Free Trade Agreements) as an alternative to global institutions.

Many nations learned from this, and quickly built up foreign exchange reserves as a hedge against attacks, including Japan, China, South Korea. Pan Asian currency swaps were introduced in the event of another crisis. However, interestingly enough, such nations as Brazil, Russia, and India as well as most of East Asia began copying the Japanese model of weakening their currencies, restructuring their economies so as to create a current account surplus to build large foreign currency reserves. This has led to an ever increasing funding for U.S. treasury bonds, allowing or aiding housing (in 2001–2005) and stock asset bubbles (in 1996–2000) to develop in the United States.

建立地区性的或双边的自由贸易协定来取代国际机构。

这场金融危机也给许多国家上了一课，并迅速建立起自己的外汇储备来抵御风险，如日本、中国和韩国。在另外一场金融危机之后，亚洲共同货币互换被引进。有意思的是巴西、俄罗斯、印度和大多数东亚国家也在模仿日本模式，弱化本国货币来实现贸易盈余（经常账户盈余）以积累大量外汇储备，这也大大地增加了对美国国债的需求，使得美国的房地产泡沫（2001年到2005年）和股票资产泡沫（1996年到2000年）开始形成。

非常点拨

1. 石油输出国组织（Organization of the Petroleum Exporting Countries，OPEC；

简称欧佩克）是一个国际组织。世界主要石油生产国为共同对付西方石油公司和保护石油收入，于1960年9月10日由伊拉克、伊朗、科威特、沙特阿拉伯和委内瑞拉代表在巴格达开会商议成立一个协调机构，9月14日"石油输出国组织"正式宣告成立。

2. **华盛顿共识**（Washington Consensus）　1989年所出现的一整套针对拉丁美洲国家和东欧转轨国家的新自由主义的政治经济理论。当华盛顿共识逐渐显现出失败，宏观经济理论界提出了与此相对的北京共识。

1989年陷入债务危机的拉丁美洲国家急需进行国内经济改革。美国国际经济研究所邀请国际货币基金组织、世界银行、美国开发银行和美国财政部的研究人员以及拉丁美洲国家代表在华盛顿召开了一个研讨会，旨在为拉丁美洲国家经济改革提供方案和对策。美国国际经济研究所的约翰·威廉姆斯（John Williamson）对拉丁美洲国家的国内经济改革提出了已与上述各机构达成共识的10条政策措施，称为华盛顿共识。

3. **坎昆**（Cancún）　又名康昆，是墨西哥东南部的一个城市，位于加勒比海沿岸，是世界著名的度假胜地。

Net Bank

Unit 11

Net Bank
网络银行

主题札记

网络银行，前名为亚特兰大互联网银行，主要经营零售银行、房屋贷款、小型商业融资、自动取款及其他商业服务。网络银行于1996年2月成立并在1997年7月完成它的首次公开募股。它被认为是网络银行的先驱。

网络银行于1996年建立,是当时美国唯一的网络银行。通过网上业务这种新型商业模式，网络银行建立初期取得了不错的回报。

2007年7月3日，网络银行收到纳斯达克证券交易所的通知，因为该银行股票价格在过去30天内已经接近最低竞价（1美元）。8月3日，网络银行从纳斯达克证券交易所撤出。

2007年9月28日，储蓄监管局宣布关闭网络公司，这也是自20世纪80年代贷款储蓄危机以来最大的储蓄贷款机构倒闭。14亿美元的储蓄和一些贷款资产以1亿4千万美元被卖到ING公司。

网络银行于2007年9月28日被储蓄监管局和联邦储蓄保险公司勒令停业。几名持股人联合对网络银行提起上诉，称该银行在重组时谎报公司价值。

网络银行公司申请破产保护，宣布将其哥伦比亚和南卡罗来纳州的房地产卖给它的子公司M.G.转保公司。联邦储蓄和贷款协会被禁止进行破产保护，只能由联邦储蓄保险公司对其进行结业清算。

Net Bank

Net Bank, formerly named Atlanta Internet Bank (1996), was a financial company engaged primarily in retail banking, mortgage banking, business finance and providing ATM and merchant processing services. Net Bank was founded in February 1996 and completed its initial public offering of stock in July 1997. It was one of the pioneers[90] of the Internet banking industry, and recognized as one of the first internet-only banks.

Net Bank was closed on September 28, 2007, by the Office of Thrift Supervision (OTS) in conjunction with the Federal Deposit Insurance Corporation (FDIC). FDIC insured deposits were acquired by another on-line bank ING Direct. Several shareholders have filed class action lawsuits against Net Bank claiming

网络银行

　　网络银行，前名为亚特兰大互联网银行（1996），主要经营零售银行、抵押贷款、商业融资、自动取款及其他商业服务。网络银行于1996年2月成立并在1997年7月完成它的首次公开募股。它被认为是网络银行的先驱，并被公认为是一家只通过网络经营业务的银行。

　　网络银行于2007年9月28日被储蓄监管局（OTS）和联邦储蓄保险公司（FDIC）勒令停业。联邦储蓄保险公司担保的储蓄事实上由另外一家网上银行ING Direct收购。几名持股人联合对网络银行提起上诉，称该银行在重组时谎报公

---

[90] pioneer: [ˌpaiəˈniə] *n.* 先锋，拓荒者，开辟者

misrepresentation[91] of the company value during the restructuring period.

Net Bank was founded in 1996 as one of the nation's first Internet-only banks. Using a new business model, Net Bank paid higher interest rates for computer-savvy customers in exchange for not having physical bank branches. This model made sense and the bank early on paid very nice interest rates.

Net Bank, like all banks, made its money from a mortgage and lending operation. The majority of home loans were offered through traditional channels and a small percentage of loans were offered through the same internet channels as the banking offerings.

Net Bank obtained customers by offering some sort of "sign on" bonus. A $50 bonus was a common bonus[92]. Net Bank signed many agreements with other companies to promote itself and the companies would offer[93] gift certificate or credit to their loyalty programs (i.e., frequent flyer programs) equivalent to around $50. These customer acquisition programs proved beneficial and Net Bank gained many customers in this manner.

Starting in the early 2000s, Net Bank

司价值。

网络银行于1996年成立,是当时美国第一家只通过网络经营业务的银行。网络银行通过向网上客户提供较高的利率来弥补其没有真正分支的劣势。通过网上业务这种新型商业模式,网络银行建立初期取得了不错的回报。

和所有银行一样,网络银行也通过借贷盈利。大部分住房贷款还是通过传统方式提供,只有一小部分贷款通过网络银行提供。

网络银行通过发放"签名"红利的方式招徕顾客,最常见的如50元红利等。此外,网络银行还与许多公司签署协议,向它们的忠实顾客(如经常飞行的乘客)发放价值50美元左右的代金券等方式,推销网络银行的业务。这种经营方式取得成功并为网络银行带来了许多客户。

21世纪初,网络银行合并了几

---

[91] misrepresentation: ['misreprizen'teiʃən]n. 误称(错误表现)
[92] bonus: ['bəunəs]n. 红利,奖金
[93] offer: ['ɔfə]v. 提供,出价,企图

acquired a number of financial-related companies to diversify and improve the bottom line.In 2000, Net Bank added the following products and services: Online safe deposit boxes for safe storage of electronic records, individual retirement accounts, and expanded customer support (online chat and 24 × 7 availability).

家金融公司并将其业务多元化同时提高了它的底线。2000年，网络银行还增加了几项产品和服务：网上储蓄箱，个人退休账户，同时还有全天候在线客户支持。

In 2001, Net Bank acquired Resource Bancshares Mortgage Group, a leading provider of mortgage banking services. An online currency program was launched. And, Net Bank acquired Market Street Mortgage, a leading provider of home mortgage to American consumers. The same year also brought a change in management to Net Bank. A new CEO, Douglas K. Freeman, was appointed to head and manage the company. Freeman came from RBMG and had a background in mortgages rather than banking.

2001年，网络银行兼并了抵押贷款银行服务业的"领头羊"（资源银行股份贷款集团）和美国住房抵押贷款市场的"领头羊"（市场街）。同年，网络银行的管理层也迎来了一些变化，新的首席执行官道格拉斯·弗里曼走马上任，尽管他的背景不是银行业而是抵押贷款业务。

In 2003, Net Bank added a number of business and product lines: Net Bank expanded into automobiles by offering auto insurance through sister company Net Insurance and direct consumer auto loans through Florida auto dealerships. Net Bank also acquired Financial Technologies, Inc., a provider of off-premise ATM and merchant processing services. A number of ATMs were acquired in this acquisition. Finally, Net Bank also launched a small business banking program.

2003年，网络银行新增加了一些业务和生产线，例如，进军汽车市场与姊妹公司——网络保险公司通过佛罗里达的经销商提供保险和抵押贷款服务。此外，网络银行还兼并了几家自动提款业务服务商，如金融技术公司。网络银行还启动了它的小型商业银行项目。

In 2004, Net Bank continued adding new product lines and acquired additional companies. Net Bank acquired the assets of Beacon Credit Services, a leading provider of RV, boat and aircraft financing. They added business credit cards, internet payroll services, prepaid Visa gift cards, and expanded financial planning services. In response to customer concerns about mailing in deposits, Net Bank launched the QuickPost system where deposits are shipped overnight to Net Bank for processing.

Net Bank reached the peak of the operation at the end of 2004 and through 2005. The rapid expansion[94] into multiple lines of businesses may have proved to be too much, too soon for Net Bank and it started to lose money in 2005.

2004年，网络银行继续扩展业务和兼并对手。如兼并了为露营车轮船和飞机制造业提供融资的贝肯信贷服务公司。此外，网络银行还开展了商业信用卡、网络工资服务、提前支付信用礼品卡和金融计划等多项服务。为了打消顾客对邮寄现金的疑虑，网络公司还开创了迅速邮寄系统（隔夜邮寄现金）。

2004年年底和2005年，网络银行达到高峰，但是过快的扩张和多线作战也使它开始亏损。

财经宝库

1. 纳斯达克（NASDAQ） 是美国的一个电子证券交易系统，是由纳斯达克股票市场股份有限公司（Nasdaq Stock Market, Inc., NASDAQ）所拥有与经营。NASDAQ是全国证券交易商协会行情自动报价系统（National Association of Securities Dealers Automated

---

[94] expansion: [iks'pænʃ ən] *n.* 扩大，膨胀

Quotations system）的缩写，创立于1971年，迄今已成为世界最大的股票市场之一。

该市场允许期票出票人通过电话或互联网直接交易，而不局限在交易大厅进行，而且交易的内容大多与新技术，尤其是计算机方面相关，是世界第一家电子证券交易市场。

一般来说，在纳斯达克挂牌上市的公司以高科技公司为主，这些大公司包括微软（Microsoft）、英特尔（Intel）、戴尔（Dell）和思科（Cisco）等。

虽然纳斯达克是一个电子化的证券交易市场，但它仍然有个代表性的"交易中心"存在，该中心坐落于纽约时代广场旁的时报广场四号（Four Times Square，该大楼又常被称为"康泰纳仕大楼"，Condé Nast Building）。时代广场四号内并没有一般证券交易所常有的各种硬件设施。

NASDAQ at Four Times Square
纽约时代广场四号纳斯达克大厦

2. **首次公开募股（Initial Public Offerings，IPO）** 是指企业通过证券交易所首次公开向投资者增发股票，以期募集用于企业发展资金的过程。当大量投资者认购新股时，需要以抽签形式分配股票，又称为抽新股，认购的投资者期望可以用高于认购价的价格售出。

DIY工作室

1. What makes Net Bank expand so rapidly from 1996 to 2005?

2. What do you think is the potential risk of Net Banks' over-expansion?

3. What is your own view towards this new banking business model?

归类记忆卡片

零售银行业 retail banking
住房贷款 home loan
首次公开募股 initial public offerings (IPO)

抵押贷款银行业 mortgage banking
兼并 acquisition
网络支付服务 internet payroll service

听力广场

Net Bank（II）

In 2005, Net Bank suffered some setbacks due to the cyclical nature of the mortgage industry and did not add any businesses or products to their line, instead choosing to

网络银行（下）

2005年，网络银行由于房贷行业的不景气而遭受挫折，因此并没有继续扩张而是保持现有资本等房贷市场有所好转后才重新盈利。同

preserve[95] capital until the mortgage curve righted itself and they could resume earning profit from the mortgage businesses. They also introduced a tiered deposit system, where they paid the highest interest rates to people who also were customers of their other products (home or auto loan, savings account, or CD) and the lowest interest rate to people that only had a savings or checking account. The intent[96] was to better cross-sell the products and help transition the banking customers to the other platforms. Many customers were turned off by the tiered system because Net Bank's auto loan rates were higher than other banks and many people didn't choose to have Autoloans through Net Bank.

In 2006, Net Bank recognized that there were some significant operating deficiencies[97] and started to restructure the company in an effort to resume profitability. They shuttered a number of businesses and sold off most businesses that were not shuttered. Some of the shuttered companies included QuickPost, payroll and finance services, non-auto (RV, boat, and aircraft) loans, and the subprime[98]/ non-conforming mortgage companies. The large network of ATMs were sold off to other

时网络银行还采用分层销售的经营模式，向选择他们其他产品（如房屋贷款或汽车贷款，储蓄账户或大额存款账户）的客户提供更高的存款利率，而向那些只有储蓄账户的客户提供低利率服务。这样做的目的是为了便于网络银行销售其他产品并向其他领域过渡。然而这种分层销售模式也使得许多客户投向其他银行，因为网络银行的汽车贷款利率较高。

2006年，网络银行意识到操作上的严重缺陷开始重组公司以保持盈利。网络银行停办了一些业务并廉价出售了大多数业务，如快速邮寄，网上工资支付，非交通工具（汽车、船只和飞机）贷款和次级/不良贷款业务等。巨大的自动取款系统也被卖给其他公司。

---

[95] preserve: [pri'zə:v] v. 保护，保持，维持
[96] intent: [in'tent] n. 意图，目的，意向，含义
[97] deficiency: [di'fiʃənsi] n. 缺乏，不足
[98] subprime: ['sʌb'praim] a. 次级的（不符合一级贷款标准），负数的

companies.

During the same year, Net Bank's mortgage operations suffered greatly. Net Bank normally originates loans and resells the loans to other financial institutions on the open markets. Some of the loans that Net Bank sold did not meet the underwriting guidelines and Net Bank was forced to repurchase[99] these loans from the other banks. Since the loans that do not meet the underwriting guidelines are often past due loans, Net Bank was forced to repurchase a large number of failed loans that it had written. This loss of capital was very harmful to the company's equity position and was the first clue to the bank's poor financial position.

In 2007, Net Bank finally recognized that the restructuring attempt was unsuccessful, and the company announced an intention to shutdown the company starting in spring of 2007. In May 2007 Net Bank reached an agreement to sell its core banking operation to EverBank.

On May 1, 2007, the ATM and merchant-servicing operation (Net Bank Payment Systems Inc.) was sold to PAI ATM Services LLC, a subsidiary of Payment Alliance International Inc..

On July 3, 2007, Net Bank Inc. received

同年，网络银行的抵押贷款业务损失严重。通常，网络银行筹集贷款并将其转销到其他金融机构或直接在公开市场上卖出。然而一些没有达到基本认购要求的贷款却迫使网络银行不得不重新从其他银行购回，因此网络银行损失惨重。这也是公司糟糕的财务状况的首要原因。

By Philip Aldrick, Banking Editor
来自银行业编辑，菲利浦·阿尔德里克

2007年，网络银行重组的尝试失败并宣布将在春季关闭。2007年5月，网络银行同意将其核心银行业务卖给永远银行。

2007年5月1日，网络银行将自动提款业务和商业服务业务(网络银行支付系统公司)卖给一家国际支付联盟公司的子公司(PAI自动提款业务公司)。

2007年7月3日，网络银行收到

---

[99] repurchase: [riːˈpəːtʃis] vt. 回购（贷款），买回

a deficiency notice from the NASDAQ Stock Market because its stock for the previous 30 consecutive business days failed to close above the minimum bid price of $1 per share. On August 3, it was delisted[100] from the NASDAQ.

On September 28, 2007, the OTS announced that it had closed Net Bank. The shutdown marked the biggest failure of a savings and loan association since the savings and loan crisis in the 1980s. $1.4 billion in FDIC insured deposits, as well as some loan assets, were sold to ING Direct for $14 million. ING Direct also took on 104,000 Net Bank customers as part of the deal Customers with balances exceeding the FDIC limit have received 50% of the excess balance, and became creditors in the bank's receivership for the remainder.

Net Bank Inc., filed for (reorganization) bankruptcy protection and announced intentions to sell Columbia, South Carolina real estate it owns as well as its captive reinsurance subsidiary M.G. Reinsurance Inc.. Federal savings and loan associations are prohibited from filing for bankruptcy protection and must be liquidated by the FDIC.

The closed Net Bank's former business model had several strategies: Retail and business

纳斯达克证券交易所的拖欠通知，因为该银行股票价格在过去连续30个交易日内未能达到最低标价（每股1美元）。8月3日，网络银行被纳斯达克政权交易所摘牌。

2007年9月28日，储蓄管理局宣布关闭网络银行，这也是20世纪80年代贷款储蓄危机以来最大的储蓄贷款机构倒闭。14亿美元的储蓄和一些贷款资产以1千4百万美元被卖到ING 公司。ING Direct还吸纳了网络银行10万4千名客户作为交易的一部分。储蓄余额超过联邦储蓄保险公司的限度的客户可获得超出限度部分的50%，同时对网络银行的剩余部分所产出的现金流持有债权。

网络银行公司，申请破产保护，宣布将其哥伦比亚和南卡罗来纳州的房地产卖给它的子公司M.G.再保险公司。联邦储蓄和贷款协会被禁止进行破产保护而必须由联邦储蓄保险公司对其进行结业清算。

网络银行之前的经营模式包括零售银行和商业银行、金融中介和

---

[100] deliste: [di:'list] *v.* 退市，退，摘牌

banking, financial intermediary, and transaction processing. All of the bank's operations and assets were located within the United States of America.

The retail banking segment was comprised of personal and small business banking operations. The major products and services offered through the retail banking segment included individual and small business deposit accounts, mortgages, home equity loans and lines of credit, auto loans, financial planning and investment services, online bill payment, and Visa check and credit cards. Net Bank, through its Internet banking operations serves approximately 286 thousand customers throughout the United States and in more than 90 foreign countries.

Net Bank provided a variety of financial-related processing services to merchants, community banks and other organizations. The Company acquired an ATM and merchant transaction processing operation. During Net Bank's peak years, the company operated approximately 8,000 ATMs across the country, which the Company made available to its banking customers on a surcharge-free basis. The network of ATMs ranked as the second largest bank-operated ATM network in the country in 2003.

One of the downsides to having no physical

交易结算。而所有的这些业务都在美国境内进行。

零售银行是个人业务和小型商业银行业务的结合，其零售银行部门提供的主要产品和服务包括个人和小型商业储蓄账户、抵押贷款、房屋净值贷款、信用服务、汽车贷款、商业计划、投资服务、网上账单支付和信用卡检查服务。网络银行共为90多个国家的约28.6万客户服务。

网络银行还为广大商业银行、社区银行和其他机构提供与金融相关的服务，如自动取款和商业交易结算业务，在其辉煌时期，网络银行曾提供全美约8,000台自动取款机的业务并免收手续费，一度在2003年成为全美第二大提供自动取款业务的银行。

缺乏实际的办公地点使得网络

157

branches was the risk of deposits getting lost, damaged, or delayed in the mail. Several people complained about Net Bank losing or delaying payments to the account for a variety of reasons. The invention of deposit-taking ATMs alleviated some of this concern because customers could make the deposit in a local ATM, where the check will post and clear very quickly. The widespread nature of Net Bank's customers made it difficult to have an ATM handy for all customers, though, and many were still required to use mail-in deposits.

Net Bank attempted to alleviate the issue of lost deposits by creating QuickPost, an innovative service where a customer drops a deposit off at a UPS Store location to be shipped overnight to Net Bank. The idea behind QuickPost is one shipment could contain deposits from several customers, justifying the additional expense of overnight shipping. However, the product did not take off, and Net Bank shut down this operation in 2006.

Net Bank also encountered several complaints due to Net Bank's freezing customer accounts for security reasons. When flagged, the customers were required to send several forms of identification to Net Bank before the account would become unfrozen. It is uncertain if the requirements were due to internal Net Bank policies or the requirements imposed by the USA Patriot Act.

银行不得不面临邮寄储蓄丢失、损坏或延误的风险。一些客户抱怨网络银行总是由于各种原因延误或丢失他们的付款。尽管可存款ATM的发明使得客户可以在一个本地ATM上进行存款和迅速清算支票（通过邮寄）。但由于网络银行的客户群分布甚广，网络银行不可能为所有客户提供这种新型ATM，许多客户仍需要将他们的存款邮寄到网络银行。

网络银行试图通过开展快速邮寄项目来缓解支票丢失的问题。客户只需将支票放在任何一家联合包裹的工作站即可。这样做实际上是为了节省邮寄费用，用一笔运费运送多个客户的存款，这样节省了隔夜运输的编辑成本。然而，网络银行却在2006年停止了这项服务。

此外，网络银行客户的账户还会由于安全原因被临时冻结。客户必须将所要求的有关身份证明的表格和文件交到银行才能解冻账户，尽管这些要求不清楚是银行内部政策还是美国爱国法案中的要求。

非常点拨

1. **联合包裹服务公司**（United Parcel Service, Inc., UPS）　世界最大的包裹快递公司。总部位于美国佐治亚州亚特兰大，每天在全世界200多个国家递送的包裹超过1,480万个。最近，UPS将其业务范围扩大到了物流和其他与运输相关的领域，例如为Nike提供仓储服务和对TOSHIBA提供维修支援服务。

2. **美国联邦储蓄保险公司**（Federal Deposit Insurance Corporation，FDIC）　是一家在大萧条时期由美国政府创办、为商业银行储蓄客户提供保险的公司。目前为每家银行每个存款人普通账户最高保险额为10万美元，个人退休账户（Individual Retirement Account，IRA）最高保险额为25万美元。

3. **零售银行**　它们的服务对象是普通大众和中小企业。零售银行服务客户通常是通过银行分行、自动柜员机及网络银行进行的。与之对应的是批发银行。

An NCR Personas 75–Series interior, multi–function
ATM in the USA
美国一台NCR个人版75系列内部多功能自动取款机

Unit 12

Northern Rock

Northern Rock
北岩银行

主题札记

北岩银行（Northern Rock，LSE：NRK）是一家英国银行，于1997年在伦敦证券交易所上市，2000年加入富时100指数成分股，但于2007年12月24日从富时100指数中除名。北岩银行是英国第五大抵押贷款机构，占英国贷款市场份额的18.3%。

挤提事件

一般银行的资金来自客户的存款，而北岩银行则主要从其他金融机构借贷，然后再转借给买房子的人。北岩银行是英国次级抵押贷款市场的贷款大户，给购房者的贷款多达十足房价，有时超出购房者收入的5~6倍，还给那些购房出租的投资者提供大量贷款。2007年，北岩银行因次级抵押贷款危机而使得其国际融资市场出现停滞，难以取得资金支持其业务，为了维持银行体系的稳定，英格兰银行决定介入，注资北岩银行以解决流动资金短缺的危机。9月14日北岩银行股票价格一度下跌三成，出现挤兑现象，各分行门前排满等待提款的储户。大批储户向北岩银行各网点或通过网络服务提款，由于登录人数太多，银行网站的服务器无法负荷，网上存取款服务严重受阻。9月17日股价再跌四成，储户挤兑持续。英国2001年制定了《存款补偿计划》，规定存款2,000英镑以下的储户在银行破产时可收回全部存款，而超出2,000英镑至31,000英镑，储户能够收回90%。财政大臣阿利斯泰尔·达林（Alistair Darling）提出保证北岩银行小储户的全部存款。9月18日，在存款获得保证后，北岩银行挤兑稍为舒缓，期间储户共提走 20 亿英镑的存款，相当于北岩银行存款的 8%，而股价也回升 16%。10月19日北岩银行董事长马特·里德利（Matt Ridley）辞职，由前保柏（BUPA）及渣打银行董事长布莱恩·桑德森（Bryan Sanderson）接任。

Northern Rock logo used until 2000
2000年之前北岩银行的徽标

Northern Rock

北岩银行

Northern Rock plc. is a British bank, currently under ownership of the UK government. The bank was formed in 1997 when the society floated on the London Stock Exchange, distributing shares to members who held savings accounts and mortgages[101]. Northern Rock joined the stock exchange as a minor bank and was expected to be taken over by one of its larger rivals, but it has remained independent. In 2000, Northern Rock gained promotion to the FTSE 100 Index, but was demoted back to the FTSE 250 in December 2007 and later suspended from the LSE due to the bank's nationalisation.

On 14 September 2007, the Bank sought and received a liquidity support facility from

北岩银行是一家英国银行，目前由英国政府所有，于1997年伦敦股市动荡时成立，并将其股份分给储蓄账户的客户和抵押贷款的客户。北岩银行以一家小银行的身份进入股票市场，面临着被其他大的竞争对手接管的可能。2000年，北岩银行晋升为英国富时100指数成分股，然而却在2007年12月降至英国富时250指数成分股，随后因为国有化从伦敦股票交易市场撤出。

2007年9月14日，受美国次级抵押贷款危机的影响，北岩银行不

---

[101] mortgage: ['mɔ:gidʒ] *n.* 抵押，抵押借款，按揭

the Bank of England, following problems in the credit markets caused by the U.S. subprime mortgage financial crisis.

At 00:01 on 22 February 2008 the bank was nationalised. The nationalisation was a result of two unsuccessful bids to take over the bank, neither being able to fully commit to repayment of taxpayers' money. The government-appointed Chairman is Ron Sandler, who assumed the position on Monday 18 February. There are no plans to change the name of the bank.

Northern Rock Building Society was formed in 1965 as a result of the merger of Northern Counties Permanent Building Society (established in 1850) and Rock Building Society (established in 1865). During the 30 years that followed, Northern Rock expanded by acquiring 53 smaller building societies, most notably the North of England Building Society in 1994.

Along with many other UK building societies in the 1990s, Northern Rock chose to demutualise[102] and float on the stock exchange in order to better expand their business. Throughout this period a concern against demutualisation was that the assets of a mutual society was built up by its members throughout its history not just the present members who would benefit, and that demutualisation was a

得不寻求紧急支持，并得到了英格兰银行的流动性支持。

2008年2月22日凌晨00：01，北岩银行正式国有化。事实上，因为不能足额偿还纳税人的钱和两个不成功的收购方案，北岩银行被迫国有化。政府任命的主席罗恩·桑德勒在2月18日星期一确认了这一点，并指出没有计划对北岩银行重新命名。

北岩银行于1965年成立，由北部国家永久建筑协会（1850年成立）和岩石建筑协会（1865年成立）联合建立。在随后的30年中，北岩银行不断扩张，兼并了53家小型建筑协会，最著名的为北部英格兰建筑协会（1994年兼并）。

和其他20世纪90年代建立的建筑协会一样，北岩银行选择实行股份制并开始在股票市场上进行融资是为了更好地扩张。而这个时期人们对股份制最大的忧虑就是协会的资产不仅归现任会员所有，整个协会（前任会员）都可从中获益。出于这些考虑，北岩银行建立了北岩基金会。从1997年10月1日起，直至被政府实行国有化，北岩银行以

---

[102] demutualise: [di'mju:tʃuəlaiz] vt. 使……变成股份

betrayal[103] of the community that the societies were created to serve. Northern Rock chose to address these concerns by founding the Northern Rock Foundation. From 1 October 1997 until the government nationalisation, the bank used the symbol NRK on the London Stock Exchange.

NRK出现在伦敦股票交易市场上。

In the year 2000 Northern Rock introduced a new corporate identity consisting of a magenta square containing the company name. This replaced the NR "blocks" logo. The Red Box Design Group have designed all of the currently standing buildings at the company's headquarters in Gosforth and have contributed to many of the other design aspects of the company, such as the in-branch styling.

2000年，北岩银行更换了标志，代替了原来的"石块"标志。红盒子设计集团承担了北岩银行在哥斯福斯的总部大楼的设计，此外还承担了北岩银行其他的设计，如分行的内部设计。

Northern Rock is one of the top five mortgage lenders in the United Kingdom in terms of gross lending.

就总借款来说，北岩银行是英国五个最大的抵押贷款商之一。

As well as mortgages, the bank also deals with savings accounts[104], current accounts[105], loans and insurance. The company also promotes secured loans to its existing mortgage customers. The unsecured loans business is administered and underwritten by Ventura based in Leeds. Home and contents insurance is dealt with by AXA whilst Legal & General,

除了抵押贷款以外，北岩银行还受理储蓄账户、经常账户、贷款和保险业务。北岩银行还向其房贷客户发放抵押贷款。而无抵押贷款业务由设立在立兹的温图拉公司管理。住房和损害保险业务由AXA保险公司经营，而Legal &General 公司的抵押贷款账簿则由北岩银行接手，经营保险和股市投资项目。

---

[103] betrayal: [bi'treiəl] *n.* 出卖，辜负，暴露
[104] savings accounts *n.* 储蓄账户
[105] current accounts *n.* 经常账户

whose mortgage book Northern Rock took over, arrange insurance and stock-market-based investments.

In 2003, to free capital for its rapid growth in mortgage lending, the bank sold its credit card business to The Co-operative Bank for a profit of more than £7 million. Until November 2007 Northern Rock continued to sell credit cards under their own brand through The Co-operative Bank; the decision to stop was made before the 2007 crisis.

In 2006 the bank had moved into sub-prime lending via a deal with Lehman Brothers. Although the mortgages are sold under Northern Rock's brand through intermediaries, the risk is being underwritten by Lehman Brothers.

The company donates substantial amounts annually to its own charity, the Northern Rock Foundation. The foundation was formed when the company was floated, with an initial donation of 15% of the share capital and a covenant to donate 5% of the company's annual profit thereafter. In 2006, Northern Rock was the second largest charitable giver in the FTSE 100 after ITV.

In April 1996, when the Building Society was considering demutualisation, plans were announced by the then chairman, Robert Dickinson, for the creation of the foundation. Since the official launch of the foundation

2003年，为了从其迅速增长的抵押贷款业务中释放出更多的资本，北岩银行将它的信用卡业务转卖给合作银行从而获得700多万英镑的利润，直到2007年11月美国次贷危机才停止。

2006年，北岩银行通过雷曼兄弟公司经营次级抵押贷款业务。尽管抵押贷款业务通过金融媒介以北岩银行的名义卖出，然而风险的承担者却是雷曼兄弟公司。

北岩银行每年都向它的慈善机构北岩基金会进行捐助。除了启动的15%的公司股份，北岩银行每年都依照承诺捐赠每年利润的5%。2006年，北岩银行紧随ITV电视公司成为富时100第二大慈善家。

1996年4月，建筑协会开始考虑股份制。罗伯特·迪更森主席宣布了此计划并建立该基金会。从1998年1月该基金会正式成立以来，该基金会一直在稳步成长和扩

in January 1998, it has steadily grown and expanded its activities. In 2003, along with a new logo and the introduction of new programmes, the Foundation moved to a new building–the renovated Old Chapel in Gosforth. At the end of 2006 the foundation received £ 28.2 million investment. By the end of 2007 £ 190 million had been donated to the foundation, by Northern Rock.

Nationalisation will end the covenant requiring Northern Rock to remit a share of profits to the Foundation. Instead, for the next three years the Foundation will receive an annual £ 15 million payment from Northern Rock, whether it remains publicly-owned or returns to the private sector. The Foundation's shares will be cancelled and compensated in the same way as those of other shareholders.

大。2003年，随着新标志和新项目的开始，该基金会搬到了新改造好的老查佩大厦中（在哥斯福斯）。2006年年底，该基金会接受了2,820万英镑的投资。2007年年底，北岩银行将1亿9千万英镑捐助给北岩基金会。

国有化将停止北岩银行向北岩基金会的资助。未来三年内，北岩基金会每年还会从北岩银行收到1,500万英镑，无论北岩银行是否国有化。而该基金会的持股人也将和其他持股人一样在三年内得到补偿。

财经宝库

1. **伦敦金融时报100指数**（Financial Times Stock Exchange 100 Index，FTSE 100 Index） 创立于1984年1月3日，是在伦敦证券交易所上市的最大的100家公司的股票指数。该指数是英国经济的"晴雨表"，也是欧洲最重要的股票指数之一。相关的股票指数包括金融时报250指数（除了100家最大的公司以外接下去的250家最大的公司的股票指数）和金融时报350指数（金融时报100指数和金融时报250指数的结合）。

2. **国有化是将财产收归国家所有的行为** 通常它指的是将私人财产国有化，但是有时它也指其他级别政府（比如市政府）的财产。一般情况下国家会支付一定的金额来补偿原来的所有者，但是有的时候这个价格比市场价格要低很多,所以会造成原来所有者的损失。国有化的理由往往是因为某些产业比如公共供水供热具有重要的战略作用。相似地，国有化的对立面通常是私有化，在私有化后发生的国有化经常称为再国有化。

1. How did Northern Rock expand to capital market?

2. Why do you think Northern Rock go demutralization?

3. Do you think the British government should nationalise Northern Rock? Why or Why not?

国有化 nationalisation	抵押贷款 mortage lending
股份制 demutualization	偿还 repayment
次级贷款 sub-prime lending	股票市场投资 stock-market-based investment

听力广场

Northern Rock(II)

On 12 September 2007, Northern Rock asked the Bank of England, as lender of last resort in the United Kingdom, for a liquidity support facility due to problems in raising funds[106] in the money market to replace maturing money market borrowings. The problems arose from difficulties banks faced over the summer of 2007 in raising funds in the money markets, caused by the subprime crisis in the United States. The bank's assets were always sufficient to cover its liabilities, but it had a liquidity[107] problem because institutional lenders became nervous about lending to mortgage banks following the U.S. sub-prime crisis. Bank of England figures suggest that Northern Rock borrowed £3billion from the Bank of England in the first few days of this crisis.

---

[106] raise funds *v.* 融资，筹集资金
[107] liquidity: [liˈkwiditi] *n.* 流动性，流畅，流动资金

北岩银行（下）

2007年9月12日，北岩银行因为未能筹集到足够的资金来替换到期借款而向最终贷款人——英格兰银行求助。这也是2007年夏天美国次级抵押贷款危机以来大多数银行所面临的问题。尽管银行的资产超过负债，而自次贷危机以来，大多数机构都不愿意借款给抵押贷款银行。英格兰银行的数据显示，在危机发生的最初几天，北岩银行向英格兰银行借款达30亿英镑。

Northern Bank, Newry
北岩银行，纽理

With shares in Northern Rock plummeting by nearly a third, the British Government moved to reassure investors with the bank, with account holders urged not to worry about the bank going bust. The Treasury Select Committee chairman John McFall MP said: "I don't think customers of Northern Rock should be worried about their current accounts or mortgages."

Northern Rock is not the only British bank to have called on the Bank of England for funds since the sub-prime crisis began but is the only one to have had emergency financial support from the Tripartite Authority (The Bank of England, the FSA and HM Treasury). However, the bank is more vulnerable[108] to a credit crunch[109] as its "high risk" business model depends on funding from the wholesale credit markets, 75% of its funds coming from this source. In his address to the Treasury Select Committee, Bank of England governor Mervyn King had stated emergency funds would be made available to any British bank that needed it, but at a penalty[110] rate, to ensure that lenders who had made bad lending decisions would suffer unfair advantages relative to lenders who had made sensible lending decisions.

On Monday 17 September, as worried

当北岩银行的股价狂跌三分之一时，英国政府开始安抚投资者。财政部特别委员会新任主席约翰·麦克弗尔说："我认为北岩银行的客户不应该担心他们的经常账户和抵押贷款。"

北岩银行并不是在这场危机中向英格兰银行求助的唯一一家英国银行，但却是唯一从三方当局（英格兰银行、金融服务局和英国财政部）得到紧急金融援助的银行。然而，银行在面对信用危机的冲击时却更加脆弱，因为北岩银行主要依靠从批发信用市场上筹集资金（75%的资金来源）。英格兰银行主席默文·金在其对财政部特别委员会的讲话中强调，紧急基金将向所有英国银行开放，但要收取惩罚性的利率。这是对作出错误决定的借款者的惩罚。

9月17日星期一，挤兑现象愈

---

[108] vulnerable: ['vʌlnərəb(ə)l] a. 易受伤害的，有弱点的
[109] credit crunch n. 信用危机（信用紧缩）
[110] penalty: ['penlti] n. 惩罚性利率，罚金，惩罚

savers continued to flock to some Northern Rock bank branches to withdraw[111] their savings, it was reported that an estimated £2 billion had been withdrawn since the bank applied to the Bank of England for emergency funds. By early afternoon in London, Northern Rock's shares, which had lost 32% on the previous Friday, fell a further 40% from 438 pence to 263 pence. Later that day, the Chancellor of the Exchequer, Alistair Darling, announced that the British Government and the Bank of England would guarantee all deposits held at Northern Rock. Northern Rock shares rose by 16% after was announced.

The announcement by the Chancellor showed its intended effects the next day, as the queues outside Northern Rock's branches gradually disappeared. In addition, Northern Rock had a series of adverts published in major UK newspapers to reaffirm that their customers' money was safe.

In an interview on BBC Radio 4, Bank of England governor Mervyn King revealed that they had anticipated emergency funding to be in the £20–30 billion range.

What we want to do is to give incentives for people to behave properly, so in judging the interest rate at which we lent to Northern

演愈烈，自从北岩银行向英格兰银行申请紧急援助以来约有20亿英镑被挤兑出来。刚过中午，北岩银行股价继上周五跌幅达32%后，继续下降40%（从438便士降到263便士）。当日晚些时候，英国财政大臣阿里索德尔大林宣布英国政府和英格兰银行将担保所有在北岩银行的储蓄金，消息宣布后，北岩银行的股价上升了16%。

A Bank Run on
Northern Bank
北岩银行的挤
兑事件

第二天，财政大臣许诺所有存款者都可获得兑现后，北岩银行的股份上升16%，挤兑现象有所减弱。此外，英国各主要媒体也重申储户的钱是安全的。

英格兰银行主席默文·金在英国广播公司第四频道的采访中透露他们预计紧急支援资金将达到200亿英镑到300亿英镑。

"我们要给人们足够的激励去作出理性的举动，这也就是说，我们要让北岩银行意识到它没有像

---

[111] withdraw: [wɪðˈdrɔː] *v.* 撤回，取回，撤退

Rock we asked ourselves the question: "At what interest rate would they have to pay in borrowing from us today that would make them regret not having taken out an insurance policy as Countrywide did before the 9th of August?"

In December, the EU regulators approved Britain's actions to provide aid to the Bank by concluding that it was in line with European emergency aid rules.

By January 2008, Northern Rock's loan from the Bank of England had grown to £26 billion. On January 11, Northern Rock announced that it had sold its portfolio of lifetime home equity release mortgages to JP Morgan for £2.2 billion and that it would use this to pay off[112] a piece of the Bank of England loan.

On February 6, the Office for National Statistics announced that it was treating Northern Rock as a public corporation, similar to the BBC and Royal Mail for accounting purposes, causing the loans (approximately £25 billion) and guarantees (approximately £30 billion) extended by the Bank of England and the value of the company's mortgage book (approximately £55 billion), provisionally estimated to total around £100 billion, to be added to the National Debt. Although not

全国金融公司那样在8月9日（2007年）之前采取保险措施，是要付出代价的。（指利息）"

12月，欧盟官员通过了英国政府对北岩银行的支持，因为这样做与欧盟紧急援助条例一致。

2008年1月，北岩银行从英格兰银行的贷款增加到260亿英镑。1月11日，北岩银行宣布将其终身房屋股份抵押贷款转卖给摩根大通集团来用于偿还英格兰银行贷款的一部分。（220亿英镑）

2月6日，英国国家统计局宣布它将北岩银行作为上市公司，与英国广播公司和皇家邮政一样，这也就意味着北岩公司250亿英镑的贷款和英格兰银行300亿英镑的担保将进入北岩银行的抵押贷款账户（合计550亿英镑），这将增加1,000亿英镑的国债。尽管没有完全国有化，但实际上北岩银行只剩下名称还未国有化。这也使得国债从5,370亿英镑，或GDP的37.7%增加到45%，从而打破了所谓的黄金

[112] pay off v. 还清，报复，付清

technically a nationalisation, the decision effectively acknowledged that "In all but name, Northern Rock is now nationalised[113]". The cost of this support increased the National Debt from £537 billion, or 37.7% of GDP to around 45%, breaking the so-called Golden Rule which sets the Public Sector Borrowing Requirement threshold at below 40%. The figure is the equivalent of £3,000 for every family in Britain, or an increase in the base rate of income tax of 28 pence in the pound written before nationalisation–check accuracy. In the 2008 Budget, the Chancellor of the Exchequer announced that the government will issue £14 billion of gilts in order to cover the Northern Rock debt.

On 31 March the bank released its annual report for 2007, it showed a loss of £16.7 million. The former boss, Adam Applegarth is also to receive a £760,000 (£63,333 a month) payoff. The report also outlined further details of their proposed business plan.

定律——公共部门的借款利率应在40%以下，这相当于每个英国家庭3,000英镑，或将每英镑的所得收入税率在原来28%的基础上继续提高28个便士。在2008年的财政预算中，财政大臣宣布政府将发行140亿英镑金边债券来抵补北岩银行的负债。

The Northern Bank of the River
设在瑞沃的北岩银行

3月31日，在它的年度报告中，北岩银行披露了1亿6千7百万英镑的亏损。前任总裁亚当·艾博嘉斯得到了76万英镑（每月63,333英镑）的奖金。报告还强调了北岩银行未来的商业计划。

---

[113] nationalise: ['næʃənəlaiz] *vt.* 使成国家，使国有化

1. **财政大臣（Chancellor of the Exchequer）** 是英国内阁中主管经济与金融事务的官员，通常简称财相。财政大臣负责管理财政部，职位相当于其他国家的财政部部长。财政大臣一般被认为是重要国务官位之一，在近年来，地位更是仅次于首相。

The Treasury at White House
位于白宫附近的财政部

2. **黄金定律储蓄率** 在索罗的经济模型中，黄金定律储蓄率是指在经济稳定发展时，能够使得每期消费达到最大值的储蓄率。

Bill Clinton awarding Solow the National Medal of Science (1999)
比尔·克林顿授予索罗国家科学奖章（1999年）

Société Générale Trading
Loss Incident
Unit 13

Société Générale Trading Loss Incident
法国兴业银行交易损失事件

主题札记

法国兴业银行爆出丑闻，交易员热罗姆·凯维埃尔违反规定，秘密进行期货买卖，导致银行损失高达72亿美元(约562亿港元)。

法国兴业银行发表声明称，该交易员负责欧洲指数，他违反规定，进行期货买卖，令银行蒙受巨额损失。

另外，法国兴业银行涉及次级抵押贷款的亏损约20亿欧元，即约30亿美元或234亿港元。

法国兴业银行宣布，因欺诈及次级抵押贷款问题，损失将高达69亿欧元，银行在欧洲市场已停牌，其债券已被评级机构降级。法国兴业银行以资产计算，是法国第二大银行。

Headquaters of Société Générale
法国兴业银行总部

阅读长廊

Société Générale Trading Loss Incident

The January 2008 Société Générale trading loss incident was an incident in which the bank Société Générale lost approximately€4.9 billion closing out positions over three days of trading beginning January 21, 2008, a period in which the market was experiencing a large drop in equity indices. The bank states these positions were fraudulent transactions created by Jérôme Kerviel, trader with the company. The police stated they lack evidence to charge him with fraud and charged him with abuse[114] of confidence and illegal access to computers. Kerviel states his actions were known to his superiors and that the losses were caused by panic-selling by the bank.

Kerviel joined the middle offices in the

法国兴业银行交易损失事件

2008年1月，法国兴业银行在贸易损失事件中损失高达约49亿欧元，以致停业3天。同一时间，股票指数大幅下挫。法国兴业银行透露这是由于其交易员热罗姆·凯维埃尔诈骗性的违规交易引起的。但是警方称他们缺乏足够的证据来指控热罗姆犯有非法滥用银行机密进行诈骗的罪名。凯维埃尔称他的上级清楚他所进行的操作，损失是由法国兴业银行的恐慌性抛售引起的。

Société Générale
法国兴业银行

2000年夏季，凯维埃尔加入了

---

[114] abuse: [əˈbjuːz] *n.* 滥用，恶习

bank Société Générale in the summer of 2000, working in its compliance department. In 2005 he was promoted to the bank's Delta One products team in Paris where he was a junior trader. Société Générale's Delta One business includes program trading, exchange-traded funds (ETFs), swaps, index and quantitative trading.

Bank officials claim that throughout 2007, Kerviel had been trading profitably in anticipation of falling market prices; however, they have accused him of exceeding his authority to engage in unauthorized trades totaling as much as €49.9 billion, a figure far higher than the bank's total market capitalization. Bank officials claim that Kerviel tried to conceal the activity by creating losing trades intentionally so as to offset his early gains. According to the BBC, Kerviel generated €1.4 billion in hidden profits by the end of 2007. His employers say they uncovered unauthorized trading traced to Kerviel on January 19, 2008. The bank then closed out these positions over three days of trading beginning January 21, 2008, a period in which the market was experiencing a large drop in equity indices, and losses attributed are estimated at €4.9 billion.

The bank claimed Kerviel "had taken massive fraudulent directional positions in 2007 and 2008 far beyond his limited

法国兴业银行的中层办公室并在合规部门工作。2005年，凯维埃尔晋升到法国兴业银行在巴黎的达尔塔一团队并成为初级交易员。该团队的业务包括程序交易、交易所交易基金、互换交易，指数交易和量化交易。

法国兴业银行管理者声称，整个2007年凯维埃尔因为对市场价格下跌的正确预期而使交易盈利，但他们同时指控凯维埃尔在未被授权的情况下交易了499亿欧元，这相当于法国兴业银行的总市值。银行管理者还称凯维埃尔企图通过制造交易损失来掩盖他的行为。根据英国广播公司的报道，截至2007年年底凯维埃尔共掩盖了14亿欧元的利润，而他的行为直到2008年1月19日才被发现。此后，法国兴业银行停业三天，与此同时，股指大幅下跌，由此造成损失估计达49亿欧元。

法国兴业银行管理者还指出，2007年和2008年，凯维埃尔在未经授权的情况下私自进行欧洲股指期

authority[115]"and that the trades involved European stock index futures. Though bank officials say Kerviel apparently worked alone, skeptics[116] question how unauthorized trading of this magnitude[117] could go unnoticed. Kerviel's unassuming background and position have heightened the skepticism that he worked alone. Some analysts suggest that unauthorized trading of this scale may have gone unnoticed initially due to the high volume in low-risk trades normally conducted by his department. The bank said that whenever the fake trades were questioned, Kerviel would describe it as a mistake then cancel the trade followed by replacing that trade with another transaction using a different instrument to avoid detection[118]. Kerviel's lawyers, Elisabeth Meyer and Christian Charrière-Bournazel, said that the bank's managers "brought the loss on themselves"; accused[119] the bank's management of wanting to "raise a smokescreen to divert public attention from far more substantial losses in the last few months"; and said that Kerviel had made the bank a profit of $2 billion as of Dec. 31, 2007.

Kerviel is not thought to have profited

货交易，这远远超出了他的权限。尽管凯维埃尔独立工作，但这么巨大的交易未能引起注意确实值得怀疑，而凯维埃尔的职位和背景更加重了人们的这种怀疑。一些分析家指出这可能是因为凯维埃尔所在的部门通常进行大量的但低风险的交易。而法国兴业银行的管理者还指出，无论凯维埃尔的这种做法是否有问题，他都将这些交易称做失误然后取消，用不同的工具来替换，以此来逃避监管。凯维埃尔的律师伊利贝斯·梅耶和克里斯丁·察哈尔声称，事实上，是法国兴业银行的管理者自己造就了这场危机，这样做是试图将大众的注意力从该银行近几个月巨大的亏损上转移（放烟雾弹），而截至2007年12月31日，凯维埃尔为法国兴业银行赢得了20亿欧元的利润。

凯维埃尔并没有从被怀疑的

---

[115] authority: [ɔ:'θɔriti] *n.* 权力，权威，当局
[116] skeptics: ['skeptiks] *n.* 怀疑，怀疑主义者
[117] magnitude: ['mægnitju:d] *n.* 大小，重要，光度，（地震）级数
[118] detection: [di'tekʃən] *n.* 察觉，发觉，侦查，探测
[119] accuse: [ə'kju:z] *v.* 责备，控告

personally from the suspicious trades. Prosecutors say Kerviel has been cooperative with the investigation, and has told them his actions were also practiced by other traders in the company. Kerviel admits to exceeding his credit limits, but claims he was working to increase bank profits. He told authorities that the bank was happy with his previous year's performance, and was expecting to be paid a €300,000 bonus. Family members speaking out say the bank is using Kerviel as a scapegoat to excuse its recent heavy losses.

交易中获取私利。公审人称凯维埃尔很配合调查，此外，银行中的其他交易员也进行过这类交易。凯维埃尔承认他确实超越了信用额度，但他确实是为了增加法国兴业银行的利润。而法国兴业银行确实对他的表现很满意，并将付给他30万欧元的红利。而凯维埃尔的家庭成员也称凯维埃尔被当做一个替罪羊，来掩盖法国兴业银行最近的巨额亏损。

1. **法国兴业银行（Société Générale，简称法兴）** 是法国银行业三大巨头之一，也称三老，另外两个为法国巴黎银行（BNP Paribas，又名"巴黎国民银行"）和法国农业信贷银行（Crédit Agricole），全称为"法国促进工商业发展总公司"，创建于1864年5月，总部设在巴黎。公司的股票分别在纽约、东京以及巴黎的证券市场上市交易。它是世界上最大的投资银行之一。

2. 2008年环球股灾是2008年1月中，因市场忧虑美国经济衰退、次级抵押贷款危机失去控制，以及法国兴业银行交易员热罗姆·凯维埃尔涉嫌违规巨额交易欧洲股票指数期货后的巨额平仓活动而引发的全球金融市场震荡。1月21日，伦敦金融时报100指数、巴黎CAC40指数、法兰克福DAX指数、新加坡海峡时报指数、香港恒生指数和上证综指跌幅均超过5%。

3. 在美国，**联邦基金利率（Federal Funds Rate）** 为一家存托机构（多数是银行）

利用手上的资金向另一家存托机构借出隔夜贷款的利率。

联邦基金利率是美国各家银行间的隔夜拆借利率，代表的是短期市场利率水平。通常联邦公开市场委员会（Federal Open Market Committee，FOMC）会对联邦基金利率设定目标区间，透过公开市场操作确保利率维持在此区间内。而要观察FOMC未来利率政策的调整方向，最好的指标便是FOMC会议后所发表的"政策声明"（Policy Statement）。

1. Do you think Kerviel is working alone, totally unauthorized? Why or why not?

2. What do you think is caused Société Générale's heavy loss?

3. Whoelse do you think should also be responsible for this?

股票指数 Equity Index	互换 swap
交易所交易基金 exchange-traded fund	资本化 capitalization
股指期货 stock index futures	低风险交易 low-risk trade

听力广场

Société Générale Trading Loss Incident (II)

法国兴业银行交易损失事件（下）

The bank states that Kerviel was assigned to arbitrage discrepancies between equity derivatives[120] and cash equity prices, and "began creating the fictitious trades in late 2006 and early 2007, but that these transactions were relatively small. The fake trading increased in frequency, and in size". The Executive Chairman of Société Générale, Daniel Bouton described the pattern as like "a mutating virus" in which hundreds of thousands of trades were hidden behind offsetting faked hedge trades. Officials say Kerviel was careful to close the trades in just two or three days, just before the trades' timed controls would trigger[121] notice from the bank's internal control system, and Kerviel would then shift those older positions to newly

法国兴业银行称凯维埃尔被授权进行股票衍生产品和现金股票价格差价的套利，开始在2006年年底和2007年年初制造虚假交易，这些交易额都相对较小，但交易频率和规模都有所增长。法国兴业银行的执行总裁，丹尼尔·宝登称这种模式就像变异病毒，使成百上千笔交易隐藏在取消的虚假对冲基金后。法国兴业银行的监管者称凯维埃尔为了逃脱银行内部控制系统的监视，总是在"交易受控时间"两三天前小心地停止交易，然后把这些以前的交易变成新的交易。城市专家对银行账户的监管表示了怀疑，因为大规模的交易并不能逃脱这种"三天监管模式"。凯维埃尔只是离职，但事实上已被法国兴业银

---

[120] derivatives: [di'rivətivs] *n.* 衍生产品；衍生金融投资工具，主要指认购和认沽期权
[121] trigger: ['trigə] *v.* 触发（事件）

initiated trades[122]. City experts have expressed skepticism of the bank's account, saying that a pattern of closing out trades within the three days cycle alleged could not be accomplished given the immense sums involved. Kerviel has simply been suspended, but is in the process of being fired by the bank.

In answers to the rumors alleging Jérôme Kerviel had fled Paris following the discovery of the unauthorized[123] trading, on January 24, 2008 Kerviel's lawyer denied that he attempted to disappear and said he remained in Paris to face the accusations.

Also on January 24, 2008, Société Générale filed a lawsuit against "a 31-year-old person" for creating fraudulent documents, using forged documents and making attacks on an automated system, according to Clarisse Grillon, a spokeswoman for the Nanterre prosecutor. Le Figaro reported that in addition to the Société Générale lawsuit, a group of shareholders filed a lawsuit for fraud, breach of trust and forgery.

On January 26, 2008, the Paris prosecutors[124] office stated that Kerviel "is not on the run. He will be questioned at the appropriate time, as soon as the police have analysed documents

行解雇。

Group Société Générale
法国兴业集团

针对关于凯维埃尔在被发现违规交易后逃离巴黎的传言，2008年1月24日凯维埃尔的律师否定了这些谣传，并说他仍旧留在巴黎来面对指控。

同样是在2008年1月24日，法国兴业银行对"这位31岁的人"提起诉讼，称其制造假文件并攻击自动系统。根据克拉利斯基雷轮（南特公诉方发言人）报道。另据法国费加洛杂志报道，除法国兴业银行外，一些持股人也针对诈骗、违规信托和伪造提起诉讼。

2008年1月26日，巴黎公诉人称凯维埃尔并没有逃跑。他将在警方审理完法国兴业银行提供的文件后在合适的时间对凯维埃尔进行审

---

[122] newly initiated trades *n.* 新启用的交易
[123] unauthorized: [ʌnˈɔːθəraizd] *a.* 未经授权的
[124] prosecutor: [ˈprɔsikjuːtə] *n.* 实行者，追诉者，告发者

provided by Société Générale". He was taken into police custody later that day.

Kerviel's initial 24 hour detention was extended to 48 while French law enforcement questioned him about possible accomplices. The investigation later widened to encompass his personal cell phone records, and to explore possible links to other individuals working at rival banks and private investment firms who may be involved. The police are investigating whether he worked alone, and whether any investors outside of Société Générale may have been tipped in advance. Police are interested whether others were involved in either the trades themselves, or received notice of the bank's impending sell-off before the details of the scandal were publicly disclosed.

Kerviel was formally charged on January 28, 2008 with abuse of confidence and illegal access to computers. He was released from custody a short time after. The charges filed carry a maximum three-year prison term. On January 29, 2008 investigating judges Renaud van Ryumbecke and Francoise Desset had rejected prosecutor Jean-Claude Marin's bid to charge Kerviel with the more serious crime of "attempted fraud" and refuse bail[125].

问。第二天，凯维埃尔被带往警察局。

凯维埃尔最初的24小时拘留延长到48小时以查清凯维埃尔是否有同谋。审查者还查看了凯维埃尔的个人手机记录，对和他有联系的人进行调查，例如其他私有投资银行是否有人从中受益，或者在丑闻曝光之前得到法国兴业银行丑闻的信息。

Société Générale
法国兴业银行

1月28日，凯维埃尔正式被指控滥用银行机密和非法使用银行电脑系统。凯维埃尔随后被释放。但检方对凯维埃尔提起了至少3年监禁的上诉。1月29日，两位调查官雷纳德·范·愈贝克和佛朗克斯·迪塞没有通过公诉人詹克鲁德·马琳要给凯维埃尔加罪的要求并且拒绝保释。

---

[125] bail: [beil] *n.* 保释，把手，木勺

185

Société Générale characterizes Kerviel as a rogue trader and claims Kerviel worked these trades alone, and without its authorization. Kerviel, in turn, told investigators[126] that such practices are widespread and that getting a profit makes the hierarchy turn a blind eye. The current investigation involves what is reported to be the largest fraud in banking history.

On 11 March 2008, Société Générale announced that another of their employees had been taken into custody in connection with the investigation of the fraud, and their headquarters searched by police.

On January 21, 2008, European stock markets suffered heavy losses of about 6%. The sharp fall, which was followed by an emergency cut in the federal funds rate by the United States Federal Reserve on the following Tuesday (U.S. markets were closed on the Monday for Martin Luther King Jr Day), came as Société Générale tried to close out positions built up by Kerviel. This has led to speculation that stock market turbulence caused the Federal Reserve Board to cut the rate. A Federal Reserve spokesperson denied the central bank knew of Société Générale's situation when it made its decision.

It is estimated that over the period the total trading in futures and the cash market for the

法国兴业银行将凯维埃尔刻画为一个流氓交易员并声称凯维埃尔是在未被授权的情况下私自交易。凯维埃尔随后告知调查者这些操作范围很广而且如果获利，上级就会对违规行为视而不见。但这起事件也可能成为银行史上最大的诈骗案。

2008年3月11日，法国兴业银行宣布另外一个员工也被拘留接受调查,同时他所在的总部也接受警方的搜索。

2008年1月21日,欧洲股票市场遭受巨大损失,跌幅达6%左右。星期二（星期一美国市场因为马丁·路得·金日而关闭）美联储紧急将联邦基金利率下调，同一天，法国兴业银行临时停业。美联储的降息也引起了美国股票市场上大批的投机行为。但美联储的官员称他们在作决定时并不知道法国兴业银行将要停业的消息。

据估计，这个时期在欧洲期货和现金市场上欧洲股票前50的交易

---

126 investigator: [in'vestigeitə(r)] *n.*研究者，调查者，审查者

Euro Stoxx 50 was €544 billion. This would make the unwinding of Kerviel's position account for five per cent or less of overall activity. Société Générale's investment banking chief, Jean-Pierre Mustier, acknowledged that the three days of forced selling played a role in the market's overall decline, but characterized that impact as "minimal".

可达5,440亿欧元，也就是说大盘将近5%的被动是由凯维埃尔事件的曝光造成的。法国兴业银行投资部经理让·皮埃尔·马斯蒂尔承认银行为期三天的被迫抛售的确导致了市场的整体下滑，但影响"微乎其微"。

非常点拨

1. **股本衍生工具** 是一种金融衍生类别投资的统称。这种投资的回报率是根据一些其他金融要素的表现情况衍生出来的。比如股票或者各种股票指数等。这些要素的表现将会决定一个衍生工具的回报率和回报时间。衍生工具的主要类型有期货、期权、认股权、远期契约、利率互换等，这些期货、期权合约都能在市场上买卖。

2. **ETF**（Exchange Traded Fund） 是一种在证券交易所交易的投资工具，与股票类似，

Traders at Chicago Stock Exchange
芝加哥股票交易所的交易员

中文一般翻译为"交易所交易基金"。它是近年来金融市场上发展比较快的基金种类。

TSEC台湾证券交易所对于此ETF商品概述：中文称为"指数股票型证券投资信托基金"，简称为"指数股票型基金"，ETF即为将指数予以证券化，由于指数是衡量市场涨跌趋势的指标，因此所谓指数证券化，是指投资者不以传统方式直接进行一篮子股票的投资，而是通过持有表彰指数标的股票权益的受益凭证来间接投资；简而言之，ETF是一种在证券交易所买卖，提供投资者参与指数表现的基金，ETF基金以持有与指数相同的股票为主，分割成众多单价较低的投资单位，发行受益凭证。

The 2008 Icelandic
Financial Crisis
Unit 14

The 2008 Icelandic Financial Crisis
2008年冰岛金融危机

主题札记

冰岛共和国是北大西洋中的一个岛国，位于格陵兰岛和英国中间，首都雷克雅未克。今日的冰岛已是一个高度发展的已开发的国家。拥有世界排名第五的人均国内生产总值，以及世界排名第一的人类发展指数。

2008年冰岛金融危机是发生在冰岛的一系列环球金融危机相关的事件，这些事件直接影响了冰岛整个国家的经济和银行系统。在过去一年内，冰岛货币对欧元的汇率大跌八成。冰岛境内三家主要银行都受到了影响，它们的控制权相继被转为国有。

2008年9月下旬，冰岛政府宣布Glitnir银行被国有化。接下来一周，冰岛国家银行的控制权也被转移到冰岛金融监管局之下。不久，金融监管局又接管了冰岛最大的Kaupthing银行。

冰岛国会紧急立法并且采取行动。因为这些银行的资产是冰岛140亿欧元国内生产总值的9倍，冰岛可能要面临银行破产。总理哈德曾发出警告说，冰岛正面临"全国破产"的危机。

Iceland Emblem
冰岛徽章

PART OF LANDSBANKI, REYKJAVIK, ICELAND

The Icesave logo, advertising it as "part of Landsbanki, Reykjavik, Iceland"
冰岛储蓄银行的标志，称其为冰岛国家银行的一部分

阅读长廊

The 2008 Icelandic Financial Crisis

2008年的冰岛金融危机

The 2008 Icelandic financial crisis is a major ongoing economic crisis in Iceland that involves the collapse of all three of the country's major banks following their difficulties in refinancing[127] their short-term debt and a run on deposits in the United Kingdom. The financial crisis has had serious consequences to the Icelandic economy; the national currency has fallen sharply in value, foreign currency transactions have been virtually suspended, the market capitalisation of the Icelandic stock exchange has dropped by more than 75%, and a severe economic recession[128] is expected.

In late September, it was announced that the Glitnir bank would be nationalised. The

2008年的冰岛金融危机是发生在冰岛的重大经济危机，国家三大银行为偿还短期债务再融资困难重重，并且在英国发生了银行存款挤兑现象，因而宣布破产。金融危机给冰岛的经济造成了严重后果，国家货币大幅贬值，外汇交易几乎停止，冰岛股票交易所总市值下降超过75%，一场严重的经济衰退即将发生。

Glitnir.svg
格里特利尔银行的标志

9月下旬，政府宣布冰岛格里特利尔银行将被国有化。接下来

---

[127] refinance: [ˈrifiˈnæns] *vi.* 重新申请贷款
[128] recession: [riˈseʃən] *n.* 后退，凹入的地方，不景气

following week, control of Landsbanki and Glitnir was handed over to receivers appointed by the Financial Supervisory Authority (FME). Soon after that, the same organisation placed Iceland's largest bank, Kaupthing, into receivership as well. Commenting on the need for emergency measures, Prime Minister Geir Haarde said on 6 October "There [was] a very real danger … that the Icelandic economy, in the worst case, could be sucked with the banks into the whirlpool and the result could be national bankruptcy".

He also stated that the actions taken by the government have ensured that the Icelandic state will not actually go bankrupt. At the end of the second quarter 2008, Iceland's external debt was 9,553 billion Icelandic krónur (50 billion euros), more than 80 percent of which was held by the banking sector: This value compares with Iceland's 2007 gross domestic product of 1,293 billion krónur (8.5 billion euros). The assets of the three banks taken under the control of the FME totaled 14,437 billion krónur at the end of the second quarter 2008.

The full cost of the crisis cannot yet be determined, but already exceeds 30 percent of the country's GDP. Outside Iceland, more than half a million depositors (far more than the entire population of Iceland) found their bank accounts frozen amid a diplomatic argument over deposit insurance. German bank BayernLB

的一周，冰岛国家银行和格里特利尔银行的控制权被转移到冰岛金融监管局指定的接收人之下。不久之后，金融监管局又接管了冰岛最大的银行考普森。冰岛总理盖尔·哈尔德针对紧急措施必要性于10月6日发言，他说，"冰岛的经济，在最糟糕的情况下，极有可能与银行一起被吸入旋涡，那将造成国家破产"。

他又宣布，政府采取的措施保证了冰岛国家经济不会实质性破产。2008年第二季度末，冰岛的外债达到了95,530亿冰岛克朗（500亿欧元），80%以上为银行负债：这部分价值可与2007年冰岛国内生产总值12,930亿冰岛克朗（85亿欧元）相比。被金融监管局接收的三家银行的资产在2008年第二季度末总值达144,370亿冰岛克朗。

危机的全部成本还没有确定，但是已经超过了冰岛国内生产总值的30%。冰岛国外，在关于存款保险外交关系的争论中，50多万储户（远远超过冰岛的总人口数）发现他们的银行账号已被冻结。德国巴伐利亚银行面临着高达15亿欧元的

faces losses of up to €1.5 billion, and has had to seek help from the German federal government. The government of the Isle of Man will pay out half of its reserves, equivalent to 7.5 percent of the island's GDP, in deposit insurance.

Development

Currency

An Icelandic 1,000-krónur note. The value of the Icelandic króna has declined significantly during 2008.

The Icelandic króna had declined more than 35 percent against the euro from January to September 2008. Inflation of prices in the economy was running at 14 percent. Iceland's interest rates had been raised to 15.5 percent to deal with the high inflation, and the króna's decline is reportedly only beaten by that of the Zimbabwean dollar. This depreciation[129] in currency value put pressure on banks in Iceland, which were largely dependent on foreign debt.

On the Wednesday night, 8 October, the Central Bank of Iceland abandoned its attempt to peg[130] the Icelandic króna at 131 krónur to the euro after trying to set this peg on 6 October. By 9 October, the Icelandic króna was trading at 340 to the euro when trading in the currency

损失，不得不求助于德国联邦政府。曼恩岛政府将支出一半储备，相当于该岛国内生产总值的7.5%，用于存款保险。

发展

货币

一张1,000冰岛克朗的钞票。在2008年，冰岛克朗大幅贬值。

2008年1月到9月，冰岛克朗兑欧元汇率下降超过35%。该经济体内，价格上涨维持在14%。为了解决高通货膨胀的问题，冰岛的利率上调到15.5%，而且，据报道，冰岛克朗的下滑幅度仅有津巴布韦元可比。由于冰岛银行主要依赖于外债，所以货币贬值给冰岛银行带来很大压力。

10月8日，星期三晚上，冰岛中央银行放弃了10月6日制定的钉住欧元的汇率制度，冰岛克朗不再固定地以131克朗兑换1欧元。到10月9日，由于金融监管局接管了最后一家主要的冰岛银行，所有清空

---

[129] depreciate: [di'priːʃieit] *vi.* （货币）贬值，降价
[130] peg: [peg] *v.* 钉木椿，用椿

collapsed due to the FME's takeover of the last major Icelandic bank, and thus the loss of all króna trade "clearing houses". The next day, the central bank introduced restrictions on the purchase of foreign currency within Iceland.

The Central Bank of Iceland set up a temporary system of daily currency auctions on 15 October to facilitate international trade. The value of the króna is determined by supply and demand in these auctions. The first auction sold €25 million at a rate of 150 krónur to the euro.

Commercial króna trading outside Iceland restarted on 28 October, at an exchange rate of 240 krónur to the euro, after Icelandic interest rates had been raised to 18 percent.

Banks

Local branches of the Icelandic savings bank SPRON, which had been due to merge with Kaupthing before the financial crisis.

On 29 September 2008, a plan was announced for the bank Glitnir to be nationalised by the Icelandic government with the purchase of a 75 percent stake for €600 million. The government stated that it did not intend to hold ownership of the bank for a long period, and that the bank was expected to carry on operating as normal. According to the government the bank "would have ceased to exist" within a few weeks if there had not been intervention. It

冰岛克朗的货币交易损失惨重，冰岛克朗交易崩盘，达到340冰岛克朗兑换1欧元。第二天，中央银行开始限制在冰岛境内购买外币。

冰岛中央银行于10月15日制定了货币每日竞价临时制度以方便国际贸易。冰岛克朗的价值由竞价中的供求关系决定。第一笔交易定在150冰岛克朗兑换1欧元，价值2,500万欧元。

10月28日，在冰岛的利率上调到18%之后，冰岛境外的商业冰岛克朗交易以240冰岛克朗兑换1欧元重新启动。

银行

冰岛储蓄银行SPRON的地区分行，原本应于金融危机前与考普森银行合并。

2008年9月29日，冰岛政府宣布了将冰岛格里特利尔银行国有化的计划，并打算以6亿欧元购买该银行75%的股份。政府表示，它不打算长久拥有该银行的所有权，而且该银行预期正常运行。政府认为，如果没有政府的干预，该银行已经不复存在。后来，格里特利尔银行被发现负债7.5亿美元将于10月15日到期。但是，格里特利尔银行并没有被国有化，因为它在冰岛

later turned out that Glitnir had $750 million of debt due to mature on 15 October. However, the nationalization of Glitnir never went through, as it was placed in receivership by the Icelandic FME before the initial plan of the Icelandic government to purchase a 75 percent stake had been approved by shareholder.

The announced nationalisation of Glitnir came just as the United Kingdom government was forced to nationalise Bradford & Bingley and to sell its retail operations and branch network to Grupo Santander. Over the weekend of 4–5 October, British newspapers carried many articles detailing the nationalisation of Glitnir and the high leverage[131] of its other banks. Influential BBC business editor Robert Peston published an opinion piece on Iceland's banks, stating that debt insurance for Kaupthing, the largest bank in Iceland, required a premium[132] of £625,000 to guarantee the return of £1 million: "the worst case of financial BO I've encountered in some time" was his graphic description.

The Guardian said "Iceland is on the brink of collapse. Inflation and interest rates are raging upwards. The krona, Iceland's currency, is in freefall". These articles spooked[133] investors discussing Icesave (the brand name of

政府购买该银行75%股份的初步计划被股东批准之前就被金融监管局接收了。

冰岛格里特利尔银行国有化计划的宣布正值英国政府被迫将布拉德福德—宾利集团（英国最大的抵押贷款机构）国有化并将其零售业务和分支网络卖给西班牙桑坦德银行之际。10月4日和5日这个周末，英国报纸刊登了许多详细介绍格里特利尔银行国有化和其分行高杠杆率的文章。具有广泛影响力的英国广播公司商业版编辑罗伯特·派斯顿发表了一篇关于冰岛银行见解的文章，称为冰岛最大的银行考普森的债务进行投保需交纳625,000英镑的保险费以确保100万英镑的收益："这是很久以来我所遇到的最糟糕的金融业务对象。"他生动地描述道。

卫报写道："冰岛濒临破产。通货膨胀和利率不断攀升。冰岛货币克朗在做自由落体运动。"这些文章吓倒了在网上论坛中谈论Icesave(冰岛国家银行在英国和荷

---

[131] leverage: ['li:vəridʒ] *n.* 杠杆作用

[132] premium: ['primjəm] *n.* 额外费用，奖金，保险费

[133] spook: [spu:k] *n.* 幽灵

Landsbanki in the UK and the Netherlands) in online forums and many started moving their savings out of the Internet bank. Problems with access to the site hinted at a run on savings.

On 6 October, a number of private interbank credit facilities to Icelandic banks were shut down. Prime Minister Geir Haarde addressed the nation, and announced a package of new regulatory measures which were to be put to the Althing, Iceland's parliament, immediately, with the cooperation of the opposition parties. These included the power of the FME to take over the running of Icelandic banks without actually nationalising them, and preferential treatment for depositors in the event that a bank had to be liquidated[134]. In a separate measure, retail deposits in Icelandic branches of Icelandic banks were guaranteed in full. The emergency measures had been deemed unnecessary by the Icelandic government less than 24 hours earlier.

That evening, the Guernsey subsidiary of Landsbanki went into voluntary administration with the approval of the Guernsey Financial Services Commission. The administrators would later say that "The main reason for the Bank's difficulties has been the placing of funds with its UK fellow subsidiary, Heritable Bank". Guernsey's Chief Minister stated "the directors

兰的品牌)的投资者，许多人开始将其存款从网络银行中取出。网络登录问题暗示出存款的挤兑现象。

10月6日，许多对冰岛银行提供服务的私人银行同业信贷设施完全关闭。冰岛总理盖尔·哈尔德向全国发表演说，宣布在反对党的协助下，将立即提交给冰岛国会一系列新的调整措施。这些措施包括赋予金融监管局接管冰岛银行维持其运行但实质上并不将其国有化的权力，万一银行不得不破产，储户享有优惠待遇。其中一项独立的措施保证了冰岛银行分支机构的小额零星存款全额退还。距现在不到24小时前，应急措施还被冰岛政府认为没有必要。

那天晚上，冰岛国家银行的根西岛分行获得根西岛金融服务委员会的批准，开始实行自愿管理程序。后来，行政人员说，"这家银行困难重重的主要原因在于将资金存于英国的子公司——Heritable银行"。根西岛的首席部长说，"冰岛国家银行根西岛分行的董事将该银行纳入管理程序的

---

[134] liquidate: ['likwideit] vt. 清算，整理，破产

of Landsbanki Guernsey took appropriate steps by putting the bank into administration".

措施非常合适"。

1. financial crisis: **金融危机**　是指一个国家或几个国家与地区的全部或大部分金融指标(如短期利率、货币资产、证券、房地产)的急剧、短暂和超周期的恶化。其特征是人们基于经济前景将更加悲观的预期，整个区域内货币币值出现幅度较大的贬值，经济总量与经济规模出现较大的损失，经济增长受到打击。金融危机可以分为货币危机、债务危机、银行危机等类型。

2. bank run: **银行挤兑**　是指大量银行客户在同一时间要求提取银行存款，而银行的储备不足以应付提款。

3. clearing house: **清算所**　是指对证券或衍生工具交易各方履行责任的公司。

1. Why was Iceland the first country to announce a possible national bankruptcy in the global financial crisis? What has happened to this country in 2008?

2. What did the Icelandic government do to save the country from bankruptcy?

3. What did the British government do to protect the interest of British depositors in response to the Icelandic financial crisis?

归类记忆卡片

refinance 再融资
deposit 存款
external debt 外债，国外债务
frozen 冻结
Inflation 通货膨胀
asset 资产
credit facility 信贷融通
depreciation 贬值

short-term debt 短期债务
market capitalisation 市值
stock exchange 股票交易所
deposit insurance 存款保险
premium 溢价，保险费
liability 负债
collateral 抵押品

听力广场

The Financial Supervisory Authority (FME) placed Landsbanki, Glitnir and Iceland's largest bank, Kaupthing, into receivership

金融监管局（FME）接管了冰岛国家银行和格里特利尔银行以及冰岛最大的银行考普森

fme
Fjármálaeftirlitið

FME_logo
冰岛金融监管局的标志

The FME placed Landsbanki in receivership early on 7 October. A press release from the FME stated that all of Landsbanki's domestic branches, call centres, ATMs and internet operations will be open for business as usual, and that all "domestic deposits" were fully guaranteed. The UK government used the Banking (Special Provisions) Act 2008 first to transfer retail deposits from Heritable Bank to a

10月7日一早，金融监管局接管了冰岛国家银行。金融监管局在新闻发布会上宣布，冰岛国家银行的所有国内分行、呼叫中心、自动取款机和网络操作将会如往常一样开放，而且，所有国内存款保证全额退还。英国政府首先根据2008年银行法案（特别条款）将小额零星存款从Heritable 银行转移到财政部控股公司，接下来又将其以100万

Treasury holding company, then to sell them to Dutch bank ING Direct for £1 million.

That afternoon, there was a telephone conversation between Icelandic Finance Minister Árni Mathiesen and UK Chancellor of the Exchequer Alistair Darling. That evening, one of the governors of the Central Bank of Iceland, Davið Oddsson, was interviewed on Icelandic public service broadcaster RÚV and stated several times that "we (the Icelandic State) are not going to pay the banks' foreign debts".

The next day, the FME placed Glitnir into receivership. Alistair Darling announced that he was taking steps to freeze the assets of Landsbanki in the UK. Under the Landsbanki Freezing Order 2008, passed at 10 a.m. on 8 October 2008 to come into force ten minutes later, the Treasury went on to freeze the assets of Landsbanki and assets belonging to the Central Bank of Iceland, and the Government of Iceland relating to Landsbanki.

The freezing order took advantage of provisions in sections 4 and 14 and Schedule 3 of the Anti-terrorism, Crime and Security Act 2001, and was made "because the Treasury believed that action to the detriment of the UK's economy (or part of it) had been or was likely to be taken by certain persons who are the government of or resident of a country or

英镑卖给荷兰ING银行。

当天下午，冰岛财政部部长奥尔尼·马修森与英国财政大臣阿利斯泰尔·达林进行了电话交谈。当天晚上，冰岛中央银行官员达维兹·奥德松接受了冰岛公共服务广播公司RÚV的采访，反复声明"我们（冰岛政府）不会偿还银行外债"。

第二天，金融监管局接管了格里特利尔银行。阿利斯泰尔·达林宣布，他正在采取措施冻结冰岛国家银行在英国的资产。依据2008年10月8日上午10点通过并于十分钟后生效的2008年冰岛国家银行冻结令，财政部冻结了冰岛国家银行的资产以及冰岛中央银行和冰岛政府与国家银行相关的资产。

该冻结令，依据第4部分和第14部分的条款、关于反恐怖主义的附表3以及2001年犯罪和安全法制定而成，"因为财政部认为，英国境外的国家或地区，其政府及其居民中的某些人已经或极有可能采取了损害英国经济（或部分经济）的行为"。

territory outside the UK".

The UK Prime Minister, Gordon Brown, announced that the UK government would launch legal action against Iceland over concerns with compensation for the estimated 300,000 UK savers. Geir Haarde said at a press conference on the following day that the Icelandic government was outraged that the UK government applied provisions[135] of anti-terrorism legislation to it in a move they dubbed an "unfriendly act". The Chancellor of the Exchequer also said that the UK government would foot the entire bill to compensate UK retail depositors, estimated at £4 billion. It is reported that more than £4 billion in Icelandic assets in the UK have been frozen by the UK government.

The UK Financial Services Authority (FSA) also declared Kaupthing Singer & Friedlander, the UK subsidiary of Kaupthing Bank, in default on its obligations, sold Kaupthing Edge, its Internet bank, to ING Direct, and put Kaupthing Singer & Friedlander into administration. Over £2.5 billion of deposits for 160,000 customers were sold to ING Direct. The scale of the run on Kaupthing Edge deposits had been such that many transactions were not completed until 17 October. Although Geir Haarde has described

英国首相戈登·布朗宣布，针对大约30万英国储户受损索求赔偿的问题，英国政府将对冰岛采取法律行动。第二天，盖尔·哈尔德在新闻发布会上说，冰岛政府对英国政府援引反恐怖主义法条款的行为极为愤怒，并称其为"不友好行为"。财政大臣也表示，英国政府将赔偿英国小额零星存款储户全部存款，约为40亿英镑。据报道，英国政府冻结的冰岛在英国的资产多于40亿英镑。

The logo of the FSA
英国金融服务监管局徽标

英国金融服务监管局也宣布，考普森银行的英国分行Kaupthing Singer & Friedlander由于不能履行义务将其网络银行Kaupthing Edge卖给了荷兰直接银行，该分行接受行政管理。16万顾客的大约25亿英镑存款也卖给了荷兰直接银行。Kaupthing Edge银行出现大规模的存款挤兑现象导致许多交易直到10月17日才完成。尽管盖尔·哈尔德将英国政府对Kaupthing Singer & Friedlander采取的行为描述为"滥

---

[135] provision: [prə'viʒən] *n.* 规定，条款

the UK government's actions over Kaupthing Singer & Friedlander as an "abuse of power" and "unprecedented[136]", they were the third such actions taken under the Banking (Special Provisions) Act 2008 in less than ten days, after interventions in Bradford & Bingley and Heritable Bank.

On the same day, the Sveriges Riksbank, Sweden's central bank, made a credit facility of 5 billion Swedish krona (€520 million) available to Kaupthing Bank Sverige AB, the Swedish subsidiary of Kaupthing. The loan was to pay "depositors and other creditors".

On 9 October, Kaupthing was placed into receivership by the FME, following the resignation of the entire board of directors. The bank said that it was in technical default on its loan agreements after its UK subsidiary had been placed into administration[137]. Kaupthing's Luxembourg subsidiary asked for, and obtained, a suspension of payments in the Luxembourg District Court. Kaupthing's Geneva office, which was a branch of its Luxembourg subsidiary, was prevented from making any payments of more than 5,000 Swiss francs by the Swiss Federal Banking Commission. The directors of Kaupthing's subsidiary on the Isle

用职权"、"前所未有",这是不到十天内英国政府根据2008年银行法案(特别条款)继干预布拉德福德—宾利集团和Heritable银行以来的第三次干预行为。

同一天,Sveriges Riksbank、瑞典中央银行向考普森银行的瑞典分行Kaupthing Bank Sverige AB提供了50亿瑞典克朗(5.2亿欧元)的贷款。这笔贷款用于支付储户和其他债权人。

10月9日,在全部董事辞职后,考普森被金融监管局接管。考普森银行表示,在其英国分行被英国行政部门接管后,该行对其贷款协议存在技术性违约。考普森在卢森堡公国的分行要求并征得了卢森堡地区法院的允许暂停支付的同意。考普森的日内瓦办事处,隶属于卢森堡分行,被瑞士联邦银行监理委员会禁止支付5,000瑞士法郎以上的付款。考普森马恩岛分行董事在与马恩岛官方协商后,决定关闭该行。

---

[136] unprecedented: [ʌnˈpresidəntid] *a.* 空前的
[137] administration: [ədminisˈtreiʃən] *n.* 行政,管理,中央政府

of Man decided to wind up the company after consultation with the Manx authorities.

On the same day, the UK Treasury[138] issued a licence under the Landsbanki Freezing Order 2008 to allow the London branch of Landsbanki to continue some business. A second licence was issued on 13 October, when the Bank of England provided a £100 million secured[139] loan to Landsbanki "to help maximise the returns to UK creditors".

On 12 October the Norwegian government took control of Kaupthing's Norwegian operations, including "all of the bank's assets and liabilities in Norway".

On 21 October, the Central Bank of Iceland asked the remaining independent financial institutions for new collateral against their loans. This was to replace the shares in Glitnir, Landsbanki and Kaupthing which had been pledged as collateral previously and which were now of much lower value, if not worthless. The value of the collateral was estimated at 300 billion krónur (€2 billion). One of the banks, Sparisjóðabanki (SPB, also known as Icebank), stated the next day that it could not provide new collateral for its 68 billion krónur (€451 million) loan, and would have to turn to the government

同一天，英国财政部依据2008年冰岛国家银行冻结令发放许可证允许冰岛国家银行的伦敦分行继续一些业务。10月13日，英格兰银行向冰岛国家银行提供了1亿英镑的抵押贷款用于帮助英国债权人获得最大回报，英国财政部再次发放许可证。

10月12日，挪威政府控制了考普森的挪威分行，包括"该银行在挪威的全部资产和负债"。

10月21日，冰岛中央银行要求剩余的独立金融机构对其贷款提供新的抵押品。这主要是为了替换格里特利尔银行、冰岛国家银行和考普森银行先前用于抵押而现在没有价值或贬值的股份。抵押品的价值估计约为3,000亿冰岛克朗（20亿欧元）。其中一家银行，Sparisjóðabanki（SPB，也被称为Icebank），第二天发表声明，它不能为其680亿冰岛克朗（4.51亿欧元）的贷款提供新的抵押品，将不得不求助于政府。"这个问题别的方式解决不了，"首席执行总裁艾

---

[138] Treasury: ['treʒəri] *n.* 财政部
[139] secure: [si'kjuə] *a.* 无虑的，安心的，安全的

for help. "This problem won't be solved in any other way," said CEO Agnar Hansson.

On 24 October, it emerged that Norway's semi-public export credit agency Eksportfinans had made a complaint to Norwegian police concerning the alleged embezzlement [140] of 415 million Norwegian kroner (€47 million) by Glitnir since 2006. The Icelandic bank had acted as an agent for Eksportfinans, administering loans to several companies: however Eksportfinans alleges that, when the loans were paid off early by borrowers, Glitnir kept the cash and merely continued with the regular payments to Eksportfinans, effectively taking an unauthorized loan itself.

格纳·汉森说道。

10月24日，挪威的次级出口信贷机构——挪威出口融资公司就2006年以来所谓的格里特利尔银行挪用4.15亿挪威克朗（4,700万欧元）事件向挪威警察局提出申诉。这家冰岛银行是挪威出口融资公司的代理，负责管理几家公司的贷款：但是，挪威出口融资公司宣称，当借款人提前偿还贷款时，格里特利尔银行保留现金，继续定期支付挪威出口融资公司贷款，相当于其有效地获得了未授权的贷款。

非常点拨

1. **国内生产总值**(GDP)（gross domestic demand ）是指一个经济体在特定时期内生产的所有货品及服务的总值，其中包括消费、政府购买、投资及贸易顺差。

2. **清算、清偿**（liquidation ） 是指若一项业务或一家公司终止运作或破产，资产将会被出售，以便向债权人偿还债务。剩余的金额将分配给股东。

3. **市值**（market capitalization ） 是指所有已发行股票的市场价值。计算方法为股票数量乘以当时的市场价格。

---

[140] embezzlement: [im'bezlmənt] *n.* 盗用，挪用，侵占

Topic Three   2008 U.S. Credit Crisis

Bear Stearns

Unit 15

Bear Stearns
贝尔斯登公司

主题札记

贝尔斯登公司(Bear Stearns Cos.) (纽约证券交易所代码：BSC)成立于1923年，是美国华尔街第五大投资银行，是全球500强企业之一，全球领先的金融服务公司，致力于为全世界的政府、企业、机构和个人提供服务。公司主要业务涵盖机构股票和债券、投资银行业务、全球清算服务、资产管理以及个人银行业务。公司总部位于纽约，在全球拥有约14,500名员工。

美资银行贝尔斯登或许不是资产规模最大的投资银行——它的规模仅仅在美国排名第五，但却是近几年华尔街最赚钱的投资银行。

根据最新的报告显示，贝尔斯登2005年第一财政季度盈利增长5%，主要是债券、结算及财富管理业务收入增长带动。在2月28日结束的第一财政季度，贝尔斯登盈利3.79亿美元，每股盈利由上年同期的2.57美元上升至2.64美元，高于市场平均预测的2.36美元。营业收入上升了6.5%，升至18.4亿美元。其中，结算业务收入增加20%，财富管理业务收入增加11%。

贝尔斯登近期大事记

2007年：

6月14日：贝尔斯登发布季报，称受抵押贷款市场疲软影响，公司季度盈利比上年同期下跌10%。

8月1日：贝尔斯登宣布旗下两只投资次级抵押贷款证券化产品的基金倒闭，投资者总共损失逾15亿美元。

8月5日：贝尔斯登公司联席总裁兼联席首席运营官沃伦·斯佩克特宣布辞职，艾伦·施瓦茨成为公司唯一总裁。

9月20日：贝尔斯登宣布季度盈利大跌68％。5月底至8月底，公司账面资产缩水达420亿美元。

12月20日：贝尔斯登宣布19亿美元资产减记。

2008年：

1月7日：贝尔斯登公司首席执行官凯恩迫于压力宣布离职，施瓦茨接任该职。

3月12日：施瓦茨在美国CNBC电视台发表讲话安抚投资者情绪，称公司目前流动性充足，并预计公司将在第一财政季度实现盈利。

3月14日：美联储决定通过摩根大通公司向贝尔斯登提供应急资金，以缓解该公司的流动性短缺危机。这是自1929年美国经济大萧条以来，美联储首次向非商业银行提供应急资金。

3月16日：摩根大通证实，将以总价约2.36亿美元（每股2美元）收购贝尔斯登。

愈演愈烈的贝尔斯登收购案在美国东部时间3月24日上午再次发生戏剧性转折，作为收购方的摩根大通同意将收购价从每股2美元提高到每股10美元，使得协议并购总价达到10亿美元。

Bear Stearn
贝尔斯登公司

383 Madison Ave Bear S tearns
麦迪逊大街383号的贝尔斯登公司

阅读长廊

Bear Stearns(I)

贝尔斯登(上)

The Bear Stearns Companies, Inc., based in New York City, was one of the largest global investment banks[141] and securities trading[142] and brokerage firms[143]. The main business areas, based on 2006 net revenue distributions, were: capital markets (equities, fixed income, investment banking; just under 80%), wealth management (under 10%) and global clearing services (12%).

　　贝尔斯登公司是全球最大的投资银行与证券交易和经纪公司之一。公司的主营业务包括：资本市场（股票、固定收入、投资银行，不到80%），资产管理（不到10%）和国际清算业务（12%）。

Beginning in 2007, the company was badly damaged by the nationwide credit crisis. In March 2008, the Federal Reserve Bank of New York provided an emergency loan to try to avert a sudden collapse of the company. The company could not be saved, however, and was sold to JP Morgan Chase for ten dollars per share, a price

　　从2007年开始，贝尔斯登遭受了蔓延全球的信贷危机。2008年3月，纽约联邦储备银行向贝尔斯登提供紧急援助，试图将其从危机中挽救出来，然而还是失败了。贝尔斯登被摩根大通公司以每股10美元的价格收购（低于危机前的股价，但比最初的2美元高）。

---

[141] investment banks *n.* 投资银行
[142] securities trading *n.* 证券交易
[143] brokerage firms *n.* 券商

far below what the stock had traded for before the crisis, although not as low as the two dollars per share originally agreed upon by Bear Stearns and JP Morgan Chase.

Bear Stearns was founded as an equity trading house in 1923 by Joseph Bear, Robert Stearns, and Harold Mayer with $500,000 in capital. The firm survived the stock market crash of 1929 without laying off[144] any employees and by 1933 opened its first branch office in Chicago. In 1955, the firm opened its first international office in Amsterdam. In 1985, Bear Stearns became a publicly traded company.

It served corporations, institutions, governments and individuals. The company's business included corporate finance, mergers and acquisitions, institutional equities and fixed income sales, trading and research, private client services, derivatives, foreign exchange and futures sales and trading, asset management and custody services. Through Bear Stearns Securities Corp., it offered global clearing services to broker dealers, prime broker clients, and other professional traders, including securities lending. Bear Stearns was also known for one of the most widely read market intelligence pieces on the street, known as the "Early Look at the Market - Bear Stearns Morning View".

贝尔斯登于1923年由约瑟夫·贝恩、罗伯特·斯特恩和哈罗德·麦耶成立，成立之初是一家拥有50万美元的股票交易所。公司奇迹般地在1929年经济大萧条时幸存下来，并且没有裁掉一名员工。1933年在芝加哥开设了第一家分公司。1955年，公司在阿姆斯特丹开设了第一家国际分公司。1985年，贝尔斯登成为上市公司。

贝尔斯登公司为公司、机构、政府和个人提供服务。它的经营范围很广，包括公司理财、兼并与收购、公共股份和固定资产销售、贸易和研究、私人客户服务、金融衍生产品、外汇和期货交易、资产管理和监管服务。此外，贝尔斯登证券公司还为主要股票经纪人和其他专业交易员提供跨国清算服务和证券借贷服务。贝尔斯登还以其超前的理念著称于世，有着"贝尔斯登清晨视角"的美誉。

---

[144] lay off *v.* 解雇，休息

In 2005–2007, Bear Stearns was recognized as the "Most Admired" securities firm in Fortune's "America's Most Admired Companies" survey, and second overall in the security firm section. The annual survey is a prestigious ranking of employee talent, quality of management and business innovation. This was the second time in three years that Bear Stearns had achieved this "top" distinction.

On March 17, 2008, JP Morgan Chase offered to acquire Bear Stearns at a price of $236 million or $2 per share. On March 24, 2008 that offer was raised to $1.1 billion or $10 per share in an effort to pacify angry shareholders. JP Morgan Chase completed its acquisition of Bear Stearns on May 30, 2008 at the renegotiated price of $10 per share.

As of November 30, 2006, the company had total capital of approximately $66.7 billion and total assets of $350.4 billion. According to the April 2005 issue of Institutional Investor magazine, Bear Stearns was the seventh-largest securities firm in terms of total capital. See Bear Stearns' 2007 SEC 10k filing, on page 80.

As of November 30, 2007 Bear Stearns had notional contract amounts of approximately $13.40 trillion in derivative financial instruments, of which $1.85 trillion were listed futures and option contracts. In addition Bear Stearns was carrying more than $28 billion in

2005～2007年，贝尔斯登被《财富》杂志评为"最让人敬佩的证券公司和证券界的第二名。这个年度排名是一个关于员工智慧、管理和商业创新的权威排名。这也是三年中贝尔斯登第二次荣登榜首。

2008年3月17日，摩根大通集团开出标价，以2美元/股（或2.36亿美元）的价格收购贝尔斯登。3月24日，为了安抚愤怒的持股者，该标价升至10美元/股（11亿美元）。5月30日，摩根大通集团以10美元每股的价格完成了对贝尔斯登的收购。

截至2006年11月30日，贝尔斯登公司的资本达到667亿美元，资产总额为3,504亿美元。根据2005年4月《机构投资者》杂志的报告，贝尔斯登是全球第七大证券公司。

截至2007年11月30日，贝尔斯登持有13.4万亿美元的金融衍生产品,其中1.85万亿美元为期货和期权合约。此外，贝尔斯登账面上还持有价值280亿美元的"三级"资产，但股票净资产只有117亿美

"level 3" assets on its books at the end of fiscal 2007 versus a net equity position[145] of only $11.7 billion. This highly leveraged balance sheet, consisting of many illiquid and potentially worthless assets, led to the rapid diminution of investor and lender confidence, which finally evaporated as Bear was forced to call the New York Federal Reserve to stave off the looming cascade of counterparty risk which would ensue from forced liquidation.

元。这个高度杠杆化的资产负债表中有大量流动性差的和毫无潜在价值的资产，这也是日后投资者对贝尔斯登的信心迅速削减的原因，尤其是纽约联邦储备银行决定对贝尔斯登实行强制停业清算的时候。

财经宝库

    1. **证券经纪人**　是与证券自营商相区别的。证券经纪人可以代客户买卖证券、基金、认股证及其他衍生产品，从而获得费用或佣金收益。

    在证券交易中，买卖双方通常需由证券经纪人在交易所代表客户进行交易，一般人不能擅自私下与他人进行买卖。证券经纪人也可为客户提供投资股票及基金等意见。

    2. **资本市场**　是金融市场的一部分，它包括所有关系到提供和需求长期资本的机构和交易。长期资本包括公司的部分所有权，如股票、长期公债、长期公司债券、一年以上的大额可转让存单、不动产抵押贷款和金融衍生工具等，也包括集体投资基金等长期的贷款形式，但不包括商品期货。

---

[145] equity position *n.* 股东、权益头寸

DIY工作室

1. Why could Bear Stearns hardly survive during the early stage of sub-prime crisis?

2. Despite the failure, what has made Bear Stearns' recent success?

3. Do you think Bear Steans' business model is fundamentally wrong? Why/Why not?

归类记忆卡片

（金融）衍生产品 derivative
期货与期权 futures and options
机构投资者 institutional investor

固定收益 fixed income
兼并与收购 merge and acquisition
权益净值 net equity

听力广场

Bear Stearns(II)

贝尔斯登（下）

On June 22, 2007, Bear Stearns pledged a collateralized loan of up to $3.2 billion to "bail out" one of its funds, the Bear Stearns High-Grade Structured Credit Fund, while negotiating with other banks to loan money against collateral[146] to another fund, the Bear Stearns High-Grade Structured Credit Enhanced Leveraged Fund.

The funds were invested in thinly traded collateralized debt obligations (CDO) found to be worth less than their mark-to-model value. Merrill Lynch seized $850 million worth of the underlying collateral but only was able to auction $100 million of them. The incident sparked concern of contagion as Bear Stearns might be forced to liquidate its CDOs, prompting a mark-down of similar assets in

2007年6月22日，贝尔斯登用一笔价值32亿美元的贷款做抵押来救助它的基金——贝尔斯登高级结构信用基金。同时，贝尔斯登还在与其他几家银行协商，来挽救它的另外一只基金——贝尔斯登高级结构信用加强杠杆基金。

由于该基金集中投资于担保债务凭证，而该凭证的价值低于估值。美林公司所持有的价值8.5亿美元的凭证只能竞价抛售价值1亿美元的凭证。这也加剧了贝尔斯登的恐惧，贝尔斯登可能将被迫清仓手中的凭证。而这也将导致其手中其他资产组合缩水。6月29日，贝尔斯登高级执行官理查德·A.马林被雷曼兄弟公司的前副主席杰弗

---

146 collateral: [kə'lætərəl] *n.* 支票，副保，附属担保物

other portfolios[147]. Richard A. Marin, a senior executive at Bear Stearns Asset Management responsible for the two hedge funds, was replaced on June 29 by Jeffrey B. Lane, a former Vice Chairman of rival investment bank, Lehman Brothers.

On July 16, 2007, Bear Stearns disclosed that the two subprime hedge funds had lost nearly all of their value amid a rapid decline in the market for subprime mortgages.

On August 1, 2007, investors in the two funds took action against Bear Stearns and its top management. The law firms of Jake Zamansky & Associates and Rich & Intelisano both filed arbitration claims with the National Association of Securities Dealers alleging that Bear Stearns misled investors about its exposure to the funds. This was the first legal action made against Bear Stearns, though there have been several others since then.

Co-President Warren Spector was forced to resign on August 5, 2007, as a result of errant trades that led to the collapse of two hedge funds backed primarily by subprime loans. A September 20 report in the New York *Times* noted that Bear Stearns posted a 61 percent drop in net profits due to their hedge fund

里·B.雷恩取代。

2007年7月16日，贝尔斯登公司透露它的两只次级对冲基金在整个次级房贷市场衰落的背景下几乎损失了它们全部的价值。

2007年8月1日，这两只基金的投资者们对贝尔斯登和它的高层采取行动。两家律师行杰克扎玛斯基和雷志，因特里萨诺单方起诉贝尔斯登，同时国家证券交易委员会声称贝尔斯登误导了投资者，隐瞒了这两只基金的风险。这也是贝尔斯登公司第一次被起诉，尽管随后它又受到几起起诉。

2007年8月5日，贝尔斯登的副总裁沃伦·斯皮科特被迫辞职，因为交易失误导致两只次级抵押贷款支持的对冲基金亏损。9月20日，纽约《时代》杂志指出贝尔斯登因为这两只基金损失了高达61%的净利润。

---

[147] portfolio: [ˈpɔːtˈfəuliəu] *n.* 文件夹，证券投资组合

losses.

Matthew Tannin and Ralph R. Cioffi, both former managers of hedge funds at Bear Stearns Companies, were arrested June 19, 2008. They are facing criminal charges and are suspected of misleading investors about the risks involved in the subprime market.

Barclays Bank PLC claimed that Bear Stearns knew that certain assets in the Bear Stearns High-Grade Structured Credit Strategies Enhanced Leverage Master Fund were worth much less than their professed values. The suit claimed that Bear Stearns managers devised[148] "a plan to make more money for themselves and further to use the Enhanced Fund as a repository[149] for risky, poor-quality investments". The lawsuit said Bear Stearns told Barclays that the enhanced fund was up almost 6% through June 2007 — when "in reality, the portfolio's asset values were plummeting".

On March 14, 2008, JP Morgan Chase, in conjunction with the Federal Reserve Bank of New York, provided a 28-day emergency loan to Bear Stearns in order to prevent the potential market crash that would result from Bear Stearns becoming insolvent[150]. Two days later,

2008年6月19日，贝尔斯登的两名前任经理被捕，同时被指控有误导投资者的嫌疑，而忽略次级房贷市场上的风险。

巴克莱银行称贝尔斯登知道其基金的真实价值远远低于它所声称的价值。诉讼指出贝尔斯登的管理者企图为自己赚取更多的利润，同时将该基金作为高风险、低质量投资的容器。诉讼还指出，贝尔斯登声称基金在2007年6月升值6%，而"实际上却在狂跌"。

2008年3月14日，摩根大通集团与纽约联邦储备银行合作，为贝尔斯登提供了为期28天的短期紧急贷款。为了防止贝尔斯登破产后市场的进一步倒塌，两天后，贝尔斯登签署了一份与摩根大通集团的合并协议，同意将其股份以2美元

---

[148] devise: [di'vaiz] *v.* 设计
[149] repository: [ri'pɔzitəri] *n.* 储藏室（博物馆，资源丰富地区）
[150] insolvent: [in'sɔlvənt] *a.* 无力偿还的，破产的

Bear Stearns signed a merger agreement with JP Morgan Chase in a stock swap worth $2 a share. In addition, the Federal Reserve agreed to issue a non-recourse loan to JP Morgan Chase, thereby assuming the risk of Bear Stearns's less liquid assets.

On March 24, 2008, a class action lawsuit was filed on behalf of shareholders, challenging the terms of JP Morgan's recently announced acquisition of Bear Stearns. That same day, a new agreement was reached that raised JP Morgan Chase's offer to $10 a share, up from the initial $2 offer. The revised deal was aimed to quiet upset investors and any subsequent legal action brought against JP Morgan Chase as a result of the deal. The Bear Stearns bailout was seen as an extreme-case scenario, and continues to raise significant questions about Fed intervention. On May 29, Bear Stearns shareholders approved the sale to JP Morgan Chase at the $10 per share price.

每股转让。同时，美联储也为摩根大通集团提供了一笔无追索权的贷款，因此也承担了贝尔斯登资产缺乏流动性的风险。

3月24日，贝尔斯登的持股人通过仲裁起诉摩根大通集团对贝尔斯登最近的收购。同一天，摩根大通集团新的收购方案出炉，为了平息持股人的不满，同意以10美元每股的价格收购。贝尔斯登收购案被看做一个极端的案例，因为有美联储的介入。5月29日，贝尔斯登持股者同意了10美元每股的收购方案。

非常点拨

1. **对冲基金**（Hedge Fund） 是指由金融期货（financial futures）和金融期权（financial options）等金融衍生工具（financial derivatives）与金融组织结合后以高风险投机为手段并以盈利为目的的金融基金。

2. **次级抵押贷款** （subprime lending） 是为信用评级较差、无法从正常渠道借贷的人所提供的贷款。次级贷款的利率一般比正常贷款高，而且常常是可以随时间推移而大幅上调的浮动利率，因而对借款人有较大风险。由于次级贷款的违约率较高，对于贷款商也有较正常贷款更高的信用风险。

3. **担保债务凭证**（Collateralized Debt Obligation，CDO） 资产证券化家族中重要的组成部分。它的标的资产通常是信贷资产或债券。这也就衍生出了它按资产分类的重要的两个分支：CLO(Collateralised Loan Obligation)和CBO(Collateralised Bond Obligation)。前者指的是信贷资产的证券化，后者指的是市场流通债券的再证券化。但是它们都统称为CDO。

担保债务凭证(Collateralized Debt Obligation, CDO)是一种固定收益证券，现金流量的可预测性较高，不仅为投资者提供多元化的投资渠道以及增加投资收益，更强化了金融机构的资金运用效率，转移不确定风险。凡具有现金流量的资产，都可以作为证券化的标的。通常，创始银行将拥有现金流量的资产汇集群组，然后将资产包装及分割，转给特殊目的的实体（SPV），以私募或公开发行的方式卖出固定收益证券或收益凭证。CDO的背后为一些债务工具，如高收益的债券、新兴市场公司债或国家债券、银行贷款或其他次顺位证券。传统的ABS其资产池可能为信用卡应收账款、现金卡应收账款、租赁租金、汽车贷款债权等，而CDO背后支撑的则是一些债务工具，如高收益的债券(high-yield bonds)、新兴市场公司债或国家债券(Emerging Market Corporate Debt、

Sovereign），也可包含传统的ABS（Assets Backed Securities）、住宅抵押贷款支持证券（Residential Mortgage-Backed Securities, RMBS）及商用不动产抵押贷款支持证券（Commercial Mortgage-Backed Securities, CMBS）等资产证券化商品。

IndyMac Bank
Unit 16

IndyMac Bank
加州银行

主题札记

美国史上第二大银行倒闭

11天挤兑13亿美元

次贷危机影响信心，美国爆史上第二大银行倒闭案

新快报综合报道，信贷危机威胁未除，加上美国楼市不景气，越来越多人断供，美国金融业备受冲击，影响银行客户的信心。加州IndyMac Bank(IMB)的客户6月底以来共提走13亿美元存款，银行因此倒闭，需由联邦政府接管，是历来在美国政府监管下而破产的最大型存贷款银行，也是美国史上第二大倒闭的金融机构。

周转不灵宣布破产

美国储蓄管理局(OTS)上周五表示，IMB没能达到存款要求，遂将其业务转托予联邦储蓄保险公司(FDIC)继续营运。OTS局长赖克称，IMB因周转不灵宣布破产。

FDIC计划于下周一重新开始运营这家银行，预期会削减3,800个职位，占全银行过半的员工。

IMB截至2009年3月31日，资产总额为320亿美元，存款金额为190亿美元。

在楼价下跌和断供宗数上升的情况下，IMB共录得9亿美元的亏损。

美国史上第二大倒闭银行

FDIC估计，接管IMB的成本介乎40亿美元至80亿美元，可能是历来收购银行成本最高的一宗。

FDIC介入事件，全因为参议员舒默上月26日的一封信。他在信中敦促银行监管机构采取措施，以防IMB倒闭。消息传出后，该行客户纷纷到银行提款，引起挤提。信件公开后11天内，客户提款共13亿美元。

OTS指责舒默的信件引发恐慌，导致银行周转不灵。他前天发表书面声明，表示IMB破产倒闭是因为银行的积习，而并非近期的个别事件。他指出："如果OST尽力监管，阻止IMB继续以宽松的态度放债，便不会弄到今天的田地。"

据FDIC数据，IMB是美国史上第二大倒闭的银行，仅次于1984年破产的Continental Illinois National Bank，后者资产接近400亿美元。

IndyMac Bank
加州银行

IndyMac Bank Center
加州银行中心

IndyMac Bank (I)

IndyMac Bank is the second largest financial institution to fail in U.S. history. Regulators feared the California-based bank did not have enough cash to cope after panicked investors withdrew more than $1.3billion in 11 days and seized its assets. The business will reopen on Monday as IndyMac Federal Bank, under supervision of the Federal Deposit Insurance Corporation, which will try and find a buyer.

IndyMac was founded in 1985 by David Loeb and Angelo Mozilo, who also founded Countrywide, another big mortgage lender whose loans helped fuel the housing boom.

Countrywide was taken over last week by Bank of America Corp.. IndyMac collapsed as shares in two of America's home loan institutions–Freddie Mac and Fannie Mae-saw their share prices slashed in half.With the collapse of IndyMac and the recent concerns

加州银行(上)

次贷危机还在加剧，IndyMac银行的倒闭成为美国历史上第二大金融机构倒闭案。管理者担心这家加州的银行没有足够的现金来应对恐慌的投资者，因为投资者们要在11天之内提取13亿美元存款，将自己的资产变现。（下个）星期一，IndyMac公司将重新开业，不过它的名字将改为IndyMac 联邦银行，因为它将在联邦储蓄保险公司的监管下找到买家。

IndyMac银行于1985年由大卫·罗布和安格鲁·莫兹罗建立。此外，他们两人还建立了全国金融公司(另一家大型房贷供应商)，旨在向建房热潮中的人们提供贷款。

全国金融公司于上周被美国银行接管。IndyMac银行的倒闭以及美国两家住房贷款机构——房利美和房地美的股价缩小了一半使得这场次贷危机的阴影进一步加重，目前我们仍不清楚这场危机还将持

related to Fannie and Freddie[151], it seems clear we may not yet know the full impact and scope of this crisis.The continuing financial uncertainty in the marketplace will focus the U.S. voters on the crisis and force the two presidential candidates–both weak in this area of finance–to come up with a real plan to stabilise the U.S. economy.This is one of those "events" that may play an unexpected role in determining the outcome of the November Election[152].

On July 2, Sen. Charles E. Schumer publicly taunted[153] bank regulators last week about IndyMac Bancorp's financial condition, which helped trigger a sudden outflow of deposits from the Pasadena thrift.

As noted here on Monday, Schumer sent letters to the Office of Thrift Supervision, the Federal Deposit Insurance Corp. and the Federal Home Loan Bank of San Francisco, saying he was "concerned that IndyMac's financial deterioration poses significant risks to both taxpayers and borrowers".

"IndyMac, which has suffered huge losses on defaulted mortgage loans, could face a failure if prescriptive[154] measures are not taken quickly." Schumer wrote.

续多久，影响面有多大。但毫无疑问，这场危机将给两位总统候选人带来一个很棘手的问题：谁能够找到真正解决这场危机的方法将会在11月的大选中占得先机。

7月2日，森·查尔斯·舒默就IndyMac 银行的财务状况公开指责银行监管者的监管无力，这引发了帕萨迪纳（加州南部城市）的挤兑风潮。

正如其周一所言，舒默给国家储蓄监管局、联邦存款保险公司、联邦住房贷款银行（旧金山）写信，表达他对IndyMac银行财务状况恶化以及由此带来的风险（对纳税人和借款者）的担忧。

"IndyMac 银行已经因为收不回住房低押贷款而遭受巨额损失，如果不采取及时的措施将会倒闭。"舒默写道。

---

151 Fannie and Freddie 房利美和房地美，俗称"两房"
152 election: [i'lekʃ(ə)n] *n*. 选举
153 taunt: [tɔːnt] *n*. 辱骂，嘲弄
154 prescriptive: [pri'skriptiv] *a*. 规定的（指示的，命令的，约定俗成的，惯例的）

How could Schumer know that? And since when are regulators supposed to tell the public in advance that a particular institution has been earmarked for possible failure? All that would do is guarantee a collapse. If depositors are within FDIC insurance limits they have nothing to worry about, anyway.

That pretty much sums up the content of a letter to Schumer today from John M. Reich, director of the Office of Thrift Supervision.

"As a regulator of insured depository institutions, we do not publicly comment on the financial condition or supervisory activities related to open and operating institutions," Reich wrote,"We believe it is critically important to maintain the confidentiality of examination and supervision information."

He went on: "Dissemination[155] of incomplete or erroneous information can erode public confidence, mislead depositors and investors, and cause unintended consequences, including depositor runs and panic stock trades. Rumors and innuendo cause damage to financial institutions that might not occur otherwise and these concerns drive our strict policy of privacy."

舒默怎么知道的呢？监管者又应该在什么时候事先向公众披露一家银行有可能破产呢？然而，这样做只能加快它的破产。如果存款人是FDIC（联邦存款保险公司）的客户，他们就没有什么可担心的。

以下的话概括了约翰·M.瑞迟（国家储蓄监督的主管）给舒默的信的内容。

"作为联邦储蓄的监管部门，我们不应该对正在营业的机构和财务状况作出评论。我们相信维护监管信息的保密性是非常重要的。"瑞迟写到。

"不完全的和错误信息的散布会打击公众信心、误导储户和投资者并导致意想不到的后果，如股市恐慌和银行挤兑现象。谣言会对金融机构造成伤害，这也是我们为什么严格执行保密政策的原因。"瑞迟继续写道。

---

[155] dissemination: [di,semi'neiʃən] *n.* 传播，宣传，传染（病毒）

John D. Hawke, the U.S. comptroller of the currency (regulator of national banks) from 1998 to 2004, had more pointed words for Schumer in a story in the American Banker newspaper today.

"If Schumer continues to go public with letters raising questions about the condition of individual institutions, he will cause havoc in the banking system," Hawke said.

"Leaking his IndyMac letter to the press was reckless and grossly irresponsible[156]. I don't see how he can be trusted with confidential information in the future. What this incredibly stupid conduct does is put at risk the willingness of regulators to share any information with the congressional oversight committees."

The senator's office didn't respond to a request for comment today. On Monday, Schumer aide Brian Fallon offered this explanation for Schumer's action: "The home loan bank system has an obligation to lend responsibly and police its members. But it has not been doing its job. We have found the only way to get the home loan bank system to act appropriately and positively is to make public the concerns we've already expressed privately."

约翰·D.霍克，从1998年到2004年担任美国货币监理官（国家银行的监管者），于今日的《美国银行家》报纸上对舒默的话发表评论。

"如果舒默继续将他对一家金融机构的评论公布于众的话，他将给整个银行系统带来浩劫。"霍克说。

"舒默将他关于IndyMac的信公布于众是极为不负责任的做法，他是个让人无法信任的人。最愚蠢的是，这将使监管者在和国会监管委员会交流信息时存在风险。"

议会并未对此事作出评论。星期一，布莱恩·弗伦对舒默的评论作出了解释："住房贷款银行系统有义务和责任对它的成员进行管制。然而，他们并没有这样做。我们发现唯一能使他们积极正确地应对公众担忧的方法就是我们所做的这样。

---

[156] irresponsible: [ˌirisˈpɔnsəbl] *a.* 不负责任的，不可靠的

住房贷款银行集团为美国金融集团提供住房贷款、中小企业贷款、农业农村贷款及其他经济发展贷款，是美国最大的联合住房贷款和社区贷款组织。该银行集团只向其他银行提供贷款而不面向个人。

1. What is the direct reason for Indy Mac's collapse?

2. What did regulators do in this regard?

3. Who do you think is responsible for investors and depositors?

储户 depositor   股价 share price

225

挤兑 depositor run
住房贷款 home loan

国有银行 national bank
储蓄监管 thrift supervision

听力广场

IndyMac Bank(II)

IndyMac Bancorp, Inc. was the holding company for IndyMac Bank, FSB (Federal Savings Bank) and the seventh largest mortgage originator in the United States. The collapse of IndyMac Bank on July 11, 2008, was the second largest bank failure in United States history.

IndyMac Bank, operating as a combined thrift and mortgage[157]bank, provided lending for the purchase, development, and improvement of single-family housing. IndyMac Bank also issued secondary mortgages secured by such housing, and other forms of consumer credit[158].

The company was founded as Countrywide

加州银行（下）

IndyMac 银行集团为IndyMac 银行和联邦储蓄银行共同所有，是美国第七大抵押贷款借款人。2008年7月11日，该公司宣布破产，这是美国历史上第二大银行破产。

IndyMac银行将抵押贷款与储蓄相结合,为个人和家庭购房提供贷款。此外，IndyMac 银行还为个人和家庭提供次级抵押贷款和其他形式的消费信贷服务。

1985年，由于全国金融公司

---

[157] mortgage: [ˈmɔːgidʒ] *n.* 抵押贷款
[158] consumer credit *n.* 消费信贷

Mortgage Investment in 1985 by David Loeb and Angelo Mozilo as a means of collateralizing Countrywide Financial loans too big. In 1997, Countrywide spun off IndyMac as an independent company. In July 2000, IndyMac Mortgage Holdings, Inc. acquired SGV Bancorp, then changed its name to IndyMac Bank and became the ninth largest bank headquartered[159] in California.

IndyMac Bancorp expanded its business and national presence by acquiring[160] Financial Freedom, an originator and servicer of reverse mortgage loans, on July 16, 2004, New York Mortgage Company, an East Coast mortgage bank, on April 2, 2007, and Barrington Capital Corporation, a West Coast mortgage bank, in September 2007.

December 28, 2007, Jim Cramer, TheStreet. com's founder published on article on TheStreet. com's pay site RealMoney.com entitled: "IndyMac and MBIA Headed For The Chute." Excoriating the management of both firms, Mr. Cramer predicted for IndyMac: "slow bleeding until, well, the abyss."

May 12, 2008, IndyMac gives its last-ever quarterly earnings report. Among other things, the bank states that a fall below adequate

的贷款数额太大，大卫·罗卜和安吉洛·莫滋罗成立了全国抵押贷款投资公司作为抵押，即IndyMac银行的前身。1997年IndyMac从全国金融公司中分离出来，成为独立的公司。2000年，IndyMac房贷公司收购了SGV银行，然后改名为IndyMac银行，成为美国第九大银行，总部设在加州。

IndyMac银行在2007年连续收购了几家金融机构：金融自由公司（反向房贷的发起者和提供者，2004年7月16日）、纽约房贷公司（东海岸的房贷银行，2007年4月2日）和巴林顿资产公司（西海岸的房贷银行，2007年9月），将它的业务进一步向房贷市场扩展。

2007年12月28日，Street.com的建立者吉姆·克雷默在他创立的网站上发表文章"IndyMac 和MBIA进入滑坡"，指责两家公司的管理不力，最后，克雷默预测，"IndyMac公司将慢慢地走向衰亡。"

2008年5月12日，IndyMac银行发布了它的最后季度盈利报告，指出公司资产远低于平均水平属于正

---

[159] headquarter: [ˌhedˈkwɔːtə] vt. 总部设立于
[160] acquire: [əˈkwaiə] vt. 收购

regulatory capitalization is a "possible scenario" and that it is seeking to raise capital[161] through its investment bankers.

May 13, 2008, in an article entitled: "Indymac Seeks To Preserve Capital", Philip Van Doorn noted IndyMac's precipitous[162] decline in capital revealed in the quarterly report. As a consequence of this decline, Van Doorn concluded: "It appears that capital-raising efforts will need to be stepped up. IndyMac Bank's risk-based capital ratio dropped to 10.26% as of March 31, from 10.81% last quarter. This ratio, which factors in asset quality and loan-loss reserve coverage, needs to be at least 10% for an institution to be considered well-capitalized under regulatory guidelines."

June 26, 2008, the release of several letters by Senator Charles Schumer (D-NY) said "The possible collapse of big mortgage lender IndyMac Bancorp Inc. poses significant financial risks to its borrowers and depositors, and regulators may not be ready to intervene to protect them".

The letters set off a bank run: IndyMac depositors, fearing for the worst, sought to withdraw their funds from the ailing bank. Regulators and others in the financial sector quickly criticized Senator Schumer for publicly

常范畴，公司将通过它的投资银行筹集资本。

2008年5月13日，飞利浦·范·杜恩在一篇名为"IndyMac试图保留资本"的文章中，指出Indymac的资本迅速流失在季报中有所披露。范·杜恩指出，Indymac需要加大融资力度，因为截至3月31日，其风险资产比例已由上一个季度的10.81%下降到10.26%。而只有当这个反映资产质量的指标在10%以上时才被认为是符合监管要求的机构。

2008年6月26日，查尔斯·舒默议员在他的几封信中披露："大型抵押贷款提供者IndyMac银行可能将倒闭，这将给借款者和广大储户带来巨大的金融风险。同时，管理者可能还没有准备好介入来保护他们。"

这几封信掀起了轩然大波，IndyMac银行门前排起了长长的队伍。而银行监管者却对舒默展开了批评，认为他的言论加剧了银行的危机。此外，监管者还指出联邦

---

[161] capital: ['kæpitə] *n.* 资金，资本
[162] precipitous: [pri'sipitəs] *a.* 突然的，陡然的

releasing his letter, which acted to further destabilize the bank. They added that the Federal Deposit Insurance Corporation (FDIC) and Office of Thrift Supervision (OTS) "do not comment on open and operating institutions", and "Dissemination of incomplete or erroneous information can erode public confidence, mislead depositors and investors, and cause unintended consequences, including depositor runs and panic stock trades. Rumors and innuendo cause damage to financial institutions that might not occur otherwise and these concerns drive our strict policy of privacy".

In the eleven days that followed the letter's release, depositors took out more than $1.3 billion, regulators said. This sudden withdrawal of insured funds caused a liquidity crisis at the bank. In ordinary times, a bank would borrow money to keep itself liquid, using the Federal Reserve and capital markets to raise the ready cash to meet depositors' demands.

July 7, 2008 IndyMac announced on the company blog that it has failed to raise capital between that date and its May 12, 2008, report, that its regulators have notified the bank that it is no longer considered "well-capitalized" and that it must submit a new business plan. Facing liquidity, capital and regulatory constraints, IndyMac announced that it had closed both its retail lending and wholesale divisions, halted new loan submissions, and cut 3,800 jobs. The bank reported a sharp increase in the number of

储蓄保险公司和储蓄监管局"不对正在经营的金融机构进行评论，片面的和错误的信息会打击公众投资信心，误导储蓄者和投资者并造成不可预见的结果，如加剧了银行挤兑和股市恐慌。关于金融机构的流言造成的损失是无法弥补的，因此我们的信息披露政策要非常严格保密"。

在这之后的11天里，存款者从IndyMac银行提走13亿美元。监管者认为这造成了银行的流动性危机。通常银行通过从美联储和资本市场借调现金来满足取款者的需要。

2008年7月7日，IndyMac银行在它的网站上宣称银行没能在5月12日以后筹集足够的资本，所以它已不再被认为是具有"良好资本"的银行，必须要提交一份新的商业计划。面对资本、现金和监管的约束，IndyMac银行宣布它将关闭借款部门，开始新的贷款计划，这将会裁减掉3,800个职位。同时，IndyMac银行承认舒默议员的评论加剧了它的抵押贷款危机。

depositor withdrawals following its announcements in the wake of Senator Schumer's remarks on the bank's ability to survive the mortgage crisis.

On July 8, IndyMac announced the sale of its Retail Lending Group to Prospect Mortgage. That day, the bank's shares closed at $0.44 in trading on the New York Stock Exchange, a loss of over 99% from its high of $50 in 2006. Additionally, analyst Paul J. Miller Jr. cut his price target on IndyMac to $0 from $1, rating the company's share price "Underperform".

On July 9, Standard & Poor's cut IndyMac's counterparty credit risk rating to "CCC", just a few steps above default, from "B", and said it may cut them again. The following day, the bank's shares reached a 52-week closing low of $0.31.

On July 11, 2008, citing liquidity concerns, IndyMac Bank was placed into conservatorship by the FDIC. A bridge bank, IndyMac Federal Bank, FSB, was established to assume control of IndyMac Bank's assets and secured liabilities (such as insured deposit accounts), and the bridge bank was put into conservatorship under the control of the FDIC.

The FDIC plans to reopen IndyMac Federal Bank, FSB on Monday July 14, 2008. Until then, depositors can access their insured deposits through ATMs, their existing checks, and their existing debit cards. Telephone and Internet account access will be restored on Monday,

7月8日，IndyMac 银行宣布将它的零售借贷部转让给未来房贷公司。同一天，IndyMac银行的股票价格在纽约股票交易市场以0.44美元/股的价格收盘，与它2006年50美元/股的高点相比，跌幅达到99%。此外，分析员保罗·J.米勒将IndyMac银行的股价降低到0~1美元，将IndyMac银行的股价评级为"差强人意的"。

7月9日，标准普尔将IndyMac银行的信用风险评级从"B"级降至为"CCC"级，仅仅高于违约，而且可能将进一步降低其信用评级。第二天，IndyMac银行股价跌至52周来的最低点0.31美元/股。

2008年7月11日,由于流动性担忧 IndyMac银行已进入联邦储蓄保险公司的保护体系。临时成立的过渡银行（IndyMac 联邦银行）保证了IndyMac银行的资产和安全负债都能受到联邦存款保险公司的保护。

2008年7月14日，联邦存款保险公司（FDIC）重新开始了IndyMac联邦银行的业务。储户们可以重新提取现金，使用支票、借记卡、电话和网上银行业务。

when the bank reopens.

The FDIC guarantees the funds of all insured accounts up to US$100,000, and has declared a special advance dividend to the roughly 10,000 depositors with funds in excess of the insured amount, guaranteeing 50% of all funds over the insured $100,000.

With $32 billion in assets, IndyMac Bank is one of the largest bank failures in American history, after the 1984 failure of Continental Illinois National Bank, with $40 billion of assets, and the 1988 failure of American Savings & Loan Association of Stockton, California. due to large losses in mortgage-backed securities.

联邦储蓄保险公司保证所有10万美元以下的账户都能得到兑现。此外，FDIC还向资金超过保额的约10,000名存款人提供一项额外预付红利，来保证50%的10万美元以上的账户都可得以兑现。

320亿美元资产的IndyMac银行成为美国历史上最大的银行倒闭案之一，仅次于1984年伊利诺州国民银行（400亿美元资产）倒闭案和1988年美国加州斯托克顿的存款和贷款协会因抵押贷款支持证券的巨额亏损引发的倒闭。

非常点拨

标准普尔是世界权威金融分析机构，由普尔先生（Mr. Henry Varnum Poor）于1860年创立。标准普尔由普尔出版公司和标准统计公司于1941年合并而成。标准普尔为投资者提供信用评级、独立分析研究、投资咨询等服务，其中包括反映全球股市表现的标准普尔全球1,200指数和以美国投资组合指数为基准的标准普尔500指数等一系列指数。其母公司为麦格罗·希尔（McGraw-Hill）。

Bankruptcy of
Lehman Brothers
Unit 17

Bankruptcy of Lehman Brothers
雷曼兄弟公司破产

主题札记

在寻找买家未果后，曾为美国第四大投资银行的雷曼兄弟公司于2008年9月15日凌晨发表声明说，公司将于当日递交破产保护申请。消息一出，美元和美国股指期货齐声下跌，预示了当天纽约股市的大跌。

破产保护

根据声明，将于15日上午向纽约南区的美国联邦破产法庭递交破产保护申请的将是雷曼兄弟控股公司，而不包括旗下金融企业。包括雷曼兄弟资产管理公司、经营资产管理和投资咨询的纽伯格·伯曼公司等雷曼兄弟旗下子公司都将继续营业，不受破产重组影响。

雷曼兄弟公司董事会在14日苦寻买家未果后作出了申请破产保护的决定。当日，英国第三大银行巴克莱银行在美国政府拒绝提供财政担保后决定退出拯救雷曼兄弟公司的行动。大约3小时后，美国银行也宣布退出，转而收购美林公司。

在政府拒绝救济、收购退路全断之后，雷曼兄弟公司最终决定，根据美国《破产法》第11章申请破产保护。一旦申请得到批准，雷曼兄弟控股公司将在破产法庭监督下走上重组之路。这也将是继垃圾债券专门公司德崇证券商品公司1990年破产之后美国金融界最大的一宗破产案。

凄凉周日

拥有158年历史的雷曼兄弟公司在美国抵押贷款债券业务上连续40年独占鳌头。但在信贷危机冲击下，公司持有的巨额与住房抵押贷款相关的"不良资产"在短时间内价值暴跌，将公司活活压垮。

面临公司破产的凄凉前景，在14日夜间雷曼兄弟公司位于曼哈顿纽约时报广场附近第七大道的总部门口人来人往，不少公司员工携带着纸盒子、大手袋、行李袋或拉杆箱走出大楼，一些人拿着印有公司名字的雨伞和装在画框内的美术品，一些人眼睛湿润，更有一些人低声哭泣，相互拥抱道别。大楼对面，各电视台的直播车排成一排。

除了公司员工，面对雷曼兄弟公司破产，心中最为焦急的可能是投资者与在公司开户交易的客户。美国证券交易委员会说，雷曼兄弟公司的客户账户将得到保护，委员会人员将在未来数周内继续在公司"蹲点"。

证券交易委员会主席克里斯托弗·考克斯14日发表声明说，雷曼兄弟公司的客户账户由证券投资者保护公司提供的保险保护。根据惯例，美国破产券商一般由证券投资者保护公司负责处理，指定托管人开展清算并保护客户权益。

股市海啸

作为华尔街巨无霸之一，雷曼兄弟公司破产可能冲击整个金融市场。被全球最大债券投资基金——太平洋投资管理公司称为"债券之王"的明星投资经理比尔·格罗斯说，雷曼兄弟公司破产将引发"金融海啸"。

雷曼兄弟公司将申请破产保护的消息15日凌晨一经宣布，标准普尔500指数期货立刻下挫3.6%，预示着当天上午的美股面临大跌。同时，美元与欧元的比价也应声下跌。印度等亚洲国家股市也大跌。

The New York City headquarters
雷曼兄弟公司的纽约总部

在美联储建议下，国际互换与衍生工具协会开设的金融衍生产品交易市场于14日临时开市，以方便各类交易商对冲相关风险。总共218家银行、代理商、保险公司和其他金融机构参与了交易。

阅读长廊

Bankruptcy of Lehman Brothers (I)

雷曼兄弟公司倒闭（上）

Lehman Brothers filed for Chapter 11 *Bankruptcy Protection* on September 15, 2008. The bankruptcy of Lehman Brothers is the largest bankruptcy filing in U.S. history with Lehman holding over $600 billion in assets.

雷曼兄弟公司于2008年9月15日根据《破产法》第11章申请了破产保护。雷曼兄弟公司持有6,000亿美元的资产，这也成了美国历史上最大规模的破产申请。

Background

In August 2007, Lehman closed its subprime lender, BNC Mortgage, eliminating 1,200 positions in 23 locations, and took a $25-million after-tax charge and a $27-million reduction in goodwill. The firm said that poor market conditions in the mortgage space "necessitated a substantial reduction in its resources and capacity in the subprime space".

In 2008, Lehman faced an unprecedented loss due to the continuing subprime mortgage crisis. Lehman's loss was apparently a result of having held on to large positions in subprime

事态背景

2007年8月，雷曼兄弟公司关闭了它的次级房贷部门BNC 抵押贷款有限责任公司，并裁减了23个办公地点中的1,200个职位。公司的关闭产生了2,500万美元的税后费用和2,700万美元的账面损失。公司表示恶化的抵押贷款市场形势已迫使雷曼兄弟公司减少在次贷市场的财力和人力投入。

2008年，因为次贷危机的继续加深，雷曼兄弟公司出现了史无前例的亏损。很明显，其巨大损失是因为雷曼兄弟公司在住房抵押贷

and other lower-rated mortgage tranches[163] when securitizing the underlying mortgages; whether Lehman did this because it was simply unable to sell the lower-rated bonds, or made a conscious decision to hold them, is unclear. In any event, huge losses accrued[164] in lower-rated mortgage-backed securities throughout 2008. In the second fiscal quarter, Lehman reported losses of $2.8 billion and was forced to sell off $6 billion in assets. In the first half of 2008 alone, Lehman stock lost 73% of its value as the credit market continued to tighten.In August 2008, Lehman reported that it intended to release 6% of its work force, 1,500 people, just ahead of its third-quarter-reporting deadline in September.

On August 22, 2008, shares in Lehman closed up 5% (16% for the week) on reports that the state-controlled Korea Development Bank was considering buying Lehman. Most of those gains were quickly eroded[165] as news emerged that Korea Development Bank was "facing difficulties pleasing regulators and attracting partners for the deal". It culminated on September 9, 2008, when Lehman's shares plunged 45% to $7.79, after it was reported that the state-run South Korean firm had put talks on hold.

款证券化业务中持有大量的次级和较低等级的住房抵押贷款。但是目前还不清楚雷曼兄弟公司这么做仅仅是因为无法出售较低等级的债券还是想故意持有。无论怎样，2008年公司在较低抵押贷款证券方面的损失剧增。第二季度财报显示，雷曼兄弟公司的损失为28亿美元，这不得不使雷曼兄弟公司廉价出售60亿美元的资产来融资。仅2008年上半年，由于信贷市场的继续收紧，雷曼兄弟公司的股价暴跌了73%。2008年8月，雷曼兄弟公司宣布将在下个季度财报前削减6%的员工，也就是1,500名雇员。

2008年8月22日，有报道说韩国开发银行正在考虑收购雷曼兄弟公司，这使雷曼兄弟公司股价以上涨5%的幅度收盘（这一周的涨幅为16%）。但不久雷曼兄弟股价又快速下跌，新消息指称韩国开发银行对雷曼兄弟公司的收购受到了监管机构的阻碍，并且和雷曼兄弟公司难以达成协议。收购进程在2008年9月9日告终，有报道声称韩国开发银行中止了与雷曼兄弟公司的收购谈判，雷曼兄弟公司股价因此又暴跌了45%，每股仅为7.79美元。

---

[163] tranche: [trɑːnʃ] *n.* 部分
[164] accrue: [əˈkruː] *v.* 自然增值
[165] erode: [iˈrəud] *v.* 腐蚀，侵蚀

Investor confidence continued to erode as Lehman's stock lost roughly half its value and pushed the S&P 500 down 3.4% on September 9, 2008. The Dow Jones lost nearly 300 points the same day on investors' concerns about the security of the bank. The U.S. government did not announce any plans to assist with any possible financial crisis that emerged at Lehman.

On September 10, 2008, Lehman announced a loss of $3.9 billion and their intent to sell off a majority stake in their investment-management business, which includes Neuberger Berman. The stock slid 7% that day.

On September 13, 2008, Timothy F. Geithner, the president of the Federal Reserve Bank of New York called a meeting on the future of Lehman, which included the possibility of an emergency liquidation of its assets. Lehman reported that it had been in talks with Bank of America and Barclays for the company's possible sale. The *New York Times* reported on September 14, 2008, that Barclays had ended its bid to purchase all or part of Lehman and a deal to rescue the bank from liquidation collapsed. Leaders of major Wall Street banks continued to meet late that day to prevent the bank's rapid failure. Bank of America's rumored involvement also appeared to end as federal regulators resisted its request for government involvement in Lehman's sale.

由于雷曼兄弟公司股价下降了近一半，标准普尔500(S&P 500)指数在2008年9月9日下降了3.4%，投资者的信心也在不断下降。当天，道·琼斯指数也将近下降了300点。但是，美国政府仍未声明要援助雷曼兄弟公司来应对可能出现的金融危机。

2008年9月10日，雷曼兄弟公司宣布第三季度的亏损达39亿美元，并打算出售旗下包括纽柏格·伯曼在内的投资管理业务中的多数来获得融资。这时雷曼股票下跌了7%。

2008年9月13日，美联储主席蒂莫西·盖特纳召开会议商讨雷曼兄弟公司的前途问题，这包括是否对雷曼兄弟公司的资产进行紧急清算。雷曼兄弟公司声称曾与美国银行和巴克莱银行谈论过收购的事项。《纽约时报》于9月14日报道说，巴克莱银行已经放弃购买雷曼兄弟公司部分或全部股权来避免雷曼兄弟公司走向破产。华尔街一些大银行的领导当天晚上又聚到一起讨论如何来避免雷曼兄弟公司破产。有关美国银行会介入的传言也被打破，因为政府监管者明确拒绝了雷曼兄弟公司希望政府介入救援的请求。

Bankruptcy filing[166]

Lehman Brothers filed for Chapter 11 *Bankruptcy Protection* on September 15, 2008.

Breakup process

On September 20, 2008, a revised proposal to sell the brokerage part of Lehman Brothers holdings of the deal, was put before the bankrupcy court, with a $ 1.35 billion ($700 million) plan for Barclays Plc to acquire the core business[167] of Lehman Brothers (mainly Lehman's $ 960 million Lehman's Midtown Manhattan office skyscraper, with responsibility for 9,000 former employees), was approved. Manhattan court bankruptcy Judge James Peck, after a 7 hour hearing, ruled: "I have to approve this transaction because it is the only available transaction. Lehman Brothers became a victim[168], in effect the only true icon to fall in a tsunami that has befallen the credit markets. This is the most momentous bankruptcy hearing I've ever sat through. It can never be deemed precedent for future cases. It's hard for me to imagine a similar emergency."

Luc Despins, the creditors committee counsel, said: "The reason we're not objecting is

申请破产

2008年9月15日，雷曼兄弟公司根据《破产法》第11章申请了破产保护。

破产过程

2008年9月20日，雷曼兄弟公司将修订过的提议交给了纽约南部的联邦破产法庭并获得了批准。该提议要求出售雷曼兄弟控股公司中的经纪业务，并以13.5亿美元（7亿英镑）的价格向巴克莱银行出售其核心业务（主要是价值9.6亿美元的曼哈顿市中心的办公楼，巴克莱负责对9,000多名雷曼兄弟公司员工的前途作出安排）。经过7小时的听证，曼哈顿破产法院法官詹姆斯·佩克在判定时说："我必须批准这项交易，因为这是唯一可行的交易。雷曼兄弟公司是唯一一家成了这次次贷危机牺牲品的偶像级公司。这是我听证过的最重大的一起破产案，希望不是将来一些案例的先例。我不敢去设想会有同样的案例发生。"

债券委员会的顾问卢卡·迪斯宾斯发表评论说："我们不反对

---

[166] file: [fail] *v.* 列队行进，归档，申请
[167] the core business *n.* 核心业务
[168] victim: ['viktim] *n.* 受害者

really based on the lack of a viable alternative[169]. We did not support the transaction because there had not been enough time to properly review it." In the amended agreement, Barclays would absorb $ 47.4 billion in securities and assume[170] $ 45.5 billion in trading liabilities. Lehman's attorney Harvey Miller of Weil, Gotshal & Manges, said "the purchase price for the real estate components of the deal would be $ 1.29 billion, including $960 million for Lehman's New York headquarters and $ 330 million for two New Jersey data centers. Lehman's original estimate valued its headquarters at $ 1.02 billion but an appraisal[171] from CB Richard Ellis this week valued it at $900 million". Further, Barclays will not acquire Lehman's Eagle Energy unit, but will have entities known as Lehman Brothers Canada Inc., Lehman Brothers Sudamerica, Lehman Brothers Uruguay and its Private Investment Management business for high net-worth individuals. Finally, Lehman will retain $20 billion of securities assets in Lehman Brothers Inc. that are not being transferred to Barclays. Barclays had a potential liability of $ 2.5 billion to be paid as severance, if it chooses not to retain some Lehman employees beyond the guaranteed 90 days.

的原因是这没有可行的选择了。我们不支持这交易是因为没有足够的时间去审评。"在修正的协议中，巴克莱银行将吸纳价值474亿美元的证券业务并承担455亿美元的交易债务。雷曼兄弟公司聘用的美国威嘉律师事务所的律师哈维·米勒说道："这项交易中房地产业务的收购总价为12.9亿美元，其中纽约总部资产为9.6亿美元，新泽西州的两个数据中心为3.3亿美元。雷曼兄弟公司原先对其总部的估价是10.2亿美元，但是本周，世邦魏理仕公司对其估价仅为9亿美元。"此外，巴克莱银行不能收购雷曼兄弟公司的能源投资业务，但可以收购雷曼加拿大有限公司、雷曼兄弟公司南美洲分公司、雷曼兄弟公司乌拉圭办事处的股权以及对高净值资产个人的私人投资管理业务。最后，雷曼兄弟公司将保留雷曼兄弟控股公司中未转给巴克莱银行的200亿美元证券资产。如果巴克莱银行在90天的保证期后不保留一些雷曼兄弟公司员工，那它可能在将来需要支付25亿美元的解雇金。

---

[169] alternative: [ɔːlˈtəːnətiv] *n.* 两者取一

[170] assume: [əˈsjuːm] *vt.* 承担债务

[171] appraisal: [əˈpreizəl] *n.* 估计，估量，评价

财经宝库

1. **商业抵押贷款支持证券**（Commercial Mortgage-Backed Securities, CMBS） 是资产证券化的一种。它是兴起于美国的一种成熟的房地产金融产品。这是一种将传统商业住房抵押贷款组成资产池,通过资产证券化技术,以资产支持证券形式向投资者发行,并以物业的租金收入还本付息的结构性融资活动。CMBS与普通ABS之间最大的区别在于,前者的基础资产是商业物业抵押贷款, 而不是一般资产。适合于发行CMBS的物业形态包括: 写字楼、酒店、出租公寓、商业零售项目和工业厂房等。它们的共性是能产生稳定的现金流的有形不动产。

2. **货币市场基金**（Money-market Fund） 是指投资于货币市场上短期有价证券的一种基金。该基金资产主要投资于短期货币工具,如国库券、商业票据、银行定期存单、政府短期债券、企业债券等短期有价证券。货币型基金是投资银行定存、商业本票、承兑汇票等风险低、流通性高的短期投资工具,因此具有流通性佳、低风险与收益率较低的特性。

DIY工作室

1. What lead to the substantial loss for Lehman in 2008?

2. Why did the Manhattan court approve the acquisition of Lehman's core business by Barclays?

3. What happened to those companies that have business relations with Lehman after its filing for bankruptcy?

归类记忆卡片

应计利息 accrued interest
去杠杆化 de-leverage
勾销/注销 write off

无担保借贷 unsecured lending
次级信用借款人 subprime lender
回购（股份）repurchase

听力广场

Impact of Bankruptcy Filing

The Dow Jones closed down just over 500 points on September 15, 2008, the largest drop in a single day since the days following the attacks on September 11, 2001.

Lehman's bankruptcy is expected to cause some depreciation in the price of commercial

雷曼兄弟公司申请破产带来的影响

2008年9月15日，道·琼斯指数收盘时仅为500多点，这是自2001年的"9·11"恐怖袭击以来当日最大跌幅。

雷曼兄弟公司的破产也会引起商业房地产的房价贬值。雷曼兄

real estate. The prospect for Lehman's $4.3 billion in mortgage securities getting liquidated sparked a selloff in the Commercial Mortgage-Backed Securities (CMBS) market. Additional pressure to sell securities in commercial real estate is feared as Lehman gets closer to liquidating its assets. Apartment-building investors are also expected to feel pressure to sell as Lehman unloads its debt and equity pieces of the $22 billion purchase of Archstone, the third-largest United States Real Estate Investment Trust (REIT). Archstone's core business is the ownership and management of residential apartment buildings in major metropolitan areas of the United States. Jeffrey Spector, a real-estate analyst at UBS said that in markets with apartment buildings that compete with Archstone, "there is no question that if you need to sell assets, you will try to get ahead" of the Lehman selloff, adding "Every day that goes by there will be more pressure on pricing".

Several money-market funds[172] and institutional cash funds had significant exposure to Lehman with the institutional cash fund run by The Bank of New York Mellon and the Primary Reserve Fund, a money-market fund, both falling below $1 per share, called "breaking the buck", following losses on their holdings

弟公司在抵押贷款支持证券方面的43亿美元被清算时将在商业抵押贷款支持证券市场中进行抛售。随着清算资产时间的临近，雷曼兄弟公司担忧在抛售商业房地产的证券时会感到更多的压力。当雷曼兄弟公司卖掉以220亿美元的收购价买来的美国第三大房地产投资信托公司Archstone的债务和股权资产时，住房投资者也会感到有压力。Archstone的核心业务是美国一些大城市的公寓住宅的所有权的掌管和管理。一个在瑞士银行工作的房地产分析师杰佛雷·斯皮科特讲述道："在与Archstone竞争的公寓房产市场中，你要先于雷曼兄弟公司的出售卖掉资产,这不会有什么问题。"并补充说，日子每过去一天，价格的竞争压力将更大。

New York City headquarters on Third Avenue
纽约第三大道的雷曼兄弟公司总部

一些货币市场基金和机构的现金资本将受到雷曼兄弟公司破产的巨大影响,主要是美林的现金资本和作为货币市场基金的初步储备基金，随着它们持有的雷曼兄弟公司股份遭受损失，两者跌到每股1美元。美林说已经把占它们1.13%资金的雷曼兄弟公司资产隔离起来。

---

[172] money-market funds *n.* 货币市场基金

of Lehman assets. In a statement The Bank of New York Mellon said its fund had isolated the Lehman assets in a separate structure. It said the assets accounted for 1.13% of its fund. The drop in the Primary Reserve Fund was the first time since 1994 that a money-market fund had dropped below the $1-per-share level.

自1994年货币市场基金跌落于每股1美元之下，这是初步储备基金第一次出现跌落。

Putnam Investments, a unit of Canada's Great-West Lifeco, shut a $12.3 billion money-market fund as it faced "significant redemption pressure" on September 17, 2008. Evergreen Investments said its parent Wachovia Corporation would "support" three Evergreen money-market funds to prevent their shares from falling. This move to cover $494 million of Lehman assets in the funds also raised fears about Wachovia's ability to raise capital.

2008年9月17日，面对巨大的赎回压力，加拿大人寿金融公司旗下的普特南投资关闭了123亿美元的货币市场基金。Evergreen Investments宣称其母公司Wachovia Corporation将帮助Evergreen 的三类货币市场基金来避免其股价下跌。但是将4.94亿美元的雷曼兄弟公司资产用于基金救助也使人们担心Wachovia能否筹集到资金。

About 100 hedge funds used Lehman as their prime broker and relied largely on the firm for financing. As administrators took charge of the London business and the U.S. holding company filed for bankruptcy, positions held by those hedge funds at Lehman were frozen[173] As a result the hedge funds are being forced to de-lever[174] and sit on large cash balances inhibiting[175] chances at further growth.

大约有100种对冲基金是以雷曼兄弟公司为主要经纪商并主要依靠雷曼兄弟公司来融资。正当一些管理人员掌管伦敦业务，雷曼兄弟公司申请了破产，对冲基金持有的雷曼兄弟公司的股份被冻结了。因此，对冲基金不得不下调和搁置会阻止未来增长的大量现金余额。

---

[173] frozen: ['frəuzn] *v.* 冻结
[174] de-lever: [di'li:və,di'levə] *vi.* 失去杠杆作用
[175] inhibit: [in'hibit] *v.* 禁止，抑制

In Japan, banks and insurers announced a combined 249 billion yen ($2.4 billion) in potential losses tied to the collapse of Lehman. Mizuho Trust & Banking Co. cut its profit forecast by more than half, citing 11.8 billion yen in losses on bonds and loans linked to Lehman. The Bank of Japan Governor Masaaki Shirakawa said "Most lending to Lehman Brothers was made by major Japanese banks, and their possible losses seem to be within the levels that can be covered by their profits," adding "There is no concern that the latest events will threaten the stability of Japan's financial system." During bankruptcy proceedings a lawyer from The Royal Bank of Scotland Group said the company is facing between $1.5 billion and $1.8 billion in claims against Lehman partially based on an unsecured guarantee from Lehman and connected to trading losses with Lehman subsidiaries, Martin Bienenstock.

Lehman was a counterparty[176] to mortgage financier Freddie Mac in unsecured lending transactions that matured on September 15, 2008. Freddie said it had not received principal payments of $1.2 billion plus accrued interest. Freddie said it had further potential exposure to Lehman of about $400 million related to the

在日本，银行和保险公司宣称雷曼兄弟公司破产会给他们带来2,490亿日元（24亿美元）的损失。瑞穗信托银行将盈收额的预算又砍掉了一半多，解释说雷曼兄弟公司破产将牵扯到它们价值118亿日元的债券和贷款损失。日本银行行长白川方明分析说："给予雷曼兄弟公司借款的是一些大的日本银行。它们可能遭受的损失在利润范围内。"并补充说，"不用担心最近的事会影响到日本金融市场的稳定"。在破产听证中，一位代理苏格兰皇家银行的律师称："我们将向雷曼兄弟公司索取15亿美元到18亿美元的债务，索债的部分原因在于雷曼兄弟公司提供无担保抵押，也与雷曼子公司Martin Bienenstock交易亏损相关。"

在无担保贷款交易上，雷曼兄弟公司与其交易对手——抵押贷款巨头房地美一样都是在9月15日到期。房地美称还没收到12亿美元的本金和应计利息。并说它们将可能遭受因雷曼兄弟公司破产而带来的与单个家庭贷款服务业务有关的4亿美元的损失，这其中包括回购

---

[176] counterparty: ['kauntəpɑːti] *vi.* 与之相对应

servicing of single-family home loans, including repurchasing obligations. Freddie also said it "does not know whether and to what extent it will sustain a loss relating to the transactions" and warned that "actual losses could materially exceed current estimates". Freddie was still in the process of evaluating its exposure to Lehman and its affiliates[177] under other business relationships.

After Constellation Energy was reported to have exposure to Lehman, its stock went down 56% in the first day of trading having started at $67.87. The massive drop in stocks led to the New York Stock Exchange halting trade of Constellation. The next day, as the stock plummeted as low as $13 per share, Constellation announced it was hiring Morgan Stanley and UBS to advise it on "strategic alternatives" suggesting a buyout. While rumors suggested French power company Électricité de France would buy the company or increase its stake, Constellation ultimately agreed to a buyout by MidAmerican Energy, part of Berkshire Hathaway (headed by billionaire Warren Buffett).

The Federal Agricultural Mortgage Corporation or Farmer Mac said it would have to write off $48 million in Lehman debt it owned

义务。房地美还说不知道公司是否能经受得起这交易的损失，也不知道能承受得住多少的损失。然后又告诫说实际的损失会比目前估算的大。房地美仍在估算由雷曼兄弟总公司和分公司带来的可能损失。

联合能源公司报道说受到了雷曼兄弟公司破产的影响，它的股价在交易当天从开盘67.87美元下跌了56%。过大的跌幅让纽约证券交易所停止了联合能源公司的交易。第二天，因为股票暴跌到13美元每股，联合能源公司宣布它们正雇佣摩根士丹利和瑞银集团给它们出谋划策，暗示可能要被收购。虽然传言说法国电力公司将买下联合能源公司或增加对其股份的持有。联合能源公司最终同意被亿万富豪巴菲特领导的伯克式尔·哈萨维旗下的中美能源收购。

联邦农业抵押贷款集团（或称Farmer Mac）宣称公司必须因雷曼兄弟公司破产注销掉4,800万美

---

[177] affiliate: [ə'filieit] *n.* 联号（联播台，同伙），附属机构，分公司

as a result of the bankruptcy. Farmer Mac said it may not be in compliance with its minimum capital requirements at the end of September.

元的雷曼兄弟公司债务。这将使公司在9月底的最低资本需求不足。

非常点拨

1. 美国金融危机升级 雷曼兄弟公司申请破产保护

美英金融机构两天来发生了一系列"地震"。英国巴克莱银行14日宣布，撤出对雷曼兄弟公司的竞购行动。当地时间2008年9月15日凌晨，拥有158年历史的雷曼兄弟公司宣布申请破产保护。

美国财政部部长保尔森、证券交易委员会主席考克斯以及来自花旗集团、摩根大通、摩根士丹利、高盛、美林公司的高层连续三天云集位于曼哈顿的纽约联邦储备银行总部，研究如何拯救面临破产的雷曼兄弟公司，以阻止信贷危机进一步恶化。但财政部部长保尔森反对动用政府资金来解决雷曼兄弟公司的财务危机，会议没有取得成果。

受此影响，与会的英国第三大银行巴克莱银行宣布，由于美国政府不愿提供财政支持，决定退出拯救计划。当地时间15日凌晨，雷曼兄弟公司宣布申请破产保护。

拥有158年历史的雷曼兄弟公司曾是美国第四大投资银行，它的破产将对美国金融市场产生明显冲击。有人预测，美国金融市场可能迎来"黑色星期一"。

2. 雷曼兄弟公司破产申请显示负债6,130亿美元

雷曼兄弟控股公司(LEH)周一上午提交的破产申请显示其目前负债超过6,000亿美元。

该行现有总计6,130亿美元的负债，而其总资产为6,390亿美元。

该行向纽约南区联邦破产法院提交的申请显示其有超过10万个债权人，其中最大的是花旗集团和纽约麦伦银行，后者是雷曼兄弟公司大约1,380亿美元的高级债券的契约受托人。

纽约银行还被列为雷曼兄弟公司的第二和第三大债权人，对120亿美元的高级债务和50亿美元的初级次顺位债务拥有索偿权。

　　这份破产申请还显示，法国安盛人寿、基金管理公司和富达投资的母公司FMR是雷曼兄弟公司最大的3个股东。

The Lehman Brother's building
雷曼兄弟公司大厦

History of Lehman Brothers

Unit 18

History of Lehman Brothers
雷曼兄弟公司的历史

主题札记

亨利·雷曼（Henry Lehman）为卖牛商人之子，1844年，23岁的亨利从德国巴伐利亚州的Rimpar市移民到美国，定居在亚拉巴马州的蒙哥马利，在那里开了一家名为"H. Lehman"的干货商店。1847年，因伊曼纽尔·雷曼（Emanuel Lehman）到来，商号更名为"H. Lehman and Bro"。当1850年家中最小的弟弟迈尔·雷曼（Mayer Lehman）也到此地后，商号再次变更，定名为"Lehman Brothers"。

在19世纪50年代美国南部地区，棉花是其最重要的作物。利用对棉花的高市场价值，三兄弟开始定期接受由客户付款的原棉贸易，最终开始第二次棉花的商业交易。几年间，这项业务的增长成为他们的运作之中最重要的一部分。在1855年，亨利因黄热病而过世之后，其余的兄弟继续关注他们的商品交易或经纪业务。

1858年，因众多因素，棉花贸易中心由美国南方转移到纽约。雷曼在纽约市曼哈顿区自由大街119号开设第一家分支机构，当年32岁的伊曼纽尔负责办事处业务。1862年遭逢美国内战，公司和一个名为约翰·杜尔的棉商合并，组建了雷曼杜尔公司（Lehman, Durr & Co.）。

内战结束后，公司为亚拉巴马州提供财务支持以协助重建。公司总部最终也搬到1870年创建纽约棉花交易所的纽约市。1884年伊曼纽尔设置了公司理事会，公司还在新兴市场从事铁路债券业务并进军金融咨询业务。

早在1883年，雷曼已成为咖啡交易所成员之一，到了1887年公司还加入纽约证券交易所。1899年，则开始首次公开募股生意，为国际蒸汽泵公司招募优先股和普通股。

尽管提供国际蒸汽，但一直到1906年，公司才从一个贸易商真正转变成为证券发行公司。同一年在菲利普·雷曼的掌管下，雷曼公司与高盛公司合作，将西尔斯·罗巴克公司和通用雪茄公司上市。

随后的二十年间，差不多有上百家新公司的上市都由雷曼兄弟协助，其中多次都和高盛公司合作。这些公司中有：沃尔沃斯公司（零售）、5月百货公司、基姆贝尔兄弟公司、梅西公司、斯杜德贝克公司、股德雷特公司以及恩迪科特强森公司。

菲利普·雷曼于1925年退休，由他儿子罗伯特·雷曼（昵称"波比"）接手担任公司领导。波比领导期间，公司在股票市场复苏时因侧重于风险资本而度过了大萧条。1928年，公司搬到现在鼎鼎有名的威廉一街。

雷曼兄弟公司是传统的家族生意。但在1924年，约翰·M.汉考克以首位非家庭成员身份加入雷曼兄弟公司，接着在1927年门罗·C.古特曼和保罗·马祖尔也相继加盟。

20世纪30年代，雷曼兄弟签署了第一电视制造商杜蒙的首次公开募股，并为美国广播公司（RCA）提供资金协助。它也为快速增长的石油工业提供金融协助，其中包括了哈利伯顿公司（Halliburton）和科麦奇公司（Kerr-McGee）。

20世纪50年代，雷曼兄弟签署了数字设备公司的首次公开募股（IPO）。稍后，它又协助了康柏公司上市。罗伯特·雷曼于1969年去世，当时已经没有雷曼家族任何一位成员在公司任职。罗伯特的过世给公司留下了领导真空，加之当时经济不景气，公司进入困难期。1973年，贝尔豪威尔公司主席和首席执行官皮特·彼得森受聘挽救公司。

investment bank Lehman Brothers
雷曼兄弟投资银行

History of Lehman Brothers (I)

雷曼兄弟公司的历史（上）

Lehman Brothers

Lehman Brothers Holdings Inc.(Pink Sheets:LEHMQ) was a global financial-services firm. The firm does business in investment banking, equity and fixed-income sales, research and trading, investment management, private equity, and private banking. It is a primary dealer in the U.S. Treasury securities market. Its primary subsidiaries include Lehman Brothers Inc., Neuberger Berman Inc., Aurora Loan Services, Inc., SIB Mortgage Corporation, Lehman Brothers Bank. The firm's worldwide headquarters are in New York City, with regional headquarters in London and Tokyo, as well as offices located throughout the world.

On September 15, 2008, the firm filed for Chapter 11 bankruptcy protection; the filing marks the largest bankruptcy in U.S. history.

雷曼兄弟公司

雷曼兄弟控股公司是一家全球性的金融服务公司,公司的业务包括投资银行业务，权益和固定收益产品的销售、研究和交易，投资管理业务，私人股权以及私人银行业务。雷曼是美国首家涉足国库券市场的公司。首批分公司包括雷曼兄弟控股公司，纽柏格·伯曼, 奥罗拉贷款服务公司，SIB房贷公司和雷曼兄弟银行。公司的总部设在纽约，在伦敦和日本还有地区总部。此外，分公司遍布世界各地。

2008年9月15日，雷曼兄弟控股公司申请了破产保护，成为美国史上最大数额的破产案。第二天，

The following day, Barclays plc announced its agreement to purchase, subject to regulatory approval, Lehman's North American investment-banking and trading divisions along with its New York headquarters building. On September 20, 2008, a revised version of that agreement was approved by Judge James Peck.

History

Under the Lehman family (1850–1969)

In 1844, 23-year-old Henry Lehman, the son of a cattle merchant, emigrated[178] to the United States from Rimpar, Bavaria. He settled in Montgomery, Alabama, where he opened a dry-goods store, "H. Lehman".In 1847, following the arrival of Emanuel Lehman, the firm became "H. Lehman and Bro." With the arrival of their youngest brother, Mayer Lehman, in 1850, the firm changed its name again and "Lehman Brothers" was founded.

In the 1850s Southern United States, cotton was one of the most important crops. Capitalizing on cotton's high market value, the three brothers began to routinely accept raw cotton from customers as payment for merchandise, eventually beginning a second business trading in cotton. Within a few years this business grew to become the most

巴克莱银行宣布已经得到监管部门的批准购买雷曼兄弟公司北美投资银行贸易分公司和雷曼兄弟公司的纽约总部。9月20日，修正后的协议得到了法官詹姆斯·皮克的批准。

历史回顾

雷曼家族掌管时期（1850~1969年）

亨利·雷曼为卖牛商人之子，1844年，23岁的亨利从德国巴伐利亚州的Rimpar市移民到美国，定居在亚拉巴马州的蒙哥马利，在那里开了一家名为"H. Lehman"的干货商店。1847年，因伊曼纽尔·雷曼到来，商号更名为"H. Lehman and Bro"。1850年,家中最小的弟弟迈尔·雷曼也到此地后，商号再次变更，定名为"Lehman Brothers"。

在19世纪50年代美国南部地区，棉花是其最重要的作物。利用对棉花的高市场价值，三兄弟开始定期接受客户用原棉付款，最终开始了新的涉及棉花的商业交易。几年间，这项业务的增长成为他们的业务运作中最重要的一部分。1855年，亨利因黄热病而过世之后，其余的兄弟继续关注他们的商品交易

---

[178] emigrate: ['emigreit] v. 移民，移居

significant part of their operation. Following Henry's death from yellow fever in 1855, the remaining brothers continued to focus on their commodities-trading/brokerage operations.

或经纪业务。

Emanuel and Mayer Lehman

By 1858, the center of cotton trading had shifted from the South to New York City, where factors and commission houses were based. Lehman opened its first branch office in New York City's Manhattan borough at 119 Liberty Street, and 32-year-old Emanuel relocated there to run the office. In 1862, facing difficulties as a result of the Civil War, the firm teamed up with a cotton merchant named John Durr to form Lehman, Durr & Co. Following the war the company helped finance Alabama's reconstruction. The firm's headquarters were eventually moved to New York City, where it helped found the New York Cotton Exchange in 1870; Emanuel sat on the Board of Governors until 1884. The firm also dealt in the emerging market for railroad bonds and entered the financial-advisory[179] business.

Lehman became a member of the Coffee Exchange as early as 1883 and finally the New York Stock Exchange in 1887. In 1899, it underwrote its first public offering[180], the

伊曼纽尔·雷曼和迈尔·雷曼掌管时期

1858年，因为纽约有着良好的发展环境并驻扎着好几家佣金行，棉花贸易中心已由美国南方转移到纽约。雷曼在纽约市曼哈顿区自由大街119号开设了第一家分支机构，当年32岁的伊曼纽尔负责办事处业务。1862年遭逢美国内战，公司和一个名为约翰·杜尔的棉商合并，组建了雷曼杜尔公司。内战结束后，公司为亚拉巴马州提供财务支持以协助重建。公司总部最终也搬到纽约市，在那里公司帮助当地于1870年创建了纽约棉花交易所。1884年，伊曼纽尔设置了公司理事会，公司还在新兴市场从事铁路债券业务并进军金融咨询业务。

早在1883年，雷曼已成为咖啡交易所成员之一，到了1887年公司还加入纽约证券交易所。1899年，则开始首次公开募股生意，为国际

---

[179] the financial-advisory *n.* 金融咨询业务
[180] first public offering *n.* 也称initial public offering，即首次公开发行股票

preferred and common stock of the International Steam Pump Company.

Despite the offering of International Steam, the firm's real shift from being a commodities house to a house of issue did not begin until 1906. In that year, under Philip Lehman, the firm partnered with Goldman, Sachs & Co., to bring the General Cigar Co. to market, followed closely by Sears, Roebuck and Company. During the following two decades, almost one hundred new issues[181] were underwritten by Lehman, many times in conjunction with Goldman, Sachs. Among these were F.W. Woolworth Company, May Department Stores Company, Gimbel Brothers, Inc., R.H. Macy & Company, The Studebaker Corporation, the B.F. Goodrich Co. and Endicott Johnson Corporation.

Following Philip Lehman's retirement in 1925, his son Robert "Bobbie" Lehman took over as head of the firm. During Bobbie's tenure, the company weathered the capital crisis of the Great Depression by focusing on venture capital while the equities market recovered. By 1928, the firm moved to its now famous One William Street location.

Traditionally, a family-only partnership[182], in 1924 John M. Hancock became the first non-

蒸汽泵公司招募优先股和普通股。

尽管提供国际蒸汽，但一直到1906年，公司才从一个贸易商真正转变成为证券发行公司。同年，在菲利普·雷曼的掌管下，雷曼公司与高盛公司合作，帮助西尔斯·罗巴克公司和通用雪茄公司上市。随后的二十年间，差不多有上百家新公司的上市都由雷曼兄弟协助，其中多次都和高盛公司合作。这些公司中有：沃尔沃斯公司（零售）、5月百货公司、基姆贝尔兄弟公司、梅西公司、斯杜德贝克公司、股德雷特公司以及恩迪科特强森公司。

1925年菲利普·雷曼退休后，由他儿子罗伯特·雷曼（昵称"波比"）接手担任公司领导。波比领导期间，公司在股票市场复苏时因侧重于风险资本而度过了大萧条。1928年，公司搬到现在著名的威廉一街。

雷曼兄弟公司是传统的家族生意公司。但在1924年，约翰·M.汉考克

---

[181] new issues *n.* 新发行股票
[182] partnership: ['pɑ:tnəʃip] *n.* 合伙，合作

family member to join the firm, followed by Monroe C. Gutman and Paul Mazur in 1927.

In the 1930s, Lehman underwrote the initial public offering of the first television manufacturer, DuMont, and helped fund the Radio Corporation of America (RCA). It also helped finance the rapidly growing oil industry[183], including the companies Halliburton and Kerr-McGee.

Pete Peterson

In the 1950s, Lehman underwrote the IPO of Digital Equipment Corporation. Later, it arranged the acquisition of Digital by Compaq. Robert Lehman died in 1969, and since that time, no member of the Lehman family has led the company. Robert's death left a void in the company, which, coupled with a difficult economic environment, brought hard times to the firm. In 1973, Pete Peterson, Chairman and Chief Executive Officer of the Bell & Howell Corporation, was brought in to save the firm.

Merger with American Express (1969–1994)

Under Peterson's leadership as Chairman and CEO, the firm acquired Abraham & Co. in 1975, and two years later merged with the venerable, but struggling, Kuhn, Loeb & Co.

以首位非雷曼家庭成员身份加入了雷曼兄弟公司，接着在1927年门罗·C.古特曼和保罗·马祖尔也相继加盟。

20世纪30年代，雷曼兄弟签署了第一电视制造商杜蒙的首次公开募股，并为美国广播公司提供资金协助。公司还为快速发展的石油行业提供融资，其中包括了哈利伯顿公司和科麦奇公司。

皮特·彼得森时期

20世纪50年代，雷曼兄弟签署数字设备公司的首次公开募股。不久，它又协助了康柏公司收购数字设备公司。罗伯特·雷曼于1969年去世，自那时候起，雷曼家族的成员再也没有在公司任职过。罗伯特的过世给公司留下了领导真空，加之当时经济不景气，公司陷入困境。1973年，贝尔豪威尔公司主席和首席执行官皮特·彼得森受聘挽救公司。

被美国运通并购（1969～1994年）

在兼任主席和首席执行官的皮特·彼得森的领导下，1975年，雷曼公司收购了亚伯拉罕投资银行。两年后又并购了处于挣扎中的库

[183] oil industry n. 石油产业

[22], to form Lehman Brothers, Kuhn, Loeb Inc., the country's fourth-largest investment bank, behind Salomon Brothers, Goldman Sachs and First Boston. Peterson led the firm from significant operating losses to five consecutive years of record profits with a return on equity among the highest in the investment-banking industry.

However, hostilities between the firm's investment bankers and traders (who were driving most of the firm's profits) prompted Peterson to promote Lewis Glucksman, the firm's President, COO and former trader, to be his co-CEO in May 1983. Glucksman introduced a number of changes that had the effect of increasing tensions, which when coupled with Glucksman's management style and a downturn in the markets, resulted in a power struggle that ousted Peterson and left Glucksman as the sole CEO.

Upset bankers, who had soured over the power struggle, left the company. Steve Schwarzman, chairman of the firm's M&A committee, recalled in February 2003 interview with Private Equity International that "Lehman Brothers had an extremely competitive internal environment, which ultimately became dysfunctional[184]". The company suffered under the disintegration, and Glucksman was

恩·罗卜公司，由此成立了雷曼兄弟—库恩·罗卜公司。雷曼从此成为继所罗门兄弟公司、高盛公司和第一波士顿公司后的美国第四大投资银行。彼得森领导公司从亏损走向连续五年的破纪录盈余，股权业务的收益在投资银行业中最高。

但是，因为公司的银行家和交易商（交易商挖走了公司大部分的收益）纠纷不断，1983年5月，彼得森不得不提携公司里的董事长、首席运营官及前任经销商刘易斯·哥锡文和他一起担任CEO。哥锡文对公司进行了大量的改革，结果却使公司里的关系更加紧张。加上哥锡文的管理方式和公司业绩的下滑，公司最终爆发了一场权力斗争，彼得森被驱逐出去，哥锡文独揽大权。

看着权力斗争的恶化，不堪忍受的银行家们离开了雷曼。作为公司并购委员会的主席的史蒂夫·施瓦兹曼在2003年2月接受国际私人股权报的采访中回忆说："雷曼兄弟内部的钩心斗角很严重，这最终使得公司瘫痪"。公司陷入瓦解，所以哥锡文迫于压力以3.6亿美元将公司卖给美国运通旗下的金融服务公司西尔森。5月11日，公

---

184 dysfunctional: [dis'fʌŋkʃənəl] *n.* 官能不良，官能障碍

pressured into selling the firm to Shearson, an American Express-backed electronic transaction company, in 1984, for $360 million. On May 11, the combined firms became Shearson Lehman/American Express. In 1988, Shearson Lehman/American Express and E.F. Hutton & Co. merged as Shearson Lehman Hutton Inc.

Divestment and independence (1994–present)

In 1993, under newly appointed CEO, Harvey Golub, American Express began to divest itself of its banking and brokerage operations. It sold its retail brokerage and asset management operations to Primerica and in 1994 it spun off Lehman Brothers Kuhn Loeb in an initial public offering, as Lehman Brothers Holdings, Inc.

Despite rumors that it would be acquired again, Lehman performed quite well under CEO Richard S. Fuld, Jr.. In 2001, the firm acquired the private client services, or "PCS", business of Cowen & Co. and later, in 2003, aggressively re-entered the asset-management business, which it had exited in 1989. Beginning with $2 billion in assets under management, the firm acquired the Crossroads Group, the fixed-income division of Lincoln Capital Management and Neuberger Berman. These businesses, together with the PCS business and Lehman's private-equity business, comprised the Investment Management Division, which generated

司更名为西尔森—雷曼—美国运通公司。1988年，因为哈顿公司的加入，公司又改名为西尔森—雷曼—哈顿公司。

脱离与独立（1994年至今）

1993年，在新任CEO哈维·戈卢布的领导下，美国运通开始脱离银行业务和经纪业务。随后将零售经纪业务和资产管理业务卖给普美利加公司。1994年，美国运通在一次公开上市时将雷曼兄弟—库恩·罗卜公司分解出去，使其变为雷曼兄弟控股公司。

尽管传言说雷曼兄弟公司会被美国运通回购，在CEO理查德·富尔德的领导下，雷曼兄弟公司却运营得非常好。2001年，雷曼兄弟公司收购了柯文公司的私人客户服务业务（或者叫PCS）。稍后，又大刀阔斧重新进军1989年退出的资产管理业务。以20亿美元的管理资产开始，雷曼兄弟公司收购了林肯资本管理公司和纽伯格·伯曼下的固定收益部门。这些业务加上私人客户业务和雷曼兄弟公司的私人股权业务组成了投资管理部门，此部门在2007年创造了大约31亿美元的净收入以及接近8亿美元的税前收入。在破产之前，公司拥有超过

approximately $3.1 billion in net revenue and almost $800 million in pre-tax income in 2007. Prior to going bankrupt, the firm had in excess of $275 billion in assets under management. Altogether, since going public in 1994, the firm had increased net revenues over 600% from $2.73 billion to $19.2 billion and had increased employee headcount over 230% from 8,500 to almost 28,600.

Response to September 11 terrorist attacks
The New York City headquarters

On September 11, 2001, Lehman occupied three floors of One World Trade Center where one employee was killed. Its global headquarters in Three World Financial Center were severely damaged and rendered unusable by falling debris, displacing over 6,500 employees. The bank recovered quickly and rebuilt its presence. Trading operations moved across the Hudson River to its Jersey City, New Jersey, facilities, where an impromptu trading floor was built and brought online less than forty-eight hours after the attacks. When stock markets reopened on September 17, 2001, Lehman's sales and trading capabilities were restored.

In the ensuing months, the firm fanned out its operations across the New York City metropolitan area in over forty temporary locations. Notably, the investment-banking

2,750亿美元的资产。总的来说，自从1994年上市以来，雷曼的净收入增加了600%，从27.3亿美元上升到192亿美元。职员人数也增加了230%，从原先的8,500人增加到接近28,600人。

对"9·11"恐怖袭击的反应
纽约总部

雷曼机构在世贸中心有三层楼的办事处，在2001年9月11日的袭击中，有一名员工遇难。在世界金融中心的世界总部严重受损，导致雷曼兄弟公司的运营也被中断，6,500名员工要转移。这家银行恢复得很快，不久就开始营业。在袭击后的48小时内，雷曼兄弟公司就恢复了网上交易，交易跨过哈德孙河到它的新办公地新泽西的泽西市。9月17日，股市开盘的时候，雷曼兄弟公司的销售和交易也同时恢复了。

在接下来的几个月里，公司暂时在纽约四十多个地方广开业务。出了名的是，这投资银行业务部门将喜来登、曼哈顿酒店的一层集休

division converted the first-floor lounges, restaurants, and all 665 guestrooms of the Sheraton Manhattan Hotel into office space. The bank also experimented with flextime (to share office space) and telecommuting via virtual private networking. In October 2001, Lehman purchased a 32-story, 1,050,000-square-foot office building for a reported sum of $700 million. The building, located at 745 Seventh Avenue, had recently been built, and not yet occupied, by rival Morgan Stanley. With Morgan Stanley's world headquarters located only two blocks away at 1585 Broadway, in the wake of the attacks the firm was re-evaluating its office plans which would have put over 10,000 employees in the Times Square area of New York City. Lehman began moving into the new facility in January and finished in March 2002, a move that significantly boosted morale throughout the firm.

The firm was criticized for not moving back to its former headquarters in lower Manhattan. Following the attacks, only Deutsche Bank, Goldman Sachs, and Merrill Lynch of the major firms remained in the downtown area. Lehman, however, points to the facts that it was committed to stay in New York City, that the new headquarters represented an ideal circumstance where the firm was desperate to buy and Morgan Stanley was desperate to sell, that when the new building was purchased, the

息室、饭店和665个客房为一体的地方改建成了自己的办公室。公司也尝试过让员工通过虚拟的网络上班和交流。2001年10月，雷曼以7亿美元买下了位于第7大道745号已经被建好但还没搬进去的竞争对手摩根士丹利的办公大厦。大厦占地1,050,000平方英尺，有32层。摩根士丹利的总部在离此处仅两个社区距离的百老汇1585号。"9·11"之后，雷曼重新评估了其办公计划，将10,000多名员工安排在纽约的时代广场。之后开始于1月搬进新办公楼，并在2002年3月完成搬迁。这次搬迁增强了公司的士气。

雷曼兄弟公司因为没有搬回曼哈顿的总部而遭到了社会的批评。"9·11"袭击之后，只有一些大公司像德意志银行、高盛和美林仍待在市中心。但是雷曼说："我们仍会待在纽约，但是新的总部能提供更理想的环境。况且雷曼不得不买而摩根士丹利不得不卖。购得新办公大厦时，世界金融中心的总部还没恢复调整过来。不管怎样,世界金融中心的整修要到2002年5月才能完成。"

structural integrity of Three World Financial Center had not yet been given a clean bill of health, and that in any case, the company could not have waited until May 2002 for repairs to Three World Financial Center to conclude.

After the attacks, Lehman's management placed increased emphasis on business continuity planning. Unlike its rivals, the company was unusually concentrated for a bulge-bracket investment bank. For example, Morgan Stanley maintains a 750,000-square-foot trading-and-banking facility in Westchester County, New York. The trading floor of UBS is located in Stamford, Connecticut. Merrill Lynch's asset-management division is located in Plainsboro Township, New Jersey. Aside from its headquarters in Three World Financial Center, Lehman maintained operations-and-backoffice facilities in Jersey City, space that the firm considered leaving prior to 9/11. The space was not only retained, but expanded, including the construction of a backup-trading facility. In addition, telecommuting technology first rolled out in the days following the attacks to allow employees to work from home was expanded and enhanced for general use throughout the firm.

"9·11"恐怖袭击之后，雷曼兄弟公司管理层越来越重视保证业务不间断的计划制定。不像其竞争对手，雷曼因其广泛扩大而受到人们的高度关注。比如，摩根士丹利在纽约威彻斯特郡仍有750,000平方英尺的交易银行业务办公楼。瑞银集团的办公楼位于康涅狄格的斯坦福德。美林的资产管理部门位于新泽西平原市的乡镇。除了世界金融中心的总部，雷曼在新泽西市也有办事处。在"9·11"恐怖袭击前公司还曾考虑过搬离此处。这办事处现在不但留住了，而且还扩大了，包括建立了后备交易设施。此外，电信通讯技术被广泛普及开来，使得员工可以在家上班。

财经宝库

1. **罗伯特·雷曼**（Robert Lehman） 出生于纽约，菲利普·雷曼之子。1925年开始接管雷曼公司。在他的领导下，公司安稳度过了1929年股市崩盘和随后的大萧条时期。第二次世界大战后，他开始扩展国际业务，成为美国最富有的人之一。

2. **国际互换与衍生产品协会**（International Swaps and Derivatives Association） 经营柜台交易衍生产品的贸易组织。总部设在纽约。为进入衍生产品交易市场制定了标准协议。标准协议有1992年和2002年两个版本。除了法律政治活动外，该协会还负责管理金融产品标记语言，即场外衍生产品的标准用语。

3. **金融衍生产品**（Financial derivatives） 是指其价值依赖于基础资产价值变动的合约。这种合约可以是标准化的，也可以是非标准化的。标准化合约是指基础资产的交易价格、交易时间、资产特征、交易方式等都是事先标准化的，因此此类合约大多在交易所上市交易，如期货。非标准化合约是指以上各项由交易的双方自行约定，因此具有很强的灵活性，比如远期协议。

4. **粉单市场**（Pink Sheets） 或粉红单市场，或粉纸交易市场，创建于1904年，由美国国家报价机构设立。在没有创立柜台交易市场之前，绝大多数场外交易的证券都在粉单市场进行报价。该市场对订阅用户定期制作刊物，发布场外交易的各种证券的报价信息，在每天交易结束后向所有客户提供证券报价，使证券经纪商能够方便地获取市场报价信息，并由此将分散在全国的做市商联系起来。粉单市场的创立有效地促进了早期小额股票市场的规范化，提高了市场效率，解决了长期困扰小额股票市场的信息分散问题。

1. What were Lehman's main businesses under the management of Lehman family? How did it make shifts between different businesses?

2. Lehman had suffered from a power struggle in the 1980s as a result of the hostilities between the firm's investment bankers and traders. What was its impact on the firm?

3. How did Lehman respond to September 11 terrorist attacks? Give your comments on its responses.

新兴市场 emerging market

私募股权 private equity

转让股份/撤销投资 divestment

清算所 clearinghouse

公开募股 public offering

风险资本 venture capital

交易商/证券商 dealer

产权 property right

听力广场

History of Lehman Brothers（II）

2003 SEC litigation

In 2003, the company was one of ten firms which simultaneously entered into a settlement with the U.S. Securities and Exchange Commission (SEC), the Office of the New York State Attorney General and various other securities regulators, regarding undue influence over each firm's research analysts by their investment-banking divisions. Specifically, regulators alleged that the firms had improperly associated analyst compensation with the firms' investment-banking revenues, and promised favorable, market-moving research coverage, in exchange for underwriting opportunities. The settlement, known as the "global settlement", provided for total financial penalties of $1.4 billion, including $80 million against Lehman, and structural reforms, including a complete separation of investment banking departments

雷曼兄弟公司的历史（下）

2003年证券交易委员会的诉讼

2003年，雷曼兄弟公司成为华尔街十大投资公司和美国证券交易委员会纽约州司法部以及其他监管机构达成和解协议的公司之一，讨论关于公司投资银行部门对公司的研究分析员误导的影响。监管机构特别指控这些公司将分析员的补偿和公司的投资银行收益扯到一起是不适当的，并希望是由客观的市场动向的研究报告代替承销机会。这项被视为全球性的和解，引出了14亿美元的财政罚款，其中雷曼被罚8,000万美元。同时，也引起了金融结构的改革，包括将投资银行部门从研究部门完全脱离出来。禁止直接或间接从投资银行收益中给分析员补偿，让自由独立的第三方给客户提供研究报告。

from research departments, no analyst compensation, directly or indirectly, from investment-banking revenues, and the provision of free, independent, third-party, research to the firms' clients.

Bankruptcy

On September 13, 2008, Timothy F. Geithner, the president of the Federal Reserve Bank of New York called a meeting on the future of Lehman, which included the possibility of an emergency liquidation of its assets. Lehman reported that it had been in talks with Bank of America and Barclays for the company's possible sale. The *New York Times* reported on September 14, 2008, that Barclays had ended its bid[185] to purchase all or part of Lehman and a deal to rescue[186] the bank from liquidation collapsed. Leaders of major Wall Street banks continued to meet late that day to prevent the bank's rapid failure. Bank of America's rumored involvement also appeared to end as federal regulators resisted its request for government involvement in Lehman's sale.

The International Swaps and Derivatives Association (ISDA) offered an exceptional trading session on Sunday, September 14, 2008, to allow market participants to offset positions

破产

2008年9月13日，美联储主席蒂莫西·盖特纳召开会议商讨雷曼兄弟公司的前途问题，这包括是否对雷曼兄弟公司的资产进行紧急清算。雷曼兄弟公司声称曾与美国银行和巴克莱银行谈论过收购的事项。《纽约时报》于9月14日报道说巴克莱已经放弃购买雷曼兄弟公司部分或全部股权来避免雷曼兄弟公司走向破产。华尔街一些大银行的领导人当天晚上又聚到一起讨论如何来避免雷曼兄弟公司破产。有关美国银行会介入的传言也被打断，因为美联储明确拒绝了雷曼兄弟公司希望政府介入救援的请求。

2008年9月14日，国际互换与衍生产品协会特例提供交易，允许市场参与者在当日晚些时候雷曼兄弟公司破产时抵消在各种衍生产品中

---

[185] bid: [bid] *n.* 出价
[186] rescue: ['reskju:] *v.* 援救，救出，营救

in various derivatives on the condition of a Lehman bankruptcy later that day. Although the bankruptcy filing missed the deadline[187], many dealers are honoring the trades they made in the special session.

Lehman Brothers headquarters in New York City on September 15, 2008. In New York, shortly before 1 a.m. the next morning, Lehman Brothers Holdings announced it would file for Chapter 11 bankruptcy protection citing bank debt of $613 billion, $155 billion in bond debt, and assets worth $639 billion. It further announced that its subsidiaries will continue to operate as normal. A group of Wall Street firms agreed to provide capital and financial assistance for the bank's orderly liquidation and the Federal Reserve, in turn, agreed to a swap[188] of lower-quality assets in exchange for loans and other assistance from the government.

Lehman's bankruptcy is the largest failure of an investment bank since Drexel Burnham Lambert collapsed amid fraud allegations 18 years ago.

Later in the day the Australian Securities Exchange (ASX) suspended Lehman's Australian subsidiary as a market participant after clearing-houses terminated their contracts with the firm.

的头寸。虽然破产申请迟于截止时间,许多交易商在这次交易中兑现了衍生产品。

2008年9月15日,位于纽约的雷曼兄弟公司总部凌晨一点不久,雷曼兄弟控股公司宣布将申请破产保护,报道有6,130亿美元的债务,1,550亿美元的债券负债,资产值为6,390亿美元。随后有公开声明分公司将继续正常营业。华尔街的一些公司表示愿意为雷曼有序地清算提供资金和财物援助。美联储也愿意以低级资产来交换来自政府的贷款和援助。

雷曼兄弟公司破产是自18年前德崇证券因欺诈指控破产以来最大额的投资银行破产。

当天晚些时候,在结算所结束了与雷曼的合约后,澳大利亚证券交易所暂停了雷曼兄弟澳大利亚分公司的交易。

---

[187] deadline: ['dedlain] *n.* 截止日期
[188] swap: [swɔp] *vt.* 交换,用……作交易

Lehman shares tumbled over 90% on September 15, 2008. The Dow Jones closed down just over 500 points on September 15, 2008, the largest drop in a single day since the days following the attacks on September 11, 2001. The conditions on Lehman's trading floors that day appeared grim; one-third of the sales force were absent[189].

In the United Kingdom, the investment bank went into administration with PricewaterhouseCoopers appointed as administrators. In Japan, the Japanese branch, Lehman Brothers Japan Inc., and its holding company filed for civil reorganization on September 16, 2008, in Tokyo District Court.

On Tuesday, September 16, 2008, Barclays plc announced that they will acquire a "stripped clean" portion of Lehman for $1.75 billion. This portion includes the Lehman headquarters building in the Times Square area of New York City, two data centers and the bulk of Lehman's trading and debt security operations, which will become part of Barclays Capital, a division of Barclays plc. On September 20, this transaction was approved by U.S. Bankruptcy Judge James Peck, who stated that, "I have to approve this transaction because it is the only available

2008年9月15日，雷曼兄弟公司的股价狂跌了90%。道·琼斯指数收盘时仅500点，这是自"9·11"事件以来最大的跌幅。雷曼的交易楼也显得凄凉，三分之一的销售人员已经离开。

在英国，雷曼兄弟公司由普华永道对其进行管理。2008年9月16日，在日本分公司，雷曼兄弟日本有限公司及雷曼兄弟控股公司向东京地区法院申请了重组。

2008年9月16日，星期二，巴克莱银行宣布他们将以17.5亿美元购买雷曼兄弟的小部分资产。这包括雷曼位于纽约时代广场的总部，两个数据中心以及大量的交易和债务证券业务。9月20日，这项交易获得了美国破产法院法官詹姆斯·佩克的批准。他说："我必须批准这项交易，因为这是唯一可行的交易。"交易最后以重估后13亿美元的低价（7亿英镑）成交。

---

[189] absent: ['æbsənt] *a.* 缺席的

transaction" with a final reduced price of $1.3 billion (£700 million) after re-evaluation of asset prices.

On September 17, 2008, the New York Stock Exchange delisted Lehman Brothers. Its old symbol, "LEH", has been replaced by the new symbol, "LEHMQ" on the Pink Sheets.

On September 17, 2008, Paul Brough, Edward Middleton and Patrick Cowley of KPMG China become the provisional liquidators appointed over Lehman's two Hong Kong based units - Lehman Brothers Securities Asia Limited and Lehman Brothers Futures Asia Limited. They are also appointed as the provisional liquidators for three further Hong Kong based Lehman Brothers companies, Lehman Brothers Asia Holdings Limited, Lehman Brothers Asia Limited and Lehman Brothers Commercial Corporation Asia Limited on 18 September 2008.

Nomura Holdings, Japan's top brokerage firm, agreed to buy both European and Asian division of Lehman Brothers for a nominal fee of $2 and $225 million, respectively. It would not take on any trading assets or liabilities in the European units.

Judgment

(This documents a current event. Information may change rapidly as the event progresses.)

2008年9月17日，纽约证券交易所删除了原名为LEH的雷曼兄弟的证券代码，将其由新的代码粉单上的"LEHMQ"取而代之。

2008年9月17日，毕马威中国公司的保罗·布拉夫，爱德华·米德尔顿和帕特里·克考利被任命为雷曼香港办事处，雷曼兄弟证券亚洲公司和雷曼兄弟期货亚洲公司的临时清算员。9月18日，他们又被任命为另外三家雷曼香港办事处的临时清算员。即雷曼兄弟亚洲控股公司，雷曼兄弟亚洲公司和雷曼兄弟亚洲商业有限公司。

日本的领头经纪公司日本野村控股公司愿意分别以200万美元和2.25亿美元收购雷曼兄弟欧洲和亚洲的分公司，但无须承担欧洲分公司的任何交易资产或负债。

评论

（此篇文章记录了有关雷曼的最新动向，但随事态发展信息在不断更新。）

On September 20, 2008, a revised version of the deal, a $1.35 billion (£ 700 million) plan for Barclays Plc to acquire the core business of Lehman (mainly its $960-million headquarters, a 38-story office building in Midtown Manhattan, with responsibility for 9,000 former employees), was approved. Manhattan court bankruptcy Judge James Peck, after a 7-hour hearing, ruled: "I have to approve this transaction because it is the only available transaction. Lehman Brothers became a victim, in effect the only true icon to fall in a tsunami that has befallen the credit markets. This is the most momentous bankruptcy hearing I've ever sat through. It can never be deemed precedent for future cases. It's hard for me to imagine a similar emergency."

Luc Despins, the creditors committee counsel, said: "The reason we're not objecting is really based on the lack of a viable alternative. We did not support the transaction because there had not been enough time to properly review it." In the amended agreement, Barclays would absorb $47.4 billion in securities and assume $45.5 billion in trading liabilities. Lehman's attorney Harvey R. Miller of Weil, Gotshal & Manges, said "the purchase price for the real estate components of the deal would be $1.29 billion, including $960 million for Lehman's New York headquarters and $330 million for two New Jersey data centers. Lehman's original estimate valued its headquarters at $ 1.02

2008年9月20日，雷曼兄弟公司将修订过的提议交给了纽约南部的联邦破产法庭并获得了批准。该提议要求出售雷曼兄弟控股公司中的经纪业务，并以13.5亿美元（7亿英镑）的出价向巴克莱银行出售其核心业务（主要是价值9.6亿美元的曼哈顿市中心的办公室，巴克莱银行负责对9,000多名雷曼员工的前途作出安排）。经过7小时的听证，曼哈顿破产法院法官詹姆斯·佩克在判定时说："我必须批准这项交易，因为这是唯一可行的交易。雷曼兄弟公司是唯一一家成了这次次贷危机牺牲品的偶像级公司。这是我听证过的最重大的一起破产案，希望不是将来一些案例的先例。我不敢去设想会有同样的案例发生"。

债券委员会的顾问卢卡·迪斯宾斯发表评论说："我们不反对的原因是这没有可行的选择了。我们不支持这交易是因为没有足够的时间去审评。"在修正的协议中，巴克莱银行将吸纳价值474亿美元的证券业务并承担455亿美元的贸易债务。雷曼兄弟公司聘用的美国威嘉律师事务所的律师哈维·米勒表述道："这项交易中房地产业务的收购总价为12.9亿美元，其中总部资产为9.6亿美元，新泽西州的两个数据中心为3.3亿美元。雷曼原先对其总部的估价是10.2亿美元，但是本周，世邦魏理仕公司对其估价仅为9亿美元。"此外，巴克莱银行不能收购雷曼的能源投资业

billion but an appraisal from CB Richard Ellis this week valued it at $900 million." Further, Barclays will not acquire Lehman's Eagle Energy unit, but will have entities known as Lehman Brothers Canada Inc., Lehman Brothers Sudamerica, Lehman Brothers Uruguay and its Private Investment Management business for high net-worth individuals. Finally, Lehman will retain $20 billion of securities assets in Lehman Brothers Inc. that are not being transferred to Barclays. Barclays acquired a potential liability of $2.5 billion to be paid as severance, if it chooses not to retain some Lehman employees beyond the guaranteed 90 days.

务，但可以收购雷曼兄弟公司加拿大有限公司、雷曼兄弟公司南美洲分公司、雷曼兄弟公司乌拉圭办事处的股权以及对高净值资产个人的私人投资管理业务。最后，雷曼将保留雷曼兄弟控股公司中未转给巴克莱的200亿美元证券资产。如果巴克莱在90天的保证期后不保留一些雷曼的员工，那它可能在将来需要支付25亿美元的解雇金。

非常点拨

1. **美国银行**（Bank of America） 创建于1968年10月7日，总部设在旧金山。美国银行为环球首要的金融服务机构之一，为美国第二大银行，致力提供一应俱全的个人及商业银行服务，服务遍及美国21个州、哥伦比亚特区及全球30个国家，为多达3,300万个家庭及250万个商业客户提供最优质完善的银行服务。该企业在2007年度《财富》全球最大五百家公司排名中名列第21位。

2. **英国巴克莱银行**（Barclays plc） 英国最大商业银行之一，1862年成立，总行设在伦敦。1998年总资产为3,652亿美元。巴克莱银行是位于汇丰银行和苏格兰皇家银行之后的英国第三大银行公司。巴克莱银行在全球约60个国家经营业务，在英国设有2,100多家分行。巴克莱银行经营消费及公司银行、信用卡、抵押贷款、代管及租赁业务，此外还提供私人银行业务。美国法院于2008年9月20日批准了英国巴克莱银行收购投资银行雷曼兄弟公司的核心业务，包括投资银行业务。

Washington Mutual
Unit 19

Washington Mutual
华盛顿互惠银行

主题札记

美国联邦存款保险公司(FDIC)于当地时间2008年9月25日晚宣布了美国历史上最大的银行倒闭案，总部位于华盛顿州的华盛顿互惠银行因资不抵债立即停业，由摩根大通以19亿美元的超低价收购这家有119年历史、曾经拥有3,000亿美元资产和1,880亿美元存款的银行的部分业务和分支机构。

鉴于华盛顿互惠银行(Washington Mutual Bank)"流动性不足,无法满足公司债务的支付要求,因而该行不能安全、稳定地开展业务"，美国储蓄监管局(OTS)于当地时间25日晚勒令华盛顿互惠银行停业。这是自1984年伊利诺伊州大陆国民银行倒闭以来，美国历史上最大的银行倒闭案。

美国联邦存款保险公司(FDIC)25日晚间发表的一份声明称，由摩根大通以19亿美元的价格收购华盛顿互惠银行的存款业务、分支机构以及其他业务。尽管华盛顿互惠银行旗下的数千亿美元资产瞬间蒸发，但这笔收购对华盛顿互惠银行现有的储蓄客户以及其他客户都不会造成任何影响，华盛顿互惠银行周五将照常营业。

此间舆论今天评论说，华盛顿互惠银行的倒闭是近期华尔街金融风暴冲击下美国金融界的新型事件，这个事件影响深远，不仅改写了美国金融行业格局，也使得数千亿美元的银行股东的财富付诸东流。

受华盛顿互惠银行倒闭消息影响，早场交易中指数期货大幅走低。道·琼斯工业指数周五早间开盘大跌150点，随后逐步回升。

美国参议院于当地时间周五上午11点半，将继续就7,000亿美元救市计划展开讨论。最新消息称，最终结果，可能由一份新的计划替代原来的7,000亿美元计划，使各方意见得以妥协。

Washington Mutual Bank
华盛顿互惠银行

阅读长廊

Washington Mutual (I)

As of September 2008, this financial institution underwent the following change in status: Bankruptcy.

Washington Mutual (abbreviated[190] to WaMu) (NYSE:WM) was a chain of savings and loans owned and operated by parent company JP Morgan Chase. Prior to September 2008 "WaMu", as it was known, was a holding company and was owner of the United States' largest savings and loan association until its closure and placement into receivership, during the subprime mortgage crisis. Despite its name, it ceased being a mutual company in 1983 when it began to trade publicly on the New York Stock Exchange.

On September 25, 2008 (the 119th anniversary of WaMu's founding) the United

华盛顿互惠银行（上）

截至2008年9月，这家金融机构的地位经历了如下变化：破产。

华盛顿互惠银行（缩写为WaMu）（NYSE: WM）是由其母公司摩根大通拥有并经营一系列的储蓄和贷款业务的银行。在2008年9月以前，众所周知，华盛顿互惠银行是一家控股公司还是全美最大的储蓄和贷款协会的主人，直到它在次级抵押贷款危机中关闭并被破产清算。尽管有互惠之名，但它在1983年于纽约股票交易所公开上市交易之后就不再是一家互助公司了。

2008年9月25日，也是华盛顿互惠银行的119年成立纪念日，美

States Office of Thrift Supervision (OTS) announced that it had closed the bank, and had placed it into the receivership of the Federal Deposit Insurance Corporation (FDIC). The FDIC announced that it had sold most of the bank's assets and liabilities, including covered bonds and other secured debt to JP Morgan Chase for $1.9 billion. Claims of equity holders, senior and subordinated debt holders were not acquired by JP Morgan Chase. Washington Mutual's government takeover is the largest bank failure in American financial history. Before the collapse, it was the sixth-largest bank in the United States. According to Washington Mutual's 2007 SEC filing, it held assets valued at $327.9 billion.

The company's stock declined from a high of $45 per share in 2007 to 16 cents per share on September 25, 2008, when it went into receivership.

Washington Mutual was founded as the Washington National Building Loan and Investment Association on September 25, 1889, after a fire nearly destroyed the city of Seattle. The newly formed company made its first home mortgage loan[191] on the West Coast on February 10, 1890. Its name was changed to Washington Savings and Loan Association on June 25, 1908.

国储蓄监管局将它关闭,并将其置于联邦存款保险公司破产保护之下。 美国联邦储蓄保险公司宣布它已经出售华盛顿互惠银行的大部分资产和债务,其中包括由摩根大通担保购买的19亿美元的抵补债券和担保债券。对股东和高级债持有者和次级债持有者的索赔,摩根大通将不予受理。华盛顿互惠银行的政府接管是美国金融历史上最大的银行破产案。在倒闭之前,它是美国第六大银行。据华盛顿互惠银行2007年向美国证券交易委员会递交的档案说明,它拥有价值为3,279亿美元的资产。

华盛顿互惠银行的股票从2007年的每股45美元的高位下跌到2008年9月25日即它进入破产清算时的每股16美分。

华盛顿互惠银行于1889年9月25日继一场大火险些毁掉西雅图之后成立,当时称为华盛顿国家建设和投资协会。新成立的公司于1890年2月10日在美国西海岸发放其第一笔住房抵押贷款。1908年6月25日,更名为华盛顿储蓄和贷款协会。

---

[191] home mortgage loan *n.* 住房抵押贷款

By 1930, it was operating under the name Washington Mutual Savings Bank. The company purchased its first company, Continental Mutual Savings Bank, on July 25, 1930.

Its marketing slogan for much of its history was "The Friend of the Family". At the time of its demise, the slogan was "Simpler Banking, More Smiles".

In 1983, Washington Mutual bought the brokerage firm Murphey Favre and demutualized. By 1989, its assets had doubled.

In October 2005, Washington Mutual purchased the "subprime" credit card issuer Providian for approximately $6.5 billion.

In March 2006, Washington Mutual began moving into its new headquarters, WaMu Center, located in downtown Seattle. The company's previous[192] headquarters, Washington Mutual Tower, still stands about a block away from the new building on Second Avenue.

In August 2006, Washington Mutual began using the official abbreviation of WaMu in all but legal situations.

On September 25, 2008, federal regulators seized Washington Mutual, selling the bulk of the company's assets to JP Morgan Chase &

到1930年，业务已在华盛顿互惠储蓄银行的名义下开展，并于1930年7月25日收购了第一家公司——大陆互惠储蓄银行。

在其发展历史的大部分时间里，其营销口号为，"家庭之友"。在其倒闭之时，其口号为，"更简单的银行业务，更多的微笑"。

1983年，华盛顿互惠银行收购了墨菲·法弗雷经纪公司，从此不再是互助公司。到1989年，它的资产翻了一番。

2005年10月，华盛顿互惠银行以大约65亿美元的价格收购了次级信用卡发行商Providian。

2006年3月，华盛顿互惠银行迁入其新的总部，坐落在西雅图市中心的华盛顿互惠中心。该行前总部，华盛顿互惠塔依然屹立在距新总部大约一个街区以外的第二大道。

2006年8月，华盛顿互惠银行开始在所有非法定情况下的官方缩写：WaMu。

2008年9月25日，联邦监管者接管了华盛顿互惠银行，并将其巨额资产以19亿美元的价格卖给摩根

---

[192] previous: ['pri:vjəs] *a.* 在……之前，先，前，以前的

Co., for $1.9 billion.

In the future, all Washington Mutual branches will be renamed to Chase. WaMu credit and debit cards will also be renamed to Chase. Chase ATMs will be freely accessible for WaMu customers, and eventually WaMu customers will be able to bank at any Chase branch. However, WaMu customers will be able to continue banking at WaMu branches[193] until the merger with JP Morgan Chase & Co. is complete.

Acquisitions[194]

Since the acquisition of Murphey Favre, WaMu made numerous acquisitions with the aim of expanding the corporation. By acquiring companies including PNC Mortgage, Fleet Mortgage and HomeSide Lending, WaMu became the third-largest mortgage lender in the U.S. With the acquisition of Providian Financial Corporation in October 2005, WaMu also became the nation's 9th-largest credit-card company.

A list of WaMu acquisitions since demutualization[195] follows:

Commercial Capital Bancorp, California,

大通。

在将来，所有的华盛顿互惠银行的分支机构都将被重命名为摩根大通，华盛顿互惠银行的借贷卡也将被重命名为摩根大通。而摩根大通的自动柜员机也可以被华盛顿互惠银行的客户自由使用，最终华盛顿互惠银行的客户将可以在任何一家摩根大通分支机构进行银行业务。不过，华盛顿互惠银行的客户可以继续在其分支机构进行银行业务直到其与摩根大通的合并最终完成。

收购

自从成功收购墨菲·法弗雷经纪公司之后，为了公司扩张，华盛顿互惠银行进行了多次收购。通过对PNC房贷公司，佛利特房贷公司和家边房贷公司三家公司的收购，华盛顿互惠银行成为全美第三大抵押贷款借贷商。随着在2005年10月对普罗威登金融公司的收购，华盛顿互惠银行同时成为全美第九大信用卡发行商。

自成为非互助公司之后，华盛顿互惠银行（以下简称"华互"）的收购名单：

2006年收购加利福尼亚的商业

---

[193] branches: [brɑːntʃis] *n.* 分支机构
[194] acquisition: [ˌækwiˈziʃən] *n.* 收购，采购，取得
[195] demutualization *n.* 企业化，公司化

2006

Providian Financial Corporation, California, 2005

HomeSide Lending, Inc., Florida, a unit of National Australia Bank, 2002

Dime Bancorp, Inc., New York, 2002

Fleet Mortgage Corp., South Carolina, 2001

Bank United Corp., Texas, 2001

PNC Mortgage, Illinois, 2001

Alta Residential Mortgage Trust, California, 2000

Long Beach Financial Corp., California, 1999

Industrial Bank, California, 1998

H. F. Ahmanson & Co. (Home Savings of America), California, 1998

Great Western Bank, 1997

United Western Financial Group, Inc., Utah, 1997

Keystone Holdings, Inc. (American Savings Bank), California, 1996

Utah Federal Savings Bank, 1996

Western Bank, Oregon, 1996

Enterprise Bank, Washington, 1995

资本银行

2005年收购加利福尼亚的普罗威登金融公司

2002年收购位于佛罗里达的一家奥地利分支银行住房贷款公司

2002年收购位于纽约的一角银行

2001年收购位于南卡罗来纳的舰队抵押贷款公司

2001年收购位于得克萨斯州的美国银行公司

2001年收购位于伊利诺伊州的PNC金融服务集团

2000年收购位于加利福尼亚州的阿尔塔住宅按揭信托

1999年收购位于加利福尼亚州的长滩金融公司

1998年收购位于加利福尼亚州的兴业银行

1998年收购位于加利福尼亚州的高频阿曼森公司（美国家庭储蓄公司的子公司）

1997年收购大西银行

1997年收购位于犹他州的联合西部金融集团

1996年收购位于加利福尼亚州的基斯通控股公司（美国储蓄银行）

1996年收购犹他联邦储蓄银行

1996年收购位于俄勒冈的西部银行

1995年收购位于华盛顿的企业银行

Olympus Bank FSB, Utah, 1995	1995年收购位于犹他州的奥林巴斯银行的FSB
Summit Savings Bank, Washington, 1994	1994年收购位于华盛顿的高峰储蓄银行
Far West Federal Savings Bank, Oregon, 1994	1994年收购位于俄勒冈的远西联邦储蓄银行
Pacific First Bank, Ontario, 1993	1993年收购位于安大略州的太平洋第一银行
Pioneer Savings Bank, Washington, 1993	1993年收购位于华盛顿的先锋储蓄银行
Great Northwest Bank, Washington, 1992	1992年收购位于华盛顿的远大西北银行
Sound Savings & Loan Association, Washington, 1991	1991年收购位于华盛顿的良好储蓄和贷款协会
CrossLand Savings FSB, Utah, 1991	1991年收购位于犹他州的葛罗斯兰储蓄的FSB
Vancouver Federal Savings Bank, Washington, 1991	1991年收购位于华盛顿的温哥华联邦储蓄银行
Williamsburg Federal Savings Association, Utah, 1990	1990年收购位于犹他州的威廉斯堡联邦储蓄协会
Frontier Federal Savings Association, Washington, 1990	1990年收购位于华盛顿的前沿联邦储蓄协会
Old Stone Bank of Washington, FSB, Rhode Island, 1990	1990年收购位于罗得岛的华盛顿旧石银行

財经宝库

1. **美国储蓄监管局**（The United States Office of Thrift Supervision，OTS）　隶属于美国财政部，是联邦储蓄协会的主要监管者。监管局也负责监督储蓄贷款控股公司和一些国家特许机构。根据1989年美国金融机构改革、恢复和强化法案，监管局作为财政部附属机构由国会创立于1989年8月9日。其预算资金来源于其负责评估管理的这些机构。它负责监管的著名企业包括通用电气、美国国际集团、美国运通、摩根士丹利和美林证券等。

2. **摩根大通**（JP Morgan Chase）　摩根大通总部位于纽约，它为3,000多万名消费者以及企业、机构和政府客户提供服务。该公司拥有7,930亿美元资产，业务遍及50多个国家和地区，是投资银行业务、金融服务、金融事务处理、投资管理、私人银行业务和私募股权投资方面的领导者。

3. **高盛集团**（Goldman Sachs）　一家国际领先的投资银行和证券公司，向全球提供广泛的投资、咨询和金融服务，拥有大量的跨行业客户，包括私营公司、金融企业、政府机构以及个人。高盛集团成立于1869年，是全世界历史最悠久及规模最大的投资银行之一，总部设在纽约，并在东京、伦敦和香港设有分部，在23个国家和地区拥有41个办事处。

4. **联邦存款保险公司**（Federal Deposit Insurance Corporation, FDIC）　又译做"美国联邦储蓄保险公司"，它创立于1933年，作用在于为美国的储户提供保险机制，维护公众信心和金融系统的稳定。如果会员银行发生破产或无法偿还债务的危机时，FDIC将为这个会员银行的每个储户提供最高限额为10万美元的存款保险。

DIY工作室

1. Before Washington Mutual was taken over by the government in September 2008, how did it perform?

2. How did Washington Mutual expand since its establishment in 1889? Did its expansion beyond its traditional business contribute to the bankruptcy in 2008?

3. What efforts have been made by Washington Mutual to save itself from the sub-prime mortgage crisis?

归类记忆卡片

储蓄机构 thrift institution	保险基金 insurance fund
有担保债务 secured debt	抵补债券 covered bond
倒闭 demise	

Washington Mutual（II）

华盛顿互惠银行（下）

Demise

In December 2007, WaMu reorganized its home-loan division, closing 160 of its 336 home-loan offices and removing 2,600 positions in its home-loan staff (a 22% reduction).

In April 2008, WaMu, responding to losses and difficulties sustained as a result of the 2007–2008 subprime mortgage crisis, announced a $7 billion infusion of new capital by new outside investors led by TPG Capital. TPG agreed to pump $2 billion into WaMu; other investors, including some of WaMu's current institutional holders, agreed to buy an additional $5 billion in newly issued stock. The bank announced that 3,000 people companywide would lose their jobs, and the company stated its intent to close its approximately 186 remaining stand-alone, home-loan offices, including 23 in Washington State and a loan-processing center

倒闭

2007年12月，华互重组其房贷部，撤销了其336家中的160家房贷处，解聘了2,600名房贷部职员（相当于22%的员工缩减）。

2008年4月，受2007～2008年次级抵押贷款危机的影响，华互在持续亏损、困难重重之际，宣布总额达70亿美元的新资本注入，此次注入的资金由得克萨斯州太平洋保险集团（TPG）牵头的外部投资者提供。得克萨斯州太平洋保险集团同意对华盛顿互惠银行注资20亿美元，其他投资方，包括一些华互现有机构股东，同意对新发行股票增持50亿美元。华互银行宣布将解雇3,000名员工，并且表示要关闭其他现有独立的186家房贷处，其中包括在华盛顿州的23家和在华盛顿州贝尔维尤市的贷款处理中心。同

in Bellevue, Washington. It stopped buying loans from outside mortgage brokers — known in the trade as "wholesale lending."

In June 2008, Kerry Killinger stepped down as the Chairman, though remaining the Chief Executive Officer. On September 8, 2008, under pressure from investors WaMu's board of directors ousted[196] Kerry Killinger as the CEO. Alan H. Fishman, chairman of mortgage broker Meridian Capital Group, and a former chief operating officer of Sovereign Bank, was named the new CEO.

By mid-September 2008, WaMu's share price had closed as low as $2.00, whereas a year previous it was worth over $30.00. While WaMu publicly insisted it could stay independent, earlier in the month it had secretly hired Goldman Sachs to facilitate an auction of the bank. However, there were no takers. At the same time, customers were pulling out their deposits in large numbers. Fearing that this could lead to a massive run, the Federal Reserve and the Treasury Department stepped up pressure on WaMu to sell itself, as a takeover by the FDIC would have been a severe drain on the FDIC insurance fund. At one point, it actually went behind the backs of WaMu's management to broker a deal. Finally, on the morning of

时不再向外部抵押贷款经纪商发放被业界称为"零售贷款"的贷款。

2008年6月，克里·基林格辞去银行总裁职务，虽然保留了其首席执行官的位置。2008年9月8日，基于投资者的压力，董事会又开除了基林格首席执行官的职务。子午线资本集团的总裁艾兰·费舍曼同时也是主权银行前首席执行官，被任命为华互银行新任首席执行官。

2008年9月中旬，华互股票市值跌至将近每股2美元，然而一年前同期却超过30美元。然而华互对外宣称它能够独立运营，而本月早些时候它却私下委托高盛为其寻找买家。不过，当时却没有买方。与此同时，银行客户却在大批提走存款。由于担心这将导致大批资金外流，美联储和财政部对华互共同施压要求其出售自己，同时被联邦存款保险公司接管，但有可能对联邦存款保险公司保险基金造成严重的资金压力。联邦存款保险公司的确在华互管理层背后做中间人达成交易。最终，9月25日，也就是星期四的早上，监管者通知摩根大通，它就是最终赢家。

---

[196] oust: [aust] *v.* 逐出，夺取

Thursday, September 25, regulators informed JP Morgan Chase that it was the winner.

That night (shortly after the close of business on the West Coast), the Office of Thrift Supervision seized WaMu and placed it into receivership with the FDIC as receiver. The FDIC then sold virtually all of WaMu-including its deposits and branch network-to JP MorganChase for $1.9 billion. The transaction, arranged[197] by the FDIC, does not require drawing from the FDIC insurance fund. Normally, bank seizures[198] take place after the close of business on Fridays, but WaMu was in such dire straits that regulators felt compelled[199]to act a day early.

WaMu's management was kept completely in the dark by the regulators; indeed, Fishman was on the way to Seattle when the deal closed. JP Morgan Chase didn't acquire any of WaMu's equity (though it plans to issue $8 billion in common stock to pay for the deal), and it is believed that the company's shareholders and some bondholders will be wiped out. However, WaMu's stock was practically worthless in any case; by the close of the week's trading its stock had dropped to only $0.16 a share.

当天晚上（即西海岸交易日结束时）监管局勒令华互停止经营并交由联邦存款保险公司进入破产管理期。随后联邦储蓄保险公司事实上将华互所有资产包括其存款和分支机构以19亿美元价格卖给摩根大通。由联邦储蓄保险公司安排的这次交易并没有要求从联邦储蓄保险基金里提款。 一般来说，勒令银行停止营业会在星期五交易日结束时发生，然而由于华互处境如此糟糕以致监管者不得不提前一天行动。

华互的管理层对此事件完全不知情，实际上，当交易达成时费舍曼正在去往西雅图的路上。摩根大通没有获取华互的任何股权（即使它计划发行80亿美元普通股以偿付此次交易），因为它认为华互股东及部分债券持有人的权益将从此消除。然而，华互的股票实际上已经变得一文不值，截至本周交易日结束时，其股值已跌至每股0.16美元。

---

[197] arrange: [ə'reindʒ] v. 安排，整理，排列
[198] seizure: ['si:ʒə] n. 捕获，夺取，捕获物
[199] compel: [kəm'pel] v. 强迫，迫使

Fishman was only in the position 17 days. He received a $7.5 million sign on bonus, then received his cash severence of $11.6 million.

费舍曼在职仅17天，他得到750万美元的红利，紧接着就收到了1,160万美元的解雇费。

WaMu's seizure resulted in the largest bank failure in American financial history, far exceeding[200] the failure of Continental Illinois in 1984.

华互的倒闭成为美国金融史上最大的银行倒闭案，远远超过了1984年大陆伊利诺的倒闭。

On September 26, 2008, Washington Mutual, Inc., the bank holding company of the thrift, and its remaining subsidiary[201], WMI Investment Corp., filed for Chapter 11 bankruptcy.

2008年9月26日，华盛顿互惠银行公司，即银行节约控股公司及其子公司WMI投资公司，申请破产。

非常点拨

1. **股份制/公司化（demutualization）**　　股份化是指客户所有的互助机构法定形式发生变化，转变为股份公司的过程。有时也被称为私有化。在股份化过程中，互助组织成员通常会从转型公司中得到现金支出或派发股票。互助化是其反过程，指股份公司被互助机构接收转变为互助组织。传统的互助组织通过其客户筹集资金以便为他们提供服务（比如建筑协会，所有成员的储蓄为部分成员的房屋抵押贷款提供了资金）。

---

[200] exceed: [ik'si:d] *v.* 超过，胜过，越发
[201] subsidiary: [səb'sidiəri] *n.* 子公司，附属机构

2. **批发贷款**（wholesale lending） 按贷款数量贷款可分为批发贷款和零售贷款。批发贷款是指数额较大、对工商企业和金融机构等发放的贷款，借款者的借款目的是经营获利。批发贷款可以是抵押贷款也可以是信用贷款，借款期限也可以是短期的、中期的或长期的。

Washington Mutual Tower
华盛顿互惠银行的高楼

Federal Takeover of Fannie Mae and Freddie Mac

Unit 20

Federal Takeover of Fannie Mae and Freddie Mac
美国政府接管房利美与房地美

主题札记

面对房市低迷可能会拖垮整个经济的威胁，对此，越来越警醒的美国政府目前正着手接管"两房"以确保住房抵押贷款有足够融资的业务。

美国财政部周日宣布，计划向美国两大住房抵押贷款公司房利美(Fannie Mae)和房地美(Freddie Mac)提供多达2,000亿美元的资金，并提高其信贷额度；同时"两房"的监管机构联邦住房金融局(Federal Housing Finance Agency, FHFA)将接管两家公司的管理。财政部部长亨利·保尔森(Henry Paulson)说，这将增加购房者的可用信贷。

财政部还计划买进"两房"发行的抵押贷款支持证券，以便降低购房者的信贷成本，但并未透露具体数额。尽管美联储曾数次大幅下调利率，但在2007年的大部分时间里，普通30年期固定利率住房抵押贷款的成本仍远高于6%。

这项举措有望小幅降低消费者的利率，帮助预防不断恶化的房市——目前已到了20世纪30年代以来最严重的状况。至少短期来看，这还会巩固政府在抵押贷款行业的地位，使纳税人暴露于风险之下，面临可能高达数十亿美元的违约相关损失。长期来看，保尔森的目的在于大幅缩减"两房"持有的抵押贷款和相关证券；不过他指出，至于"两房"最终将变成什么样，要由国会和下届政府决定。

保尔森说，政府除了支撑房利美和房地美之外，已经别无选择。"两房"

由国会创建以支持住房市场，但由私人股东持股。两家公司发行了逾5万亿美元的债券和抵押贷款支持证券，由世界各地的中央银行和其他投资者持有。保尔森说，两家公司中任何一家崩溃都会导致美国乃至全球金融市场的动荡。

Bloomberg/Landov
美国财政部部长保尔森和联邦住房金融局局长洛克哈特
周日在新闻发布会上

Federal takeover of Fannie Mae and Freddie Mac (I)

美国政府接管房利美与房地美（上）

The federal takeover of Fannie Mae and Freddie Mac refers to the placing into conservatorship of government sponsored enterprises Fannie Mae and Freddie Mac by the U.S. Treasury in September 2008. It was one financial event among many in the ongoing Subprime mortgage crisis.

The director of the Federal Housing Finance Agency (FHFA), James B. Lockhart Ⅲ. on September 7, 2008 announced his decision to place two Government sponsored enterprises (GSEs), Fannie Mae (Federal National Mortgage Association) and Freddie Mac (Federal Home Loan Mortgage Corporation), into conservatorship run by FHFA. United States Treasury Secretary Henry Paulson, at the same press conference stated that placing the two GSEs into conservatorship was a decision he fully supported, and said that he advised "that

2008年9月，美国政府对房利美和房地美的接管意味着由美国政府担保的两家企业被美国财政部托管。这仅是次级抵押贷款危机中的金融事件之一。

美国联邦住房金融局局长詹姆斯·B.洛克哈特2008年7月宣布，由政府支持的两家企业——房利美（联邦国民抵押贷款协会）和房地美（联邦住房贷款抵押公司）（以下简称"两房"）由美国联邦住房金融局托管。美国财政部部长亨利·保尔森，在同场记者招待会上指出，接管"两房"是他全力支持的一项决定，并建议表示"托管是我将保证纳税人的钱用于政府支持企业的唯一形式。"他进一步说："今日行动的必要性主要在于政府

conservatorship was the only form in which I would commit taxpayer money to the GSEs." He further said that "I attribute the need for today's action primarily to the inherent[202] conflict and flawed business model embedded in the GSE structure, and to the ongoing housing correction". The same day, Federal Reserve Bank Chairman Ben Bernanke stated in support: "I strongly endorse[203] both the decision by FHFA Director Lockhart to place Fannie Mae and Freddie Mac into conservatorship and the actions taken by Treasury Secretary Paulson to ensure the financial soundness of those two companies."

Background and financial market crisis

Main articles: *Financial crisis of 2007–2008* and *Liquidity crisis of September 2008*

The combined GSE losses of $14.9 billion and market concerns about their ability to raise capital and debt threatened to disrupt the U.S. housing financial market. The Treasury committed to invest as much as $200 billion in preferred stock and extend credit through 2009 to keep the GSEs solvent and operating. The two GSEs have outstanding more than US$ 5 trillion in mortgage backed securities (MBS) and debt; the debt portion alone is $1.6 trillion.

担保企业结构固有的冲突以及商业模式的缺陷，还有出于对房地产企业进行修正的考虑"。

同一天，美联储主席本·伯南克表示支持："我强烈支持由联邦住房金融局局长洛克哈特作出的关于托管房利美和房地美的决定以及财政部部长亨利·保尔森所采取的旨在保持'两房'财政稳定的相关措施。"

相关背景以及金融市场危机

主要文章来源：《2007—2008年金融危机》，《2008年9月清算危机》

"两房"达149亿美元的总损失及市场关于其募资能力和其债务可能导致住房融资市场低迷引发担忧。财政部保证对其优先股注资2,000亿美元并延长其信贷至2009年以保证"两房"的清偿能力和正常运营。"两房"在抵押担保证券以及债务方面的未清偿额已超过5万亿美元，其中仅债务就高达1.6万亿美元。此次接管被视为"几十年来政府对私人金融市场最为全面

---

[202] inherent: [in'hiərənt] *a.* 内在的，固有的
[203] endorse: [in'dɔːs] *v.* 支持，赞同，背书于

The conservatorship action has been described as "one of the most sweeping government interventions in private financial markets in decades," and one that "could turn into the biggest and costliest government bailout ever of private companies".

With a growing sense of crisis in U.S. financial markets, the conservatorship action and commitment by the U.S. government to backstop the two GSEs with up to U.S.$ 200 billion in additional capital turned out to be the first significant event in a tumultuous month among U.S.-based investment banking, financial institutions and federal regulatory bodies. By September 15, 2008, the 158 year-old Lehman Brothers holding company filed for bankruptcy with intent to liquidate its assets, leaving its financially sound subsidiaries operational and outside of the bankruptcy filing. The collapse is the largest investment bank failure since Drexel Burnham Lambert in 1990. The 94 year-old Merrill Lynch accepted a purchase offer by Bank of America for approximately U.S.$ 50 billion, a big drop from a year-earlier market valuation of about U.S.$ 100 billion. A credit rating downgrade of the large insurer American International Group (AIG) led to a September 16, 2008 rescue agreement with the Federal Reserve Bank for a $ 85 billion dollar secured loan facility, in exchange for a warrants for 79.9% of the equity of AIG.

的干预之一", 也将成为政府对私人企业最大规模也是代价最高的一次紧急援助。

随着美国金融市场危机意识的日益增强, 美国政府对"两房"的接管行为以及对其额外注资2,000亿美元的承诺将成为在金融动荡的9月对美国众多投资银行、金融机构以及联邦管理机构中第一起意义重大的事件。到2008年9月15日, 具有158年历史的美国雷曼兄弟控股公司申请破产, 希望对其资产进行清算, 并剥离其财务良好运转正常的子公司(于破产申请之外)。这次倒闭是继1990年德崇证券公司倒闭以来最大的一次投资银行倒闭事件。具有94年历史的美林证券也接受了来自美国银行的大约500亿美元的要约收购, 这对于美林一年以前的大约为1,000亿美元的市值是一个大幅度的下滑。由于信用评级下滑, 美国国际集团于2008年9月16日与美国联邦储备银行签署援助协议, 以其79.9%的股权换取联邦储备银行的850亿美元的援助。

美国财政部部长亨利·保尔森在新闻发布会上

Worries continued about the solvency of country's largest savings bank, Washington Mutual, and it was put into receivership September 25, 2008.

Previous attempts for GSE reform

In 2003, the Bush Administration sought to create an agency to oversee Fannie Mae and Freddie Mac. While Senate and House leaders voiced their intention to bring about the needed legislation, no reform bills materialized[204]. A Senate reform bill introduced by Senator John Corzine (D-NJ) (S.1656) never made it out of the 21-member (10D/11R) Senate Banking, Housing, and Urban Affairs Committee. At the time members of the 108th congress expressed faith in the solvency of Fannie and Freddie. Congressman Barney Frank (D-MA), for example, described them as "not facing any kind of financial crisis".

In 2005, *the Federal Housing Enterprise Regulatory Reform Act*, sponsored by Senator Chuck Hagel (R-NE) and co-sponsored by Senators Elizabeth Dole (R-NC), John McCain (R-AZ) and John Sununu (R-NH), would have increased government oversight[205] of loans given by Fannie Mae and Freddie Mac. Like the 2003

同时，对于美国最大的储蓄银行——华盛顿互惠银行的清偿能力的担忧也没有停止，这家银行于2008年9月25日实行破产管理。

对政府资助企业改革的尝试

2003年，布什政府企图建立一家机构以监管房利美和房地美。然而众参两院领袖表示要事先制定相关立法，改革方案没有成形。一项由参议院议员约翰·考兹尼提出的改革方案也未能获得21个成员组的参议院银行、住房和城市事务委员会的通过。与此同时，第108届国会的议员们对房利美和房地美的清偿能力充满信心。国会议员巴尔尼·佛兰克说它们"没有面临任何形式的财务危机"。

2005年，由参议院查克·海格尔和参议员伊丽莎白·多尔以及参议员约翰·麦凯恩和约翰·苏努努联合提出的《联邦住房企业监管改革法案》旨在增强政府对"两房"发放贷款的监管。然而其命运却和2003年提出的法案一样未能通过参议院银行、住房和城市事务委员

---

[204] materialize: [məˈtiəriəlaiz] *v.* 赋予实质，使体现，物质化
[205] oversight: [ˈəuvəsait] *n.* 勘漏，失察，失败

bill, it also died in the Senate Banking, Housing, and Urban Affairs Committee, this time in the 109th Congress. A full and accurate record of the congressional[206] attempts to regulate the housing GSEs is given in the Congressional record prepared in 2005.

Gerald P. O'Driscoll, the former vice president of the Federal Reserve Bank of Dallas, stated that Fannie Mae and Freddie Mac had become classic examples of crony capitalism[207]. Government backing let Fannie and Freddie dominate the mortgage-underwriting. They returned some of the profits to the politicians, sometimes directly, as campaign funds, and sometimes as "contributions to favored constituents".

Federal Housing Finance Agency and Treasury authority

The Housing and Economic Recovery Act of 2008—passed by the United States Congress on July 24, 2008 and signed into law by President George W. Bush on July 30, 2008—enabled expanded regulatory authority over Fannie Mae and Freddie Mac by the newly established FHFA, and gave the U.S. Treasury the authority to advance funds for the purpose of stabilizing Fannie Mae, or Freddie Mac,

会的批准，这次是在第109届国会上。一份全面精确的关于国会试图监管住房领域的政府资助企业的记录在2005年国会报告中给出。

达拉斯美联储前副主席杰拉尔德·P.奥特思考指出房利美和房地美已成为裙带资本主义的典型代表。政府资助致使房利美和房地美主宰了抵押承销业务。他们将部分利润返还给政治家，有时作为竞选资金直接返还，有时作为对中意选民的捐款。

联邦住房金融局及美国财政当局

由美国国会于2008年7月24日通过的《2008年住房与经济恢复法案》经美国总统乔治·W.布什于2008年7月30日签署成为法律。这部法律使得新成立的联邦住房金融局扩大了对房利美和房地美的监管权，同时也给予美国财政部为稳定"两房"而对其进行注资的权力，注资限额仅限于整个联邦政府在法律许可范围之内。本部法律将财

---

[206] congressional: [kən'greʃənəl] *a.* 会议的，议会的，国会的
[207] crony capitalism *n.* 裙带资本主义

limited only by the amount of debt that the entire federal government is permitted by law to commit to. The law raised the Treasury's debt ceiling[208] by U.S.$ 800 billion, to a total of U.S.$ 10.7 trillion, in anticipation of the potential need for the Treasury to have the flexibility to support Fannie Mae, Freddie Mac, or the Federal Home Loan Banks.

政部的债务限额提升了8,000亿美元，使其债务总限额达到10.7万亿美元，这是考虑到财政部对房利美、房地美或其他联邦住房贷款银行的支持的灵活度的潜在需要而作出的规定。

1. 美国联邦国民抵押贷款协会（简称为房利美）(Fannie Mae) 成立于1938年，是一家股份制企业，于1968获得国会许可接受国家赞助，公司的目的是通过买卖抵押债券确保向购房者贷款的机构资金正常周转。

2. 美国联邦住房贷款抵押公司（简称为房地美）(Freddie Mac) 成立于1970年，是由美国政府为了扩大住房贷款二级市场资助建立的一家企业。与其他政府资助企业一样，房地美在二级市场购买按揭贷款，将其集中后，以资产支持证券的形式在公开市场上出售给投资者。这种二级抵押市场增加了用于抵押贷款的资金，为购买新房提供了方便。

3. 次级抵押贷款危机（Subprime mortgage crisis） 是指由于抵押贷款人违约止赎引起的一场不断升温的金融危机，严重影响了全球银行业和金融市场。这场危机起源于20世纪末期，在2007年显现出来，揭露出金融业监管制度和全球金融体系中普遍存在的

---

[208] debt ceiling *n.*债务最高限额，上限

弱点。近年来，许多美国公司发放次级抵押贷款，要求低首付或零首付，贷款给低收入、无资产、信用低的家庭。当房价在2006年到2007年开始下跌的时候，抵押贷款违约率上升，次级抵押贷款证券大幅贬值，结果导致许多银行和政府资助企业巨额资本流失，全球范围内信贷紧缩。

4. **美国联邦住房金融局**（Federal Housing Finance Agency） 是联邦住房金融委员会与联邦住房企业监督局法定合并后形成的一个独立的联邦机构，继承了两者的监管权力，扩大了法律和监管权，包括接管政府资助企业的权利。

5. **政府资助企业**（government sponsored enterprises） 是指由美国国会设立的一些金融服务公司。其职能是加快经济中某些部门的信贷流通，使资本市场更有效更透明。政府资助企业希望能够在农业、住房和教育等政府支持部门提供更多的信贷机会，并降低其信贷成本。

1. Why did the U.S. treasury take over Fannie Mae and Freddie Mac? How did the two government sponsored enterprises get into trouble?

2. How did the government attempt to reform the government sponsored enterprises before 2008? Why did all the attempts end up with a failure?

3. What did the U.S. treasury and Federal Reserve Bank plan to do to help Fannie Mae and Freddie Mac overcome their present financial difficulties?

归类记忆卡片

接受管理 conservatorship
抵押承销 mortgage-underwriting
最后担保 backstop
抵押贷款支持证券 mortgage backed securities (MBS)

次级债务 subordinated debt
债务限额 debt ceiling
融资方式 financing facilities
股本余额 outstanding capital stock

听力广场

Federal takeover of Fannie Mae and Freddie Mac (II)

美联储接管房利美与房地美（下）

Pri or GSE support measures

The September 7 conservatorship was been termed by *The Economist* as the "second" bailout of the GSEs. Prior to the enactment of *the Housing and Economic Recovery Act of 2008*, on July 13, 2008, Treasury Secretary

早先对政府资助企业的支持措施

9月7日，美国财政部的托管行为被英国《经济学家》杂志解读为对政府资助企业的"第二次"紧急援助。在制定《2008年住房与经济恢复法案》之前，2008年7

Henry Paulson announced an effort to backstop the GSEs based on prior statutory authority, in coordination with the Federal Reserve Bank. That announcement occurred after a week in which the market values of shares of Fannie Mae and Freddie Mac fell almost by half (from a previously diminished value of approximately half of year-earlier market highs). That plan contained three measures: an increase in the line of credit available to the GSEs from the Treasury, so as to provide liquidity; the right for the Treasury to purchase equity in the GSEs, so as to provide capital; and a consultative role for the Federal Reserve in a reformed GSE regulatory system. On the same day, the Federal Reserve announced that the Federal Reserve Bank of New York would have the right to lend to the GSEs as necessary.

Capital infusion by the Treasury

The agreement the Treasury made with both GSEs specifies that in exchange for future support and capital investments of up to U.S.$ 100 billion in each GSE, at the inception of the conservatorship, each GSE shall issue to the Treasury U.S.$ 1 billion of senior preferred stock, with a 10% coupon, without cost to the Treasury. Also each GSE contracted to issue common stock warrants representing an ownership stake of 79.9%, at an exercise price of one-thousandth of a U.S. cent ($ 0.00001) per

月13日，财政部部长亨利·保尔森宣布了一项与美联储立场一致基于法定权限的对政府资助企业的援助措施。这项宣布是在房利美和房地美的股票市值缩水近一半（与一年前高位市值相比下降了将近一半）一周后作出的。那项计划包括三项措施：增加政府资助企业从财政部得到的贷款额度，以提供资产流动性；财政部购买政府资助企业的股权的权力为其提供资金；以及美联储在改革了的政府资助企业的监管系统中的咨询性角色。同日，美联储宣布其下属机构纽约联邦储备银行如有必要有权向政府资助企业发放贷款。

财政部的资本注入

财政部与"两房"的协议明确规定，为换取财政部的未来支持以及金额高达1,000亿美元的对各自的资本投资，在托管之初，"两房"要向财政部发行10亿美元的高级优先股以及10%的息票并且对财政部不计成本。同时，每一家机构以合同形式发行代表79.9%所有权股份的普通股凭证，其发行价格为每股1美分（0.00001美元），并且凭证期限为20年。

share, and with a warrant[209] duration of twenty years.

The conservator, FHFA signed the agreements on behalf of the GSAs. The 100 billion amount for each GSE was chosen to indicate the level of commitment that the U.S. Treasury is willing to make to keep the financial operations and financial conditions solvent and sustainable for both GSEs. The agreements were designed to protect the senior and subordinated debt and the mortgage backed securities of the GSEs. The GSEs' common stock and existing preferred shareholders will bear any losses ahead of the government. Among other conditions of the agreement, each GSE's retained[210] mortgage and mortgage backed securities portfolio shall not exceed $850 billion as of December 31, 2009, and shall decline by 10% per year until it reaches $250 billion.

FHFA initial actions as conservator

In the September 7, 2008 conservatorship announcement, Lockhart indicated the following items in the plan of action for the Federal Housing Finance Agency conservatorship:

On September 8, 2008, the first business day of the conservatorship, business will be

托管人联邦住房金融局代表被托管公司签署协议。对"两房"各自 1,000亿美元的注资额是美国政府愿意为保持"两房"财务经营以及财务清偿能力稳定并可持续而作出的承担义务的级别。该协议旨在保护高级以及次级债务和"两房"的抵押担保证券。"两房"的普通股以及现有优先股的股东将先于持有高级优先股的美国政府承担损失。在此项协议的所有条件中，两家各自保留的抵押贷款和抵押贷款支持证券组合截至2009年12月31日不能超过8,500亿美元，每年可以降低10%，直到达到2,500亿美元。

联邦住房金融局作为托管人的初步举措

2008年9月7日，在宣布托管计划时，洛克哈特提出了在联邦住房金融局的托管计划中的以下几点：

2008年9月8日，即托管后的第一个营业日，在抵押贷款支持证券

---

[209] warrant: ['wɔrənt] v. 保证，辩解，担保
[210] retain: [ri'tein] v. 保持，保留

transacted normally, with stronger backing for the holders of Mortgage Backed Securities (MBS), senior debt and subordinated[211] debt.

The Enterprises will be allowed to grow their guarantee MBS books without limits and continue to purchase replacement securities for their portfolios, about $20 billion per month, without capital constraints.

As the conservator, the FHFA will assume the power of the Board and management. The present Chief Executive Officers (CEOs) of both Fannie Mae and Freddie Mac have been dismissed but will stay on to help with the transition.

Appointed as CEOs are Herbert M. Allison for Fannie Mae and David M. Moffett for Freddie Mac. Allison is former Vice Chairman of Merrill Lynch and for the last eight years chairman of TIAA-CREF. Moffett is the former Vice Chairman and CFO of U.S. Bankcorp. Their compensation will be significantly lower than the outgoing CEOs. They will be joined by equally strong non-executive chairmen.

Other management action will be very limited. The new CEOs agreed it is important to work with the current management teams and employees to encourage them to stay and to

持有人，高级债和次级债持有人的大力支持下，交易正常进行。

允许"两房"扩大对抵押贷款支持证券的担保额度不受限制并继续为其投资组合购进置换债券，大约每月200亿美元，并且无资本限制。

作为托管人，联邦住房金融局将履行董事会以及管理层的职责。房利美和房地美的现任首席执行官被解职，但将留在公司协助过渡。

房利美和房地美将分别由前美林公司副董事长赫伯特·M.艾利森（过去8年他一直是美国教师退休基金会的董事长）和美国合众银行前副董事长和首席财务官的大卫·M.莫菲特接掌。他们的薪资将大大低于即将离任的两个首席执行官。同时将会有同样精干的非执行主席与他们合作。

其他管理层变动将非常有限。新的首席执行官认为与现有管理团队及员工的合作将至关重要，鼓励他们留下并继续为公司

---

[211] subordinate: [sə'bɔ:dinit] a. 从属的，副职的

continue to make important improvements to the Enterprises.

To conserve over $2 billion annually in capital, the common stock and preferred stock dividends will be eliminated, but the common and all preferred stocks will continue to remain outstanding. Subordinated debt interest and principal payments will continue to be made.

All political activities, including all lobbying, will be halted immediately. Charitable activities will be reviewed.

There will be financing and investing relationship with the U.S. Treasury via three different financing facilities to provide critically needed support to Freddie Mac and Fannie Mae, and also to the liquidity of the mortgage market. One of the three facilities is a secured liquidity facility, which will be not only for Fannie Mae and Freddie Mac, but also for the 12 Federal Home Loan Banks that are regulated by FHFA.

Treasury Secretary Paulson on September 7, 2008 described four aspects of the U.S. Treasury's support of the two government sponsored enterprises[212] (GSEs) while under conservatorship of the FHFA:

"To promote stability[213] in the secondary

作出重大改善。

为了每年节省超过20亿美元的资本，普通股和优先股的派息将被取消，但两种股票将继续作为流通股票。次级债务利息和主要支付将继续实施。

所有政治活动，包括游说将被立即停止。慈善活动将被重新纳入考虑范畴。

"两房"将会与美国财政部通过三种不同的融资方式建立融资和投资关系，以提供对房利美和房地美关键性的支持。三种融资方式之一就是担保清偿，这将不仅适用于房利美和房地美，也对由联邦住房金融局监管的美国12家联邦住房贷款银行适用。

财政部部长保尔森于2008年9月7日指出，在联邦住房金融局托管下，财政部对于"两房"支持的四个方面：

"为促进次级抵押贷款市场的

---

[212] government sponsored enterprises *n.* 政府资助企业，GSEs
[213] stability: [stə'biliti] *n.* 稳定性

mortgage market and lower the cost of funding, the GSEs will modestly increase their MBS portfolios through the end of 2009. Then, to address systemic risk, in 2010 their portfolios will begin to be gradually reduced at the rate of 10 percent per year, largely through natural run off, eventually stabilizing at a lower, less risky size."

The Treasury and the FHFA has established *Preferred Stock Purchase Agreements*, contractual arrangements between the Treasury and the conserved entities. "Under these agreements, Treasury will ensure that each company maintains a positive net worth. These agreements support market stability by providing additional security and clarity to GSE debt holders-senior and subordinated- and support mortgage availability by providing additional confidence to investors in GSE mortgage backed securities. This commitment will eliminate any mandatory triggering of receivership and will ensure that the conserved entities have the ability to fulfill their financial obligations.

The Treasury established "a new secured lending credit facility available to Fannie Mae, Freddie Mac, and also Federal Home Loan Banks. This facility is intended to serve as an ultimate liquidity backstop, in essence, implementing the temporary liquidity backstop authority granted by Congress in July 2008, and

稳定以及降低融资成本，截至2009年年末，"两房"将适度增加抵押贷款支持证券组合。随后，为解决系统性风险，在2010年其证券投资组合将以每年10个百分点的额度逐步减少，主要是通过自然流失，最终稳定在一个低成本、低风险的规模上。"

财政部和联邦住房金融局达成《优先股购买协议》以及财政部与被保护实体间的契约安排。在这些协议下，财政部将确保每家公司都能保持一个正净值。这些协议通过给"两房"债权人、高级和次级债权人，提供额外的担保和明确说明支持市场稳定，并通过对"两房"不动产放宽抵押贷款支持证券投资者提供额外的信心以支持抵押贷款的可用性。这项承诺将会消除任何由于破产管理而产生的强制命令并将确保这些被保护实体有能力清偿其债务。

财政部成立了"一个新的担保借款信贷工具，房利美和房地美以及联邦住房贷款银行将可用这个工具进行贷款。作为最终清算捕手工具，该工具本质上是在实行2008年7月由国会授予的暂时清算捕手的权力，这将在此授权于2009年12月截止后被使用。"

will be available until those authorities expire in December 2009."

"To further support the availability of mortgage financing for millions of Americans, Treasury is initiating a temporary program to purchase GSE MBS ... Treasury will begin this program later this month, investing in new GSE MBS. Additional purchases will be made as deemed appropriate. Given that Treasury can hold these securities to maturity, the spreads between Treasury issuances and GSE MBS indicate that there is no reason to expect taxpayer losses from this program, and, in fact, it could produce gains. This program will also expire[214] with the Treasury's temporary authorities in December 2009.

为了进一步支持对广大美国人民抵押贷款融资的需求，财政部正在起草一项购买政府资助企业抵押贷款支持证券的暂时计划。这项计划将于本月晚些时候实行并投资于新的政府资助企业的贷款支持。追加购买将被视为恰当的。由于财政部能够对这些债券到期予以保证，国库券与政府资助企业贷款支持之间的差价表明纳税人将不会因这项计划而受损，而且事实上，这将会产生新的收益。这项计划将随着财政部的暂时清算捕手权力的到期于2009年12月同期截止。

非常点拨

1. **亨利·保尔森**（Henry Paulson） 美国财政部部长，国际货币基金组织理事会成员，曾担任高盛集团主席和执行总裁。

---

[214] expire: [iksˈpaiəˌeks-] *v.* 期满，失效，终止，断气

2. **美林公司**（Merrill Lynch） 一家总部设在纽约曼哈顿的全球性金融服务公司。该公司通过其子公司与附属公司，在全球范围内提供资本市场服务、投资银行和咨询服务，并从事于财富管理、资产管理、保险、银行及相关金融业务。2008年12月5日，美国银行和美林公司股东共同批准了美国银行收购美林公司的提议。

3. **美国国际集团**（American International Group, AIG） 是美国一家总部设在纽约的大型保险公司。在福布斯2008全球2,000强名单中排名第18位。 由于在2008年信用评级中下降到投资级AA级，该公司遭受流动性危机。2008年9月，联邦储备银行向该公司提供了850亿美元的信贷资金，以确保其偿还债务。

4. **裙带资本主义**（Crony Capitalism） 是指在所谓的资本主义经济中，企业的成功取决于企业与政府的密切关系。这主要表现在企业可以通过政府法律政策、政府补助及特别税额优惠政策等形式牟取暴利。企业与政府之间唯利是图的朋友关系和亲属关系给经济和社会带来严重的不良影响。

Evictions by Fannie Mae
房利美的房屋收回